No one has been more mi an Jesus
Christ. Mark introduces u ages of
Scripture, a Jesus who is irre

, bestselling author,
founder of A21 and Propel Women

This book isn't a roadmap for playing it safe, it's an invitation to join
Jesus for the risky adventure of your life!

**Bob Goff**, author of *New York Times* bestsellers
*Love Does, Everybody Always*, and *Dream Big*

I love the way Mark Clark turns the kaleidoscope, revealing new
dimensions of who Jesus is. This book will help you encounter Jesus
all over again!

**Mark Batterson**, *New York Times* bestselling author of *The
Circle Maker*; lead pastor of National Community Church

There is nobody like Mark Clark. He's brilliant, funny, and compelling
all at the same time. In the *Problem of Jesus*, he points to the challenges
and reasons for faith in a way that feels both honest and fresh. This is a
captivating look at Jesus and what he means for us today.

**Jud Wilhite**, author of *Pursued*; senior
pastor of Central Church

This truly is a great book. If you don't pick it up now, it will only be a
matter of time until someone hands you a copy because they enjoyed
it so much.

**Carey Nieuwhof**, author and founding
pastor, Connexus Church

If you're interested in apologetics or just find yourself pondering the
deeper aspects of your faith, this is the book for you!

**Joshua Gagnon**, lead pastor of Next Level Church
and author of *It's Not Over: Leaving Behind
Disappointment and Learning to Dream Again*

Mark Clark has a rare gift for coupling deep theological insights with clear, concise writing. No matter where you personally land when it comes to Jesus of Nazareth, this book will deepen your faith or shake your skepticism.

**Larry Osborne**, pastor and author, North Coast Church

Mark provides proper context and evidence for all of us to see and understand the real Jesus in his day and ours. I'm more inspired than ever to follow the Jesus of the Scriptures!

**Brad Lomenick**, founder, BLINC; author;
H3 Leadership & The Catalyst leader

This book is, I sense, going to be a very significant voice to this generation and others to come. It is culturally informed and sensitive without being enculturated. Like the Jesus Mark describes, you can't ignore his message in this book, and you can't be neutral to it.

**Ross Hastings**, professor of theology, Regent College

With a poet's pen, a scholar's precision, and a pastor's heart, Mark brings Jesus out of culture's usual trappings and places him front and square where he belongs—in our hearts and minds.

**Ricky Jenkins**, senior pastor of Southwest Church; author of
*What They Taught Me: Enduring Wisdom for Changing Times*

With astute insights, biblical wisdom, and cultural savvy, Mark is the perfect person to write *The Problem of Jesus*. It is a tremendous resource for the skeptic, for the new believer, and for the seasoned saint.

**Daniel Fusco**, lead pastor @ Crossroads Community Church, TV
& radio host, author of *Crazy Happy* and *Upward, Inward; Outward*

Mark does a great job helping people get a good look at our beautiful Lord Jesus and how he represents a new way of being human.

**Alan Hirsch**, author of numerous books on missional
leadership, organization, and spirituality; founder
of the Movement Leaders Collective

# THE PROBLEM OF
# JESUS

ANSWERING A SKEPTIC'S CHALLENGES

TO THE SCANDAL OF JESUS

# MARK CLARK

ZONDERVAN
REFLECTIVE

ZONDERVAN REFLECTIVE

*The Problem of Jesus*
Copyright © 2021 by Mark Clark

Requests for information should be addressed to:
Zondervan, 3900 Sparks Dr. SE, Grand Rapids, Michigan 49546

Zondervan titles may be purchased in bulk for educational, business, fundraising, or sales promotional use. For information, please email SpecialMarkets@Zondervan.com.

ISBN 978-0-310-10830-6 (softcover)
ISBN 978-0-310-10832-0 (audio)
ISBN 978-0-310-10831-3 (ebook)

Author is represented by the FEDD Agency, Inc., Post Office Box 341973, Austin, Texas 78734.

*Cover design: FaceOut Studio*
*Cover image: Christ Weeping Over Jerusalem, Ary Sheffer / Wikipedia*
*Interior design: Denise Froehlich*

*Printed in the United States of America*

20 21 22 23 24 25 /LSC/ 10 9 8 7 6 5 4 3 2 1

*To my Bobbie,*

*The first one to tell me about, and more importantly, show me Jesus. Without you I would not have written this book, nor would I know the subject of it personally. It took years for me to care about Jesus, but you never gave up on me and, even now, as you come close to meeting him face to face, you never stop pursuing him. Whenever that day comes, know that I am right behind you and will see you soon.*

*Thank you for everything.*

# CONTENTS

# Foreword

## By Ray Johnston

In every generation, in every country, and tragically, in many churches there is always one problem with Jesus. Here it is.

The Jesus of the Bible is ignored.

Years ago, I saw this firsthand. As I landed in South Africa for a two-week speaking tour, the country was in complete turmoil. The air was filled with anticipation. Everything was new! Nelson Mandela was free. The constitution was being rewritten. Decades of suffocating apartheid were ending. Nobody knew what the future would hold, and at that moment Carol and I were getting off a plane in Cape Town to spend two tension filled weeks training pastors and leaders in South Africa's Dutch Reformed Churches.

Change was everywhere—except in the church. Carol and I found ourselves growing more and more depressed as we visited one lifeless, segregated, change-resistant church after another. Tradition reigned. Pastors were frustrated. Change looked impossible. And even the leaders were telling us, "It's a nightmare. Our church is stuck. It's hopeless!" And it was—a total disaster.

Then everything changed.

On our last weekend there, I was invited to preach at the largest Dutch Reformed Church in the country. We pulled into the parking lot expecting another dead, uptight, condemning, segregated, old-fashioned, tradition-driven church.

Instead, we were stunned! The atmosphere was electric.

We walked in and saw thousands of people joyfully worshiping together. The crowd was diverse, a mix of whites and blacks, teenagers and adults, rich and poor, all standing side by side singing in English and several other languages. I couldn't believe it. This place radiated unity and joy unlike anything we had seen in the rest of the country. Still in shock, I leaned over and elbowed the pastor. "How long have you been pastor of this church?

"Ten years," he said.

"Was it this way when you got here?"

"No, it was like every other church in the country."

I had to know what had happened, and I was afraid the song was about to end, so I got right to the point. "What happened?!"

The worship team began a new song, and he shared the whole story with me. He said the change took place with just one meeting. He walked into his first church board meeting, went to the head of the table where a chair was reserved for him, and turned to his leaders.

"I'm not sitting in that chair," he said. "No one will ever sit in that chair again. That's Jesus' chair. It's supposed to be his church. From what I can tell, this church has been running without him, and that's going to stop right now. Since it's his church, why don't we give it back to him? And since it's his church, from now on we will only ask one question—*what does Jesus want us to do?*

"Any decisions that have to be made from this point on will not be determined by South African culture or our own tradition or preferences. Beginning at this moment we are recommitting our lives and our church to Jesus, and from now on we will only do what Jesus wants to do!"

When it came to worship styles, how to reach teenagers, preaching methods, and every other defining issue of the day, he told me everyone had an opinion. But they came together and decided Jesus couldn't care less what their past preferences were. They looked to Scripture to hear the voice of Jesus and committed to move that direction regardless of the consequences. Two hundred years of cultural conditioning and church history were thrown right out the window—gone now and replaced by new life, fresh growth, and dramatic impact.

The pastor put his arm around my shoulder and continued, "None of our traditions or preferences mattered anymore," he said. "We just gave the church back to Jesus." Then he swept his arm across the still worshiping congregation and added, *"And this is just what Jesus wanted to do!"*

I have never recovered from that service.

I walked away from that courageous group of South African Christ-followers more convinced than ever that the greatest need of any person is to be confronted by those two questions:

1. *Who is Jesus?* and
2. *Does he want to have anything to do with my life?*

And we ask those questions because the greatest need of any Christian is to reconnect and rediscover the power unleashed by actually following the authentic Jesus.

My friend Mark Clark's brilliant new book, *The Problem of Jesus,* just might ignite the same thing on our continent! Mark is rapidly becoming the leading Christian apologist to the emerging generation. Why? Mark isn't afraid to tackle every hard question. He does exactly that in this new book by beginning with a warning of the internal crisis that comes from the "scandal" of Jesus. Then, he brilliantly presents Jesus from the perspectives of history, geography, economics, culture, religion, and more.

Mark is unafraid to tackle questions such as:

- Can we trust what's written in the Bible about Jesus?
- Is there a problem with science and Jesus' miracles?
- What is Christianity?
- Is discipleship just a grown-up version of basic Christianity?
- What are the barriers stopping people from following him?

Who Jesus is, why he causes problems when we confront him, and why that matters are all explored and expertly laid out in this book. I pray it will ignite hope in you as you read it. Mark gives a startling answer about halfway through this book. He writes, "There are many reasons why, but they all come down to one: we don't really believe that the best is yet to come. We lack faith that the future Jesus promises is real . . ."

As a former atheist—someone who once talked a guy *out* of becoming a Christian when I was eighteen (which does not look good on a pastor's resume)—I would call this book philosophical dynamite. It will help any skeptic think more deeply about Jesus. And no one lives well, loves well, and leads well until they think well. *The Problem of Jesus* will take your thinking about Jesus—and your relationship with him—to whole new levels. I recommend you devour this book, and then buy it for every atheist you know.

---

Ray Johnston is the founding and lead senior pastor of Bayside Church, Granite Bay, California; *Wall Street Journal* bestselling author of *The Hope Quotient*; and president of Thrive Communications, Inc.

# Acknowledgments

Stephen Thomson, my professor and friend. They say there is always one teacher we can look back on in our lives who shaped us in a significant way. Without a doubt, that teacher is you. You introduced me to the study of Jesus that this book presents and showed me how to live a life worthy of following him in all you did and didn't do in the face of the unspoken challenges you faced in those years.

We couldn't have known at the time, or maybe you did, that the hours spent together over meals and coffee both late into the night and in the early morning exploring the historical Jesus, what the Gospels were all about, and how to follow Jesus in the real world, would define the direction of my life. You showed me how to think and, in the end, that may be the greatest gift of all.

Beyond that you showed me how to live, and that is a gift I have always tried to live up to. "He's the most important," you said in your office one day when I asked you why you had so many books about Jesus.

Indeed.

Those were the most formative years of my life, and I can't thank you enough for all you gave me.

Thank you.

# INTRODUCTION

*And they took offense at him.*

—MATTHEW 13:57

The demons are in your closet," he said with a concerned look.

"Sorry, *what?*"

I had flown into Toronto from Vancouver to speak at a church conference and had agreed to meet with a local pastor for coffee. Our conversation was pretty normal, talking about our churches and learning more about his ministry, until he stopped—and rather abruptly asked me an odd question.

"Hey, I don't mean to sound weird," he said, "but I feel like I'm supposed to ask you a question: How are you liking the house your family lives in? Is it concerning you at all?"

An odd question, right? But that question sent a shiver down my spine. *Concerning me?* The answer, for reasons no one in the world could have known, was unequivocally *yes.*

This was at a time before we owned our first home. We had been renting several places over the past few years, and the most recent was hands-down our favorite. It was a beautiful home with lots of space for the girls to play and for hosting staff parties and community groups. However, after living there for a few weeks—and for the first time in my life—I began to sense what could only be described as a *presence.* I might be downstairs in the basement going over my sermon on a Saturday night and something would just feel off, not right. Or

I would wake up in the middle of the night and stare at our closet for several minutes, sure that someone was in there. I was often busy at work in my office writing my first book, *The Problem of God*, and for unexplained reasons I would need to abandon my writing, feeling cold and weirded out. I knew something was really off when, for four or five nights in a row, I woke up and sensed with absolute certainty that someone was in our house. I found myself walking around the main floor with a baseball bat in the middle of the night, convinced that someone was there, stalking us.

Another evening I was downstairs watching television in our living room. On the floor directly above me, I heard a chair being dragged across the floor, from one end of our bedroom to another. I called up to Erin to see what she was doing. Chillingly, she answered from ten feet behind me, "I am right here." I turned around to see her folding laundry.

"Were you upstairs just now?"

"No, I've been sitting here for half an hour." I checked on the girls, and they were all fast asleep. I checked our bedroom, and the only way I can describe the way it felt was cold and distant. Erin and I began to earnestly talk about the weird feelings we were experiencing in the house. This had happened just before I left for the conference in Toronto, and we had even discussed looking for another place.

So, there I now sat with this pastor, and he had asked me a question that was both seemingly innocent and oddly specific. "Well," I said casually, "It's a nice house, but we have been thinking of moving recently."

At that moment, the pastor started making an odd sound—sort of like a sneeze—and tipped his body forward.

I sat back and said, "God bless you."

He replied, "I am not sneezing. I am having a reaction to your house."

I sat there, stunned and a little confused. My mind was buzzing a mile a minute. I asked him to explain what he meant.

"I don't know—you tell me," he said, lurching forward again and sneezing loudly.

I looked to my left and right and lowered my voice. "As of late, the house has been rather unsettling to us." I reluctantly told him about a few of the things that had happened.

He nodded as I spoke, gave me a sympathetic smile, and then asked softly, "Do you want to know?"

I took a minute to think about it. *Know what?* I wondered. But then, I knew. I nodded.

"They are in your closet."

I can't forget those words, because they affirmed something I think I already knew but hadn't admitted, even to myself. *They?* It was an unsettling word.

"Demons?" I asked. It was sort of a question but more of a statement.

"Yes," he answered. He asked the barista for a piece of paper, pulled a pen from his bag, and began to sketch. "This may sound odd to you," he explained, "but I can see your house in my mind, and I can tell you where they are." He proceeded to draw the upstairs level of my house as accurately as if he'd seen a floor plan. "Your bedroom is here. Your closet is here. The wall for the walk-in closet is shared with your office, isn't it?"

"Yes."

"That's where they are. They were invited," he said. "They are sexual spirits. Violent."

I'll tell the rest of this story later in the book.

You see, there are *two* worlds in which we live. Two worlds in which we contend: the world of spiritual realities—that of the question of God, salvation, heaven, hell, joy, satisfaction, et cetera, and whether any of these have any legitimacy, or should be talked about anymore in our modern world and the world of our everyday existence: the world of family, work, sex, politics, raising kids. This book is about where those two worlds collide. This book is about the idea that, contrary to the fact that every day, from a thousand different angles, we are told that only one of those worlds (the latter) is something we should think about, care about, spend time on, and give our lives to, nothing could be further from the truth. Actually, those two worlds aren't all that different, aren't all that separate. And that they both find their meaning and significance, for all people—who live today and have ever lived—in one place, indeed, one person—Jesus of Nazareth.

While you may have picked up this book because it is a book about Jesus, in a sense it is more a book about *you*. It is about finding how your deepest desires in life—to flourish, to have joy and passion and pleasure—can be satisfied. It is about both the *quantity* of your life (What if I told you that you could live forever?), and the *quality* of your life (to live as well as you can), but in ways that might surprise you. It is about finding love and giving it away, finding satisfaction, happiness, and contentment beyond anything this world can give you or ever steal away. It is about finding the kinds of things that get you up in the morning. That put steel in your spine when the darkness takes over and you don't know if you can go on. This book tells you where to find that kind of resolve—that kind of joy worth fighting for, something nobody can take and no pain or challenge can diminish. In the end, while this book will challenge and confront you, it also will help you find your place in the world and comfort you in a world that doesn't offer much of any of that.

To get there, however, we must start not with us but with Jesus.

The story of Jesus' earthly life is a scandal from beginning to end. Who he was, what he said, what he did—and how his life and teachings continue to influence our modern world—is without a doubt the greatest of all scandals. This may sound odd to us today. In the modern Western world, Jesus of Nazareth is associated with many things, but scandal isn't one of them. He is a *nice guy*, a *good leader*, a *great teacher*, an *example of love*, but most of us don't find anything particularly scandalous about him. A scandalous person stirs the pot. They do something controversial. They violate norms and upset the status quo.

They say or do something that gets people talking around the water cooler, something that offends us, causing us to lean-in with fascination or recoil in horror. Scandal is front-page news kind of stuff. And that's not Jesus.

Or is it?

You may have grown up seeing Jesus on felt boards in Sunday school. Perfect white teeth, luxuriant hair, and smiling eyes. Bestselling books promote this picture of Jesus as an ancient hippy and self-help guru. Like the founders of other religions (Muhammad, Abraham, Buddha), Jesus taught eternal principles such as the Golden Rule and showed us a better way to be human by his example. He's kind, gentle, fun, and safe. "He just putters in his garden, smiles benignly, waves now and then, and mostly spends a lot of time in his room doing puzzles . . . as though he were a half-daft old uncle . . . a bit runny about the eyes, winking at our little pranks and peccadilloes."[1] Chuck Norris meets Tony Robbins meets Mr. Rogers. After all, Madonna and Justin Timberlake wear T-shirts calling Jesus their "Homeboy," Oprah Winfrey finds him an inspiration, and Brad Pitt "respects" him. What could be more watered down, easy to digest, and safe for the whole family, than that?

But what if this is all a big mistake? What if, instead, Jesus was a problem—a walking controversy? What if, wherever he went in life, from the day he was born until the day he died, he was followed by scandal? What if, instead of a nice guy and a safe guy, he was a disturber of the peace? A man many people didn't actually like. A man who challenged the status quo and made life less safe for the family and friends who orbited around him.

Over and over again the Bible tells us this is exactly what Jesus did:

They took offense (*skandalon*) at him. (Matthew 13:57)

"You will all fall away (*skandalizō*) because of me this night." (Matthew 26:31)

Aware that his disciples were grumbling about this, Jesus said to them, "Does this offend (*skandalizō*) you?" (John 6:61 NIV)

We preach Christ . . . a stumbling block (*skandalon*). (1 Corinthians 1:23)

This book explores why Jesus was such a scandal in the ancient world and what that scandal has to do with our lives today. As we will see, if Jesus is who he said he is, the fate of everyone who ever lived, and everyone alive today, is defined not by what they think of "God" or politics or religion or success or parenting or self-actualization or whatever, but by what they think of *him*.

A scandal indeed. But this type of scandal is different from the latest politician caught in adultery, or pastor stealing money from the coffers. It's a controversy worth leaning into rather than away from, it will bring life to you rather than steal life from you.

## Two Kinds of People

Jesus confronts, challenges, and comforts modern people in much the same way as he did ancient people, but there are also a few twists unique to our time and culture that we will explore throughout this book. The first one is that in the end—and maybe you will do this only after reading this book—we have to actually pick a side. Modern people have decided that there is a third way to respond to Jesus: neutral. They don't love him, they don't hate him. In the four Gospels—the biographies of Jesus—however, we find only two kinds of people: those who love, follow, and give their lives to Jesus, and those who hate, reject, and want to kill him. Those *were* the only two options. Those *are* the only two options. There is no third way. The "I like, respect, and value Jesus as a leader/teacher/example" route isn't on the table. Why? Because he doesn't allow it. If Jesus is not God as he claimed to be, then he is not a great teacher, leader, or example. He is a man who has led astray billions of people for thousands of years. As C. S. Lewis famously said, "A man who was merely a man and said the sort of things Jesus said would not be a great moral teacher. He would either be a lunatic . . . or he would be the devil of hell. . . . But let us not come with any patronizing nonsense about his being a great human teacher. He has not left that open to us.[2] Most people would prefer to live in the uncommitted middle, but that place doesn't exist.

The scandal of Jesus is that he creates a crisis in each of us. This book is about understanding that crisis and deciding what to do about it. It's an opportunity to stop and reflect on the claims of Jesus and how they come to define our lives. We will cover a little bit of everything about Jesus: from his existence to the Gospels that introduce us to his life and ministry, his parables, the question of whether he claimed to be God, his miracles, and his death and resurrection. In looking at each of these, we will discover some new things about Jesus—crazy, upside-down, challenging things that reframe Jesus in a way that changes everything for us and our lives as we live them.

The life and teachings of Jesus are more than just historical events we dust off and examine like artifacts in a museum. They alter reality, forcing us to rethink and reconfigure everything about our lives.

Such is the risk and the adventure of the problem of Jesus.

**Problem:** a question raised for inquiry, consideration, or solution; an intricate unsettled question.

# PART I

## The Problem of
# THE HISTORICAL JESUS

*The only people for me are the mad ones,
the ones who are mad to live, mad to talk,
mad to be saved, desirous of everything at the
same time, the ones who never yawn or say a
commonplace thing, but burn, burn, burn like
fabulous yellow roman candles exploding like
spiders across the stars.*

—JACK KEROUAC, ON THE ROAD

## CHAPTER 1

## Did Jesus Really
# EXIST?

I've only broken the law a few times in my life. But this time felt worth it.

I clutched the steering wheel in my hands as I drove—let's just say faster than the speed limit—all the way home from downtown Toronto to my house (an hour away, but I didn't have an hour). I screeched around the corner of my quiet suburb, barely stopping at the stop signs, flew into my driveway, ran up the steps to my front door, swung it open, and grabbed the binder off my kitchen table. "Thanks!" I yelled to my stepdad. He shouted, "Good luck!" behind me as I dashed back into the driver's seat and began to make the long trip back to exactly where I came from. But I was running out of time.

When I arrived, the class had already started. The professor, Stephen Thomson, was at the front welcoming the students. He gave me a look as I ran into the room, sweating and shaken. And then, as the classroom hushed, he said, "So please give Mark your undivided attention, as he is teaching today." The class looked at one another confused. No one other than the professor himself had taught this class before. *So why was someone else going to teach today? And why the twenty-year-old kid who smoked in front of the college every day?*

*And why was he sweating so much?*

Rewind the clock back a month. It was midway through the semester, and I was in my second year of Bible College. The class was the Gospel of John. Every student had turned in a paper on a passage in John 15 where Jesus used the metaphor of a vine and branches: "I am the vine; you are the branches. . . . If anyone does not abide in me he is thrown away" (John 15:5–6).

The professor had just handed back the papers, and as I grabbed mine, he paused. "Can I talk to you for a second, Mark?" That didn't sound good. Once the classroom cleared, he sat down on the desk. "I loved your paper," he said with a smile. "It was original in so many ways, I can't tell you."

I stared at him, waiting for the typical "however." Instead, he continued, "I see things in your paper—ideas and connections to the larger story—that I don't want to just take from you and teach. So, I want *you* to teach it."

I laughed, a little confused. "What do you mean?" I asked.

"I want you to teach the class this passage in a couple weeks. Prepare a lecture, an hour and a half or so, and teach us."

Again, I laughed. I thanked him for the vote of confidence but declined the offer. I was not going to stand up in front of my peers and exegete the Bible for them. Who was I?

As I walked away, I heard his voice behind me. "Mark, you are misunderstanding. I am not *asking* you. I am *telling* you: you are lecturing in two weeks: John 15. See you then." And he walked away.

For the next two weeks, I could barely sit still or keep a thought in my head. I was passionate about explaining the Bible to people, and I was excited for the opportunity, so I spent every moment preparing every word of that lecture. I was not going to mess this up! This was what I wanted to do with my life: scholarship, students, theology, and teaching. So, of course, on that very day, as I left my house for the long journey to school, lo and behold, I put the wrong binder in my bag. An hour before class began, I realized I had left my lecture at home.

And that is how I found myself standing—sweaty, shaking in fear, five minutes late—before my classmates. I opened my binder—the right one—and at the top it read: "John 15: The Vine and the Branches."

What was it about that paper that impressed my professor? Well,

over the course of that year, I had read several studies on the historical Jesus and had worked tirelessly to place Jesus *in the context of his
world* versus ours. What were the beliefs, stories, expectations, and
so on of the world Jesus entered, specifically, first-century Judaism.
As I did this, Jesus' teachings, actions, and life began to take on a
whole new meaning. What once seemed like a simple teaching on a
person's spiritual life became a subversive and challenging message
to the people of his day. For instance, my understanding of "abiding
in Jesus" had always been something sentimental and individualistic/
devotional. I thought Jesus was referring to activities like praying and
walking through the day in God's presence. That is what every sermon
I had heard on this passage was about.

However, in the original language (Greek/Aramaic) the word for
"abide" means "to remain." *Remain?* What could that mean? As I read
the chapters before and after John 15, I realized that he was wasn't
encouraging his followers to spend more time praying or reading their
Bibles; he was telling them that history was reaching a fork in the road
around what it meant to be the people of God. *Now it meant believing in Jesus as the climax of their own story versus what it had meant
for thousands of years*—and he wanted them to choose to *remain the
people of God* by accepting this new way. He was the Vine now. If, on
the other hand, they rejected him, they in turn would be rejected by
him; they would not "remain" the people of God.

This reading of a seemingly simple, traditional text of the New
Testament blew up my understanding of the Bible. It caused me, like
Alice, to go down a rabbit hole. Had I misinterpreted Jesus' entire life
and teachings? I share this as we begin, because this chapter addresses
what this whole book is trying to do in a sense: see and understand
Jesus in his context in order to see and understand the *real* Jesus.
That is the only Jesus I want to follow and listen to. In the end, as we
will see, it is a portrait that in some ways will affirm what traditional
Christianity has always understood about Jesus and, in other ways,
upend it altogether.

## The Historical Jesus

In his book *Seven Types of Atheism*, London School of Economics philosopher John Gray admits, "The Victorian debate between science and religion is best forgotten. A more serious challenge to Christianity comes *from history*. If Jesus was not crucified and did not return from the dead, the Christian religion is seriously compromised. The same is true if what Jesus taught was other than what Christians later came to believe. The real conflict is not between religion and science but between Christianity and history."[1]

This is why we must start with a *historical* rather than *theological* examination of Jesus. Before we can answer the challenges skeptics raise and assess the theological and practical impact of Jesus on our lives, we must answer the problem of history and show that the answer to Gray's question is that there is no conflict between history and Christianity.

The most popular challenges in this context from the secular culture that pervades the West center on (1) whether Jesus ever actually *existed*—which won't take up too much of our time because it's a pretty well settled dispute among scholars that he did—and (2) what he actually *meant* by what he said and did. This will take a bit more space but is a fascinating journey!

## Did Jesus Exist?

You might wonder if it is even necessary to ask, or answer, the question of whether Jesus ever actually existed, but over the last century a number of skeptics have argued that he didn't, challenging the very foundation of Christianity. In his essay "Why I Am Not a Christian," the atheist philosopher Bertrand Russell asserted, "Historically it is quite doubtful whether Christ ever existed at all."[2] Nineteenth-century writer Gerald Massey, in his work on Jesus, contended that "the Gospels do not contain the history of an actual man, but the myth of the God-man, Jesus, clothed in historical dress."[3] Massey believed Jesus was a made-up religious figure based on ancient Egyptian and Greek archetypes. On a popular level people like Bill Maher have proposed the same idea over and over again on his show and his film *Religulous.*

Is this a legitimate challenge? The short answer is no. Most historians writing about Jesus don't spend any time on this argument, not because it's not important, but because Jesus' existence is a settled matter. No historian today worth their salt questions the existence of Jesus of Nazareth. In the preface to his 741-page study of the historical Jesus, respected and celebrated historian N. T. Wright says, "I have taken it for granted that Jesus of Nazareth existed . . . against people who try from time to time to deny it. It would be easier, frankly, to believe that Tiberius Caesar, Jesus' contemporary, was a figment of the imagination than to believe that there never was such a person as Jesus."[4]

Even skeptics and critics of Christianity who approach the topic through a historical lens, like Bart D. Ehrman, agree that Jesus was a historical figure who really existed.[5] Nevertheless, the question is still raised today, so we will briefly examine the evidence. We will see that there is more historical evidence for the existence of Jesus than for any other religious founder, and for most anybody living in his time, including political rulers of Rome. This case can be made from a number of angles, but we'll look at just three: (1) mentions of Jesus *outside* the Bible, (2) mentions of Jesus *within* the Bible, and (3) the *experience of the early church* and what it tells us about Jesus' existence.

## Jesus outside the Bible

At least ten writers *outside of the Bible* mention Jesus by name.[6] These were not friends of Christianity, but rather first-century Jewish and Roman historians—most of whom operated with an *anti*-Christian agenda. Here are a few examples:

Nero fastened the guilt . . . on a class hated for their abomina-
tions, called Christians by the populace. Christus, from whom
the name had its origin, suffered the extreme penalty during the
reign of Tiberius at the hands of the procurator Pontius Pilatus.
(Tacitus, *Annals* 15.44)

On the eve of the Passover Yeshu was hanged. For forty days
before the execution took place, a herald . . . cried, "He is going
forth to be stoned because he has practiced sorcery and enticed
Israel to apostasy. (*The Babylonian Talmud,* vol. 3, Sanhedrin
43a, 281)[7]

About this time there lived Jesus, a wise man, if indeed one
ought to call him a man. For he . . . wrought surprising feats. . . .
He was the Christ. When Pilate . . . condemned him to be crucified, those who had come to love him did not give up their
affection for him. On the third day he appeared . . . restored
to life . . . and the tribe of Christians . . . has not disappeared.
(Josephus, *Antiquities of the Jews* 18.63–64)

Amazingly, besides the example above, Pontius Pilate, the Roman
governor of Judea at the time of Jesus, is not mentioned in any other
nonbiblical document from antiquity. The only other surviving reference to him mentions his name only because of the death sentence
he passed on Jesus.

These writers make the same claims about Jesus that are found in
the New Testament. In fact, even if we didn't have the New Testament
writings, we would be able to construct the following picture of Jesus
from these passages from secular history alone: Jesus was a Jewish
teacher, people believed he performed miracles and exorcisms, he
believed he was the Messiah, he was tried and crucified under Pontius
Pilate as a criminal during the reign of Tiberius, and despite his death,
his followers believed he was still alive and worshiped him as God.[8]

By historical standards that is an impressive amount of corroborating *extrabiblical* evidence with no underlying Christian agenda.

## Jesus within the Bible

The New Testament, and the Gospels in particular, assume the existence of Jesus. We will explore the question of the legitimacy of the Gospels exhaustively later in the book. For now we will just answer the question skeptics raise about the Gospels in regard to the question of Jesus' existence, namely, the idea that Matthew, Mark, Luke, and John are made-up stories—legends and myths about a made-up person called Jesus that a community of people wrote down to start a religion in his name. In other words, the authors weren't trying to record history but rather were telling "religious stories" to inspire people.

For a plethora of reasons, few historians believe this is the case. One reason is that they recognize standard *historiography*—the science of historical investigation—that is applied to other ancient documents should also be applied to the biblical records, and when this is done, the Gospels fare very well in regard to the question of their legitimacy. Historian Edwin Yamauchi argues that when we compare the records of other religious figures in history—for instance, Zoroaster, Buddha, and Muhammad—we have *better historical documentation* for the existence of Jesus than for any of these founders.[9]

If you were to read books such as *The Da Vinci Code* (which sold over eighty million copies worldwide!), you'd come away thinking the New Testament is an untrustworthy joke. But as New Testament scholar N. T. Wright says, this bias against the Bible as history is nothing more than "a cultural imperialism of the Enlightenment," an attitude that assumes it is only in the last two hundred years that we have discovered what "history" really is, "while writers in the ancient world were ignorant about these matters, freely making things up, weaving fantasy and legend together and calling it history."[10] The reality is, this is the opposite of true. The gospel writers cared immensely about history and facts from beginning to end.

## What's in a Name?

One of the ways the Gospels show themselves to have an interest in reality versus myth is that they cite hundreds of historical events, personalities, and geographic locations. At first blush, this may not stand out to modern readers—but it should. Several years ago, in his book *Jesus and the Eyewitnesses*, University of St. Andrews scholar Richard Bauckham explored "one phenomenon in the Gospels that has never been satisfactorily explained. . . . It concerns names."[11] He wrote, "Many characters [in the Gospels] are unnamed, but others are named" and that changes depending on which gospel you are reading. Why, for instance, would Mark name people and their family relations? He told us a guy named Simon from Cyrene carried the cross for Jesus, and that he was "the father of Alexander and Rufus" (15:21); Matthew and Luke, however, omitted the names of the sons. The same is the case with the blind beggar Bartimaeus. Mark told us not only his name, but that he was the "Son of Timaeus" (10:46). By conducting a detailed analysis of all of the instances in which the gospel writers cited people's names, coupled with when, where, and to whom those gospels were written, Bauckham arrived at the following conclusion: "I want to suggest now the possibility that many of these named characters were *eyewitnesses* who not only originated the traditions to which their names are attached but also continued to tell the stories [of Jesus] as authoritative guarantors of their traditions."[12]

In other words, the writers named names because they expected their readers to personally know certain people within the stories they were telling. Why? To root their story around real people, thus if their audience had questions, they could themselves confirm the details and facts! This is, by definition, the opposite of how one crafts a myth.

This is the practice of *historical verification*. Uniquely among ancient texts, the Gospels put us in direct touch with the eyewitnesses of Jesus rather than anonymous people or fictitious figures of later generations. The Gospels then are "the testimony of the eyewitnesses, not via a long period of community transmission but through, in many cases, immediate access to the eyewitnesses, or in other cases, probably no more than one intermediary."[13]

## Not Wrong, Just Different

Historians also see a kind of credibility in the subtle *discrepancies* (the supposed contradictions) in the Gospel accounts. Take, for instance, the resurrection stories. German historian Hans Stier observes that when narratives like the resurrection story display agreements over basic details coupled with differences (such as how many angels were at the tomb, what exactly was said, both of which differ depending on the Gospel one is reading), this is, for the historian, a "criterion of extraordinary *credibility*" not the opposite. He explains, "For if that were the fabrication of a congregation or of a similar group of people, then the tale would be consistently and obviously completely" free of discrepancies.[14] Somewhat ironically, small discrepancies within the Gospels—reasons skeptics choose not to believe the Bible—are cited by historians as legitimate reasons to believe it!

Even Bart D. Ehrman admits it would be a mistake to conclude that any differences in the documents were made by copyists trying to fabricate stories. Most of the variations, he says, were omissions or slips of the pen, and they don't in any way affect major or even minor doctrine within Christianity.[15] Instead, we find legitimate discrepancies that lend credibility to the accounts because the Gospel authors (1) made no attempt to harmonize all the information/details, (2) included material that cast Jesus in a negative light, (3) left many difficult passages within the texts, (4) identified women eyewitnesses of the resurrection in a patriarchal culture, (5) challenged their readers to check the history for the themselves (see also 1 Corinthians 15:6), and (6) included more than *thirty* historical people in their stories who have been verified by history outside the Bible.[16] In other words, if you were creating myths and trying to lead people to adopt your personal stories as true, you would avoid all six of these things. Yet the gospel writers intentionally included them, evidence that they were reporting on true, verifiable events.

## Persecution (and Dinosaurs)

Another reason scholars trust in the existence of Jesus is the bleak reality of the *persecution of the early church*. Many of the earliest followers of Jesus were tortured and killed as a direct result of their claims about him—namely, that he was the long-awaited Messiah, a prophet, and the true Lord of the world. They were burned on stakes for these claims, torn apart by lions, sawed in half, and tortured in other ways devised by Rome to threaten enemies of the state—which is what they were seen as because of their claims. It wouldn't make much sense for the early Christians to willingly suffer this way if Jesus had never existed. What motivation would they have to die like this and for this? What reason would they have to make up Jesus, take the time and energy to establish all the stories about him as oral tradition, painstakingly write them all down and make copies, travel long distances to pass the information along, and devote their lives and resources to spread this message? If the message were false, would they have claimed its truth even unto death, submitting to brutal torture all for a lie *they* had made up?[17]

Skeptics may not believe in the resurrection. They can dismiss something because they "don't believe in miracles" or "because people don't rise from the dead." The duty of historians, however, is to honestly examine all available facts and then report them. In reporting on the early church, historians have sought to explain its rise and accurately determine what the group said about itself. And they have discovered that the early church formed itself as a community of people worshiping a man they believed was God—a claim that was scandalously offensive, both politically and religiously.

Some skeptics may consider these arguments for the existence of Jesus and say, "Well, this evidence is fragmented and inconclusive. It doesn't prove beyond a shadow of a doubt that Jesus existed." This is true in a sense, but that's true of any historical study. All history—not to mention all science, philosophy, psychology, and all knowledge itself—is fragmentary and inconclusive. That doesn't mean we abandon the pursuit of understanding and the attainment of accurate knowledge. Fragmentary knowledge of fossil evidence, for instance, does not hinder scientists from believing in dinosaurs and reconstructing an entire framework to explain our geological past. All knowledge is limited, but it can still be deemed *adequate*. The key issue when studying anything, including Jesus, is not whether evidence is fragmentary but whether it is *representative* and correctly interpreted. And if you are looking to explain the writings of the Gospels and the rise of the early church using the rules of historical inquiry, the existence of a real man named Jesus makes the most sense of the data we have. As the late I. Howard Marshall, professor emeritus at the University of Aberdeen, pointed out, "It is not possible to explain the rise of the Christian church or the writing of the Gospels and the stream of tradition that lies behind them without accepting the fact that the founder of Christianity actually existed."[18]

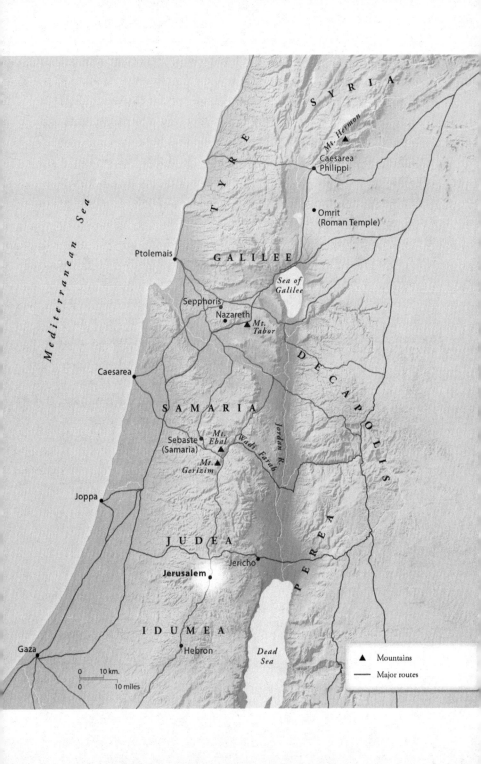

*Mediterranean Sea*

S Y R I A

T Y R E

Mt. Hermon ▲

Caesarea
Philippi ●

Omrit ●
(Roman Temple)

Ptolemais ●

G A L I L E E

Sea of
Galilee

Sepphoris ●

Nazareth ●
▲ Mt.
Tabor

D E C A P O L I S

Caesarea ●

S A M A R I A

Sebaste ● ▲ Mt.
(Samaria)   Ebal

Wadi Farah

Jordan R.

▲ Mt.
Gerizim

Joppa ●

J U D E A

Jericho ●

Jerusalem ●

P E R E A

I D U M E A

Gaza ●

Hebron ●

Dead
Sea

0    10 km.
0    10 miles

▲   Mountains

——  Major routes

# CHAPTER 2

## What Jesus Was

# ALL ABOUT

Jesus was named by his parents after an angel appeared to his father, Joseph, and said that his betrothed, Mary, would give birth to a son. "You shall call his name Jesus, for he will save his people from their sins" (Matthew 1:21), the angel instructed. The name Jesus means "God is salvation." As best we can tell, Jesus, had four brothers and a number of sisters. He was part of an agrarian society, likely part of the working or lower class, and he never traveled more than a few hundred miles from his home. "He never held a political office, never wrote a book, never married [and] never attended college."[1] Matthew and Luke agree that Jesus was born in Bethlehem, which is in Judea near Jerusalem, about an hour's drive. They also agree that Jesus grew up in a little town called Nazareth, in the northern part of Israel, in Galilee (Nazareth is sixty-four miles north of Jerusalem). It was "a dumpy, rural hick town not unlike those today where guys change their own oil, think pro wrestling is real, and eat a lot of Hot Pockets."[2]

As you read the Gospels, you will notice that Jesus spent most of his life and ministry in Galilee, a region known for fishing and rural life, and not down in Judea, the center of religious life, where Jerusalem and the temple were located, and thus where the most elite religious scholars were). This distance from Jerusalem is an interesting reality in and of itself given what Jesus was trying to do. New Testament scholar R. T. France points out: *Economically,* Galilee offered better agricultural and fishing resources than the more mountainous Judea, "making the wealth of some Galileans the envy of their southern neighbors." *Culturally,* Judeans despised their northern cousins, their lack of

Jewish sophistication compounded by their greater openness to non-Jewish influence. *Linguistically*, Galileans spoke a distinctive form of Aramaic whose "slovenly consonants (they dropped their aitches!) were the butt of Judean humor." *Religiously*, they were viewed as lax in their observance of proper ritual (a result of their distance from the temple and the theological leadership in Jerusalem). France pointed out that because all of this was true, Jesus didn't make a good candidate at all for a great religious leader, teacher, and certainly not the Messiah! "Even an impeccably Jewish Galilean . . . was not accepted among his own people; he was as much a foreigner as an Irishman in London or a Texan in New York. His accent would immediately mark him out as 'not one of us,' and all the prejudice of the supposedly superior culture of the capital city [of Jerusalem] would stand against his claim to be heard even as a prophet, let alone as the Messiah."[3]

As a Galilean, Jesus did not naturally fit in with the elites in the capital city and the culture of the religious leadership. All of this sets the stage for the key question all of us, Christians and skeptics, must face: What did this Galilean teacher say, teach, and do that so changed the world? And, just as important, what did it all actually mean? To these two questions we now turn.

## A Marginal Jew

Throughout history the church has developed a very thorough answer to the question "Why did Jesus die?" but in many ways has provided a far less helpful answer to the question "Why did Jesus live?" Modern Christians have not done much better. But the question will not go away. To simply "give some shrewd moral teaching to the world? . . . We may be forgiven for thinking [that] a little lame. It also seems quite untrue to Jesus' own understanding of his vocation and work."[4]

So why did he live? What was the meaning of his life? To best answer that question, we need to locate him within his world—that of first-century Judaism. When we do, we see everything he was saying and doing in a new light. In his groundbreaking book on Jesus' parables, Kenneth Bailey pointed out that when an Englishman tells the tale of King Arthur and Camelot to his countrymen, everyone knows exactly how the characters are expected to act. Knights obey the king, they carry out daring quests, and they rescue damsels in distress. "Likewise," said Bailey, "castles, dark forests, and so on, are never explained but are simply assumed as familiar images. This pool of shared expectations and stock figures constitutes the 'grand piano' upon which the English story teller deftly plays." He then asks his reader to imagine the following: "[Picture] an Englishman telling the same story about Sir Lancelot to Alaskan Eskimos. Obviously, the music of the 'grand piano' will not be heard, because the piano is in the minds of the English listeners who share a common culture and history with the story teller. In the case of the parables of Jesus, we are the Eskimos."[5]

What Bailey said about the parables also applies when we seek to understand the teachings of Jesus more generally. Jesus did not show up like an alien dropping out of the sky, teaching general "spiritual truths" and performing miracles to show he was different. "The historical jigsaw must portray Jesus as a credible and recognizable first-century Jew, relating comprehensively in speech and action to other first-century Jews."[6] In other words, without a proper understanding of Jesus' world, we misunderstand him in both small and significant ways. As we will see, some interpretations, long held to be self-evident, may not at all be what Jesus intended by his life or teachings.

## Nazi Jesus and the End of the World

Locating Jesus in his original context is paramount for two reasons. First, it works against a dangerous temptation we all have: making Jesus in our own image and using him for whatever agenda we need him for. This was the essential warning given by German theologian Ernst Käsemann (1906–98) during the rise of Nazism. Countering the historical reconstructions of Jesus that reflected the personalities and policies of post–World War I German culture and the Third Reich, Käsemann insisted that a Jesus not earthed in history could be pulled in any direction. Such a Jesus could be made into the hero of any theological or political program. "Käsemann had in mind especially the various Nazi theologies which had been able, in the absence of serious Jesus-study in pre-war Germany, to construct a largely *unJewish* Jesus."[7] This non-Jewish portrait helped set the course for the atrocities of World War II against the Jewish people.

In other words, if we fail to acknowledge and understand Jesus' historical setting, we will inevitably twist his agenda and message in light of our own. To medieval Catholics Jesus became the founder of the institution called "the Church," along with its established hierarchies. To Protestants he became the revolutionary against such staunch, institutional "religion." To socialists he became the one who prized community over the individual. To capitalists he became the founder of free enterprise ("give to Caesar that which is Caesar's"). To the Anabaptists he became an example of "enemy love" and pacifism. And on and on, right up to today's pet agendas and movements. Some of these are relatively benign portraits of Jesus, while others have led to grave misunderstandings and even oppression and tragedy.

We all face a similar temptation. We must do the work of locating Jesus in *his* setting so we don't make the mistake of adapting him to ours. Jesus was not a twenty-first-century, middle-class, white North American. Nor was he a rural Chinese farmer or a new age guru. He was not a communist, a capitalist, or a social justice warrior. He was not a Democrat or a Republican, a liberal or a conservative. He was a first-century Galilean Jew who spoke and lived like his contemporaries—but with an explosive message for all people, in every time and place, including you.

A second reason we must locate Jesus in his setting is because if we can't understand what his message *was*—what he was doing and saying in his time and place—we can't understand what his message actually *is*—to us in our time and place. Our first step therefore must be to *enter into his world* the best we can. That is a key interpretive move to get at what Jesus was all about. This is something often misunderstood by modern Christians, but must be: his life and teachings cannot mean something his listeners would not understand.

For example, take the destruction caused by some scholars when they misunderstand how apocalyptic literature (for instance, the book of Revelation) works, reading it like a modern Western rationalist versus a first-century Jew. Skeptics over the centuries have attempted to discredit Jesus by pointing out his mistaken prophecy regarding the end of the world (i.e., that it would occur in his lifetime or shortly after). The accusation is made that Jesus couldn't have been who he said he was because he was wrong about the end of the world. After all, during his ministry he had said, "The sun will be darkened, and the moon will not give its light, and the stars will be falling from heaven . . . the Son of Man coming in clouds. . . . *This generation* will not pass away until all these things take place" (Mark 13:24–30).

The famous and much-celebrated scholar Albert Schweitzer (1875–1965) said this was proof that Jesus was a failed prophet who believed the end of the world would come about *imminently* ("*this* generation"), and alas, it did not. I ran into this argument studying theology as a skeptic in my college days, and found it very disturbing. In response I did a deep study of every passage in which Jesus referenced the so-called end of the world (Matthew 24:4–44; Mark 13:5–27; Luke 21:10–28), and I remained bothered until I learned that the mistake was not one Jesus made—it's one we make. We project our own ways of thinking onto the words of Jesus in a way that violates their original meaning. In this passage, similar to how we read the book of Revelation, we wrongly read apocalyptic literature and apocalyptic statements. We read such passages *literally*, looking for the melting of the moon, the falling of the stars, the breakdown of the physical cosmos, and a man riding down on a cloud. However, that's not how apocalyptic literature works: instead, *it is used to invest historical events with their theological significance.*[8] Like describing the fall of the Berlin Wall as an "earth shattering event." In a thousand years from now one might mistakenly take that to mean that an earthquake had caused the collapse of the wall, which of course would be to misunderstand how language works.[9] In the passages cited above then, Jesus was predicting the destruction of the temple (answering their question; Mark 13:1–4), an event that really occurred thirty-five years later in AD 70. No first-century Jew would have interpreted Jesus' words as a prophecy about the melting of the actual space-time universe and the "end of the world" in the sense that we mean. Instead, as Oxford scholar G. B. Caird explained,

> Here as in the book of Daniel . . . the coming of the son of man on the clouds of heaven was never conceived as a primitive form of space travel, but as a symbol for a mighty reversal of fortunes *within history* and at the national level. . . . How odd of Mark, say the critics, to append to a question about a *historical* crisis [when the destruction of the temple would occur; Mark 13:4] a discourse which is an answer to an *eschatological* [end of the world] crisis! But supposing Mark was right! Supposing the prediction of the coming of the son of man on the clouds of heaven really *was* an answer to the disciple's question about the date of the fall of Jerusalem! Is it indeed credible that Jesus, the heir to the linguistic and theological riches of the prophets, and himself a greater theologian and master of imagery than them all, should ever have turned their symbols into flat and literal prose?[10]

Jesus was tapping into his prophetic role, speaking with precise metaphorical, not literal, language. His statements are a prediction of the destruction of the temple, but they are commentary on the thing behind the thing, the theological/religious meaning of that destruction. And his prediction was fulfilled in AD 70: Rome destroyed the temple, decimating the center of Israel's religious life. This event, Jesus was saying, was to be interpreted as God's judgment on unfaithful Israel, which is why it had to come on *"this* generation" (Mark 13:30, italics mine): *the generation that rejected the Son* whom God had sent (see Mark 12:1–12, the parable Jesus told just before). In other words, Jesus wasn't a failed prophet who wrongly predicted the end of the world in his generation. He was right in precisely the way he meant to be.

## Israel in Person

Once we see Jesus in light of first-century Judaism rather than modern Western thought, his whole life and all he did and taught comes alive in fresh and colorful ways.

For instance, he called his first disciples. How many were there? *Twelve.* Modern readers tend to pass over this detail, but no Jewish person reading the Gospels would miss it. The people of God had been organized into twelve tribes since Genesis 48 (Jacob, later called Israel, and his twelve sons). In choosing twelve disciples to surround him, Jesus was symbolically reconstituting the identity of God's people, Israel, around himself. He was saying to the world, "I am bringing about a renewal of Israel and thus the whole world. The story of God's people has reached its climax in me."

What did Jesus do immediately before choosing his twelve disciples? He got baptized and then underwent temptations in the wilderness (Mark 1:9–13). This sounds pretty straightforward to most of us until we look at it with first-century Jewish eyes. The central salvation story for a Jewish person was the exodus story—when God set Israel (whom he calls his "son") free from slavery in Egypt, bringing them through the waters of the Red Sea and into the wilderness to wander for forty years before reaching the promised land. We are told that when Jesus was baptized, he came *up through the waters*, a voice declared that he was God's beloved "Son," whom he called out of Egypt (Matthew 2:15); and then he went into the wilderness for *forty* days. Here is what a first-century Jewish person would understand from these details:

- Jesus was tempted in the desert by Satan, reenacting Israel's forty years of failure in the wilderness, facing constant temptation to be faithless to God.
- Jesus succeeded each time, citing a passage from Deuteronomy (the Old Testament book containing the story of Israel in the desert for forty years; see Matthew 4:1–11).
- Jesus began his ministry in Matthew with blessings (called *beatitudes*; 5:1–11) and ended it with curses (called *woes*; 23:13–36), just like Moses laid out for Israel as they entered the Promised Land (Deuteronomy 28–30).
- Jesus presented his atoning work as the true and better Passover at the Last Supper. He identified this thousands-year-old meal, which included bread and wine commemorating God setting Israel free from slavery, with himself. He said the elements were his body and his blood. He then sang a song, just as Israel did immediately following the exodus (Exodus15:1–18; Matthew 26:26–30).

In the Gospel of John, the stories of Jesus turning water into wine and cleansing the temple are told back to back (John 2:1–22). These stories are recounted together by John to make a theological point, one that is best understood in light of the context again of first-century Judaism. The water jars that held the water-turned-wine were used, John tells us, "for the Jewish rites of purification" (John 2:6). John wanted us to see the *meaning* of the event: that this stage of salvation history, the one Jesus was bringing about, was connected to but superseded Israel's story. The very next story makes the same point. Jesus went to the temple, the central symbolic place of Jewish life, and said it would be destroyed, but that three days later it would rise. John shared the deeper meaning behind Jesus' words: that "he was speaking about the temple of his body" (John 2:21). In other words, Jesus wasn't just making a random prediction. He was making a theological statement, namely, that he had come to bring the true and better temple.

Jesus presented himself as the bread and the water in the desert that Israel ate during their wandering (John 4–6); as the "light of the world" (John 8:12), which was a designation specifically for Israel since the time of the prophets (Isaiah 42:6); and as the "true vine" (John 15:1), which was how Israel saw themselves (Psalm 80:8–9). The Gospels are littered with such examples, and once one has the basic framework built, they jump off almost every page: Jesus consciously putting himself in the role of Israel. He made it clear that he was bringing Israel's story to a close, or rather, to a new and final phase, one that would be redrawn to include Jews and Gentiles alike. The long-awaited *new* Exodus, spoken of by the Jewish prophets, whereby the whole world was being offered freedom not from slavery in Egypt but from Satan, sin, and death, was now happening in and through him.

## The Kingdom of God

Knowing that we need to understand certain historical or theological frameworks about the world Jesus stepped into in order to fully understand him, we can now ask and answer an important controlling question about the life and teachings of Jesus—namely, if there was *one* thing we get right to help us better understand his life and message, what would it be? I believe the one concept that is misunderstood by modern people that holds the key to understanding most everything Jesus said and did in both his life and death is the concept of the *kingdom of God*.

Jesus was a first-century Jewish teacher (or rabbi) and a prophet. In this context Jesus remained true to most of the core convictions of Judaism. He didn't abandon them to teach a completely new religion, but rather filled them out, redefined them, expanded them, and brought them to a climax. Arguably these are the three most essential of those ideas:

- Monotheism—the idea that there is only one God
- Election—the belief that Israel is God's chosen people

- Eschatology—an understanding of the end of God's created purposes wherein God would return to Zion, defeat evil, bring about forgiveness of sin, the restoration of all things, the resurrection from the dead, healing, shalom, and the salvation of the world, including both Jews and Gentiles.[11]

The reality was that "first-century Jews looked forward to a public event in and through which their god would reveal to all the world that he was not just a local, tribal deity, but the creator and sovereign of all."[12] In other words, God's rule/reign would break into the world in a special way and through a special person (the true King/Messiah) to put the world to rights.

This long-awaited great and climactic day/moment of history (eschatology), this intervention that would redefine who the one true people of God were (election) and in a sense who God was (monotheism), could be summarized in one phrase: the coming of the "kingdom of God." And this is precisely what Jesus was claiming to bring. This was, in fact, his central message. This is where Christians today often miss what Jesus was about. Christians often say Jesus was primarily about "dying for people's sins," or people being "born again," or "doing justice," or "loving others." But taken in isolation these answers miss the mark. Jesus' life and message were primarily about *the kingdom of God*!

> [Jesus] went throughout all Galilee, teaching in their synagogues and proclaiming the **gospel of the kingdom** and healing every disease and every affliction among the people. (Matthew 4:23)

> Jesus came into Galilee, proclaiming the gospel of God, and saying, "The time is fulfilled, and **the kingdom of God** is at hand; repent and believe in the gospel." (Mark 1:14–15)

> [Jesus] said to them, "I must preach the good news of **the kingdom of God** to the other towns as well; for I was sent for this purpose." (Luke 4:43)

Jesus answered, "My **kingdom** is not of this world. . . . You say
that I am a king. For this purpose I was born and for this purpose
I have come into the world." (John 18:36–37)

New Testament scholar Norman Perrin was not overstating the
case when he concluded, "The central aspect of the teaching of Jesus
was that concerning the Kingdom of God . . . all else in his message and ministry serves a function in relation to that proclamation
and derives its meaning from it."[13] In his work on the historical Jesus,
Mortimer Arias pointed out that it is impossible to read the first three
Gospels without encountering the "kingdom of God" every few lines.
The term is repeated no less than 122 times—90 of which come from
Jesus' own lips![14] As James D. G. Dunn says, "The centrality of the
kingdom of God in Jesus' preaching is one of the least disputable,
or disputed, facts about Jesus."[15] It is the content of his teaching, his
explanation for why he heals, casts out demons, and tells parables
("The kingdom of God is like . . ."). In other words, we are on firm
ground in concluding that Jesus' primary identity was that of a prophet
proclaiming the arrival of the kingdom of God.[16]

But what did Jesus mean by the kingdom of God? Once we locate
Jesus in his first-century Jewish context, we find he wasn't talking about
"going to heaven when we die" as modern Christianity has popularized for generations. Rather, his message would have been understood
this way: First, Jesus was referring to the *reign* or *rule* of God and how
it was playing out in relationship to the world. He was telling a story
with a range of meanings, addressing the fundamental questions of the
universe and human life in general. This is a story that included God's
creation, creation's corruption by human sin, the choosing of Israel to
restore the world, the slavery of Egypt, and the events of Mount Sinai
and the Promised Land. Furthermore, it included a description of how
God was ruling through a kingship (David and the kings that followed),
God's choice of Jerusalem, the preaching of the prophets to a disobedient
Israel, the Babylonian exile, and the promise of future restoration.

The long-awaited "reign" of God would dawn on the world through the forgiveness of sins, the defeat of evil, the end of exile for Israel, and the return of God to Zion. As Ben F. Meyer says in his classic *The Aims of Jesus*, "this pithy phrase [the kingdom of God], which might easily be mistaken for a trite technical formula in Jesus' usage, was inevitably charged with his own religious intentionality: his existential understanding of God (i.e., of how he himself related to God) and his understanding of God's will for the world and his activity in it at this moment."[17]

Jesus' life and ministry was nothing less than the announcement of the arrival of *a new world*—and he was boldly saying that he was the One ushering it in. "If it is by the finger of God that I cast out demons, then the kingdom of God has come upon you" (Luke 11:20) he declared. He "believed that he was the prophet of the last day whom God had appointed to usher in the kingdom. He thought of this kingdom as continuous with the ancient covenants that God had made with Israel, but he also conceived of his activity as something new and restorative."[18]

By this point, we are beginning to answer the question we asked earlier: Why did Jesus live? *To bring about the climactic moment of salvation for the world* as the long-awaited fulfillment of history. He lived to do the work of the long-awaited Messiah, identifying himself as such through his teachings, healings, meals with sinners, actions in the temple, death on the cross, and resurrection. These actions were done as the fulfillment of "messianic expectations" but often in a fresh and unexpected way, so much so that those who knew the Bible the best rejected Jesus the hardest.

## Healing and Welcome

Jesus' understanding that he was the one bringing this kingdom reality to the world was clear in his teachings, but it was also demonstrated through his *actions and deeds*. Jesus' healings served a greater purpose than illustrating his divinity or desire to "help people," though they did that, too, of course. They were his announcement to the world that God was breaking through the veil in a special way. This is why when John the Baptist asked if he should look for another end-time prophet or if Jesus was the one he had been waiting for, Jesus quoted Isaiah 35:5–6, one of the most well-known Old Testament texts that speaks of the great end-time moment wherein "the blind receive their sight and the lame walk, lepers are cleansed and the deaf hear, and the dead are raised up, and the poor have good news preached to them" (Matthew 11:5). The healings were an indication that this great kingdom moment had at long last arrived! "Every physical healing pointed back to a time in Eden when physical bodies did not go blind, get crippled, or bleed nonstop for twelve years—and also pointed forward to a time of re-creation to come."[19]

Yet the healings were even more than restorations of sick people. Once understood in light of the Old Testament and the social world of Jesus' time, they were symbolic of outsiders being restored and welcomed back into the newly constituted people of God. "In addition to the physical burden of being blind, or lame, or deaf, or dumb, such a Jew was blemished, and unable to be a full Israelite."[20] Jesus' healings were a way of welcoming such people into the people of God. Society at that time (much like today) had many boundaries, and the authorities believed people attained (and maintained) holiness by separation from unclean people and objects. They avoided lepers, menstruating women, corpses, people with unclean spirits, impure food, and other such things.

The arrival of God's reign in Jesus shattered this orientation, for as we see, Jesus interacts with all of these categories of people and heals and reverses their afflictions. In Jesus, God was now actively spreading holiness and wholeness, redrawing covenant membership in the people of God around Jesus. This made Jesus come into direct confrontation with the leaders who were guarding the boundaries; his life declaring that God now sought to overcome and dismantle the hardened walls that were keeping people out.[21] Jesus challenged what they held dear, and implied a deep truth that modern people miss but first-century Jews would not have: "the expectation of the restored *land* [had] become focused on restored *human beings*."[22] Oh that the world would see this as one of the staggering implications of Jesus' life and ministry!

## What Is Christianity Then?

Some, upon discovering Jesus' *kingdom* focus, have argued that if this is true, it *opposes* our traditionally held Christian beliefs—things like the forgiveness of sins, substitutionary atonement, and justification by faith. They say these doctrines are not found in Jesus' teachings (that they are Paul's ideas) or at least not central to Jesus' message. But this is an overcorrection, a result of either/or thinking instead of both/and. As Cambridge University's Simon Gathercole has shown, Jesus' kingdom message includes these concepts through and through. Justification by faith, for instance, is a central teaching in Jesus' parables (Luke 10:25–37; 18:9–14), and the forgiveness of sins and substitution is littered throughout his teachings. For instance, Jesus taught that the "Son of man did not come to be served but to serve and *to give his life as a ransom for many*" (Mark 10:45, italics mine).[23] Jesus was dying "for" people, in their place, a clear reference to substitution for the forgiveness of sins. Concepts as clear as day when you are looking for them.

And when we turn to the story of Israel in the Old Testament, we find that this personal ransom to save sinners was always central to the expectations of Israel. Most of the stories where Jesus is said to be acting for the forgiveness of sinners (Mark 2:1–12; Luke 7:36–50; 15:11–32) "have to do with sinners who are not only alienated from God but also *socially* ostracized."[24] In other words, these stories are saying more than we might think if we are limiting ourselves to a Western, individualized sense of forgiveness. In context, they are signs that history has reached its climax and the people of God are no longer to be defined by ethnicity or geography. *All people* willing to come under the rule of God through the person and work of Jesus are welcome. Any difference between the teaching of Jesus and Paul can be attributed more to the idea that Jesus was declaring the arrival of the kingdom and Paul was applying the implications of such a reality to local churches and their mission in the world. Jesus was declaring the kingdom, while Paul was declaring the King!

To become a "Christian," then, is to become someone who embraces the *rulership of God* through the person and work of Jesus in their life. That rule applies to every part of us: our souls but also our thought lives, our handling of money, our sex lives, our family relationships, our work, and so on. The goal of biblical conversion in this way is holistic. As Jim Wallis has said, it's "not to save 'souls' apart from history but to bring the kingdom of God into the world with explosive force; it begins with individuals but is for the sake of the world. Conversion in the New Testament can only be understood from the perspective of the kingdom of God. . . . The call to conversion in the Gospels arose directly out of the fact of an inbreaking new order. To be converted to Christ meant to give one's allegiance to the kingdom."[25]

## Jesus as Unique among the Options

This message about the arrival of the kingdom was very controversial at the time of Jesus. What made it uniquely offensive, however, is that Jesus wasn't calling for a general sort of repentance or a call for people to "believe in God" again, like many today say is the answer to the decline in values in our culture—though that of course is important and arguably a central reason for many of the social challenges we see today (see the latest arguments from thinkers like David Berlinski, in his *The Devil's Delusion*; he is a secular Jewish philosopher/scientist who sees a connection between many of our social ills and atheism, especially in the realm of the question of meaning). Instead of a generic call like that, Jesus was offering something far more scandalous: membership in the new people of God "on his *own authority* and by *his own process*."[26] That's what made it all so scandalous and put him in direct conflict with every part of Judaism.

The Sadducees, the Essenes, the Pharisees, and the Zealots were the four major sects of Judaism during Jesus' time on earth. The Sadducees believed they could bring in God's kingdom through *political* power. Jesus rejected this outright and claimed that political power oppresses those who desire nothing more than to experience God; it is the meek who will eventually experience the kingdom. The Essenes believed they could bring about the kingdom by *removing* themselves from the sinful world around them, yet Jesus challenged Israel to be salt and light in the world, preserving the goodness and penetrating darkness and evil. His people were to be "in the world but not of it." The Pharisees thought they could usher in the kingdom by being *religiously* faithful to the Law; Jesus challenged that idea by exposing how one could be faithful to laws but still be empty and rotten inside—knowing about God but still going to hell. The Zealots' attempt was to *revolt* and commit violence toward their oppressors, yet Jesus called his followers to love our enemies and pray for those who persecute us, turning the other cheek and walking a second mile when forced to walk only one.

With so many options available to a faithful and concerned Jewish person, Jesus' ministry did what all good prophetic ministries do: it subverted the stories, beliefs, and actions of these movements and replaced them with something better. Jesus' vision offered both prophetic *critique* and prophetic *hope* that supplanted the others. Jesus and his kingdom message were unique in the marketplace of ideas—and that scandalous uniqueness proved deadly for him.

# PART II

---

## The Problem of
# THE GOSPELS

*The secret of the Great Stories is that they have no secrets. The Great Stories are the ones you have heard and want to hear again. They don't deceive you with thrills and trick endings. They don't surprise you with the unforeseen. They are as familiar as the house you live in. Or the smell of your lover's skin. You know how they end, yet you listen as though you don't. In the way that although you know that one day you will die, you live as though you won't. In the Great Stories you know who lives, who dies, who finds love, who doesn't. And yet you want to know again. That is their mystery and their magic.*

—Arundhati Roy, The God of Small Things

# CHAPTER 3

# What Are the
# GOSPELS?

O kay, don't freak out at what I'm about to tell you.

You may have memorized the Lord's Prayer and might even recite it regularly in church. If so, you are familiar with the last lines: "For yours is the kingdom and the power and the glory forever and ever. Amen." Jesus probably never said that. Someone made that up and put it in later. While we are at it, not to ruin all the signs people hold up at football games, he most likely did not say the most famous words in history that are ascribed to him either: "For God so loved the world, that he gave his only Son" (John 3:16). And it's likely Jesus healed that leper not because he was moved with pity or compassion, as most translations of our Bible say, but moved with anger or indignation (see Mark 1:41). Oh, and Christmas is totally not what you think either. There was no rejection of Jesus' parents at a local hotel, no stable full of barnyard animals, and not even three wise men. And that whole "Jesus was sweating drops of blood" thing (Luke 22:43–44) probably never happened either.

Wait, what? Aren't these claims un-Christian? Don't they mean the Gospels can't be trusted? The short answer: no. It means we as a modern audience haven't been reading them right. We haven't been reading them for what they are, and once we start to, they all begin to make sense and we find sound explanations for these and a hundred other so-called reasons to doubt their legitimacy. The Gospels, when seen in their own world and thus properly understood, become so rich and invigorating that they are hard to put down, and like any good story, they never lose their effect on us. To see them as such, however, we will have to be open to moving the furniture around in our brains.

Let's start by looking at one of the craziest things Jesus ever said and did.

## U See Baby

Back in 2006, when my wife was pregnant with our firstborn, we wanted to know the gender of our baby. We're not patient people who wait until the big day to find out what we are getting. (What is this, the eighties?) So we scheduled an ultrasound at a company called U See Baby. A generic black-and-white blob on a screen wasn't good enough for us—we needed a 3D color video of our baby looking right at us while Mozart played in the background, a video we could watch every night. And that's what we got. From May until that special day in August, we would throw on the video and watch that girl move around. While we had dinner. When we had friends over. Whenever. It was a precious time.

Now, how weird would it have been if, once our baby was born, I never looked at her or played with her, but just continued watching the DVD instead? What if the real baby had arrived but I kept holding on to the pointer—the past, the shadow of what was to come? It would be silly, but it would also be destructive.

Early in his ministry, Jesus came face-to-face with a group of mature Bible scholars and told them this was exactly what they were doing: "You search the Scriptures because you think that in them you have eternal life; it is they that bear witness about me, yet you refuse to come to me that you may have life. . . . How can you believe, when you receive glory from one another and do not seek the glory that comes from God?" (John 5:39–44)

Jesus was saying, "If you don't believe in me, you completely misunderstand the entire Bible. You keep going back to the DVD even though I'm standing here in the flesh." Remember that Jesus belonged to a Jewish culture that prided itself on knowing the Bible. They not only spent years memorizing it, but they valued understanding it, knowing what it *meant*. And here was Jesus telling them they didn't understand it despite having spent a lifetime studying it.

Before you judge these guys too harshly, you should understand that what Jesus was saying to them about their interpretation of the Bible is just as true today, whether you are a Christian or a skeptic. Both groups tend to underestimate the Bible—and specifically the Gospels. Christians tend to see what they want to see, having grown familiar with the text. And once skeptics better understand what the Gospels are and what they aren't, the skeptical challenges often fall away. What's left are four beautiful, life-giving books crafted by skilled authors about the most important subject ever written. It's presented not in cold prose or boring historical-biographical summary but through colorful and emotional portraits that "bewitch the mind and ensnare the senses," to quote Professor Snape.

It's truth but truth *on fire*.

## What a Gospel Is and Isn't

The Gospels are the primary sources that detail the life and teachings of Jesus. These four books—Matthew, Mark, Luke, and John—have been recognized as the authoritative biographies of Jesus for the last two thousand years, and we look to them to understand the Man, his message, and his ministry. But we first need to confront two questions head-on: (1) What are the Gospels exactly? and (2) Can we trust them?

The best way to understand the writings called Gospels (literally, "good news") is as *theological history*. They are, at one level, Greek-style biographies, an established genre in the first century that presented the lives of interesting people through a fact-based story. On another level, they also fit the genre of Jewish storytelling, presenting a prophet or teacher in light of his anointing by God and the resulting message for the world. Both genres prioritize the accurate retelling of facts through engaging storytelling.[1] It's a creative blending of history and theology that can sometimes be difficult for modern readers to untangle.

In that sense, the Gospels are not biographies in the way we use that term today. The writers did not feel compelled to include every detail of Jesus' life, especially if it didn't serve their authorial intentions. Craig Blomberg explains, "[They] did not feel constrained to write from detached and so-called objective viewpoints. They did not give equal treatment to all periods of an individual's life. They felt free to write in topical as well as chronological sequence. They were highly selective in the material they included. . . . In an era, which knew neither quotation marks nor plagiarism, speakers' words were abbreviated, explained, paraphrased and contemporized in whatever ways individual authors deemed beneficial for the audiences."[2]

The same is true of the Gospels. Matthew's use of the phrase "kingdom of *heaven*," instead of "kingdom of God" (as is used in Mark and Luke), is an example of a difference in how the author wants to report his story. So which one did Jesus actually say: "heaven" or "God"? The answer is yes. Scholars point out that Matthew's account may have changed out "God" for "heaven" because he had a very Jewish audience in mind and they had great reverence for the word *God* in written form. In some cases, each reading of that name might require performing a routine of washing and cleansing. So he changed it to adapt to his audience.

Another well-known passage is John 3:16: "For God so loved the world, that he gave his only Son, that whoever believes in him should not perish but have eternal life." In many modern Bibles, these words are recorded in red, an indication that Jesus said them. However, the original Greek has no quotation marks, and it's unclear whether these words were actually spoken by Jesus or if they are the writer's commentary on what Jesus said. It is quite possible that Jesus stopped talking at an earlier point and this verse is John's meditation and extrapolation to his audience. Even some conservative and evangelical scholars, such as D. A. Carson, believe this is likely the case.[3]

## Blind Men and Fig Trees

Also, a different standard existed for the way stories were used in the ancient world. Writers had the freedom to move stories around in support of the author's theological goals, not always maintaining a strict chronology. Luke, for example, tended to order events by subject, while Mark clustered together the miracles in chapter 1 and the parables in chapter 4. Is this allowed? In modern biographies we might say no, but in ancient biographies this practice was commonly accepted. There was no other known way of doing it! Eusebius pointed this out as early as the second century: "Mark, having become Peter's interpreter, wrote down accurately everything he remembered, though not in order, of the things either said or done by Christ. He had no intention of giving an ordered account of the Lord's sayings" (*Historia ecclesiastica* 3.39.15). So there's nothing terribly scandalous about this practice, though it is commonly raised by skeptics today. In fact, understanding the flexibility available to the gospel writers and the intentional way with which they ordered events and stories opens the Bible up to us in amazing new ways.

I still remember the day I first discovered this. It was the day I first realized that sometimes a blind man is not *just* a blind man, nor is a fig tree *just* a fig tree. The Gospel of Mark gives an odd account that includes a seemingly failed attempt of Jesus to heal a blind man (8:22–26). The first time I read this story, I didn't think much about it. But then it started to bother me. Jesus touched a blind man's eyes and then asked him what he saw. The man replied, "I see people, but they look like trees, walking" (v. 24). In effect, he was saying, "I half see and have been only half healed." Jesus then gave him a second touch to heal him completely (v. 25). The very next account is one in which Jesus asked the disciples about his identity—whether they understood who he was. Peter declared that Jesus was the Messiah, but when Jesus clarified that being the Messiah included suffering, Peter rejected Jesus' version of messiahship. Jesus famously rebuked him, calling him "Satan" (8:27–33).

I wrestled with how the first blind-man story made any sense until I was taught how to properly read the Gospels. I learned that these stories are connected to one another on purpose. This two-stage healing wasn't simply about Jesus' ability or inability to heal someone or the blind man's lack of faith or whatever modern skeptics (or even preachers) might think. It was about the disciples' inability to see and understand what was right before their eyes. By ordering the stories as he did, Mark exposed the gaps in how the disciples understood Jesus. They tended to see him like trees walking around—they knew enough to call him by the right title, but they didn't fully comprehend what that title meant. Like the blind man, they needed a *second touch*, which is the purpose of the second half of Mark's Gospel. It is in this latter half that Mark presented Jesus as the Suffering Servant for eight full chapters. His goal? To reform the reader's view of what Jesus had come to do. Seeing this, I realized the Gospels are bold, strategic stories with theological intent—even in the way they are organized.

Another example of this organizational freedom is found in the story of Jesus going into the temple and throwing out the money changers. In Matthew, Mark, and Luke, this incident happens at the *end* of Jesus' life, right before his trial and his death (Matthew 21:12–13; Mark 11:15–19; Luke 19:45–48). In John, however, it occurs at the beginning of his ministry (2:14–16). While scholars debate why this may be, most conclude that John moved the event to the beginning because the genre of gospel didn't force him into a chronological account, and it better fit his theological and spiritual intent to have it at the beginning. The Synoptic writers (Matthew, Mark, and Luke) recorded the event as a buildup to Jesus' trial because it is an important part of why Jesus would go to the cross: challenging the Jewish authorities' misuse of the most sacred symbol within Judaism (the temple). In contrast, the entire Gospel of John is one big trial in front of Jewish authorities, and thus John used the story differently. He put it directly following Jesus' turning of water into wine (2:1–11) because it communicates the same message: Jewish ritual symbols were being superseded by Jesus. The six jars of water used for the Jewish ritual of purification were surpassed by the new and better wine of Jesus. The temple would be destroyed and three days later rebuilt. Jesus was speaking, of course, "about the temple of his body" (John 2:21), because Jesus is the true and better temple.

Mark frequently used a literary device that has come to be known as a "Markan sandwich." He gave a piece of information (the bread), followed by another piece of seemingly disconnected information (the meat), and then finally something similar to the first piece (the second piece of bread), and connected the three in a way that made one large theological point. Take Jesus' actions in the temple and his cursing of the fig tree:

(A) Jesus cursed a fig tree upon his entry into Jerusalem (Mark 11:12–14).
(B) Jesus cleansed/cursed the temple (vv. 15–19).
(A) Disciples saw that the fig tree had withered (vv. 20–25).

Mark arranged the material this way to say that the same thing that happened to the fig tree (A and A) was going to happen to the temple (B). It would wither for the same reason: it bore no fruit because it had rejected its rightful King. To modern readers, this may seem insignificant—but it is far from that! As E. P. Sanders points out, "To evoke, even conditionally, the destruction of the temple was to touch not just stone and gold and not only the general well-being but history and hope, national identity, [and] self-understanding"[4] of all of Israel. Jesus was hinting at a profound shift in salvation history, moving the vehicle through which salvation is achieved from Jewish ritual to himself. If Israel clung to the old ways, they, like the temple and the fig tree, would wither, fall, and be destroyed.

So the skeptic must understand that it is naive and anachronistic to judge the methods used by writers of a different era. One cannot read ancient texts by modern standards. It is the height of what C. S. Lewis once called "chronological snobbery." Newer and better ways of doing things don't invalidate the approaches of the past. They simply make them a product of their time.

It's also important to remember that there is no such thing as history without an agenda. Contrary to modern skeptical critique of the Gospels, which sees something "wrong" in organizing stories to present theological points, all history is being written from a particular perspective. Some of the most reliable records of the Holocaust are from Jews, for instance, who either lived through the events or transcribed the stories of families who experienced them, such as *The Diary of Anne Frank* or Nobel Peace Prize winner Elie Wiesel's *Night*. Interestingly, *Night* is a sparse and fragmented narrative of the Holocaust, yet no one challenges its historicity. History isn't just about recording facts and events; it also relates what communities are learning from what happened and was recorded. All history is interpreted history. As Craig Blomberg summarizes, "Why bother to record and pass on the story of certain events unless there is a moral to be learned from them?"[5]

This reality shouldn't sow seeds of doubt in us, nor should it shake our confidence in the authority of the Gospels as historical sources. Rather, it helps us respect the Gospels as some of the highest quality documents of their time, the best of what they are trying to be, not what we try to make of them. The Gospels deserve to be treated at least as generously as any other historical narrative from the ancient world, but they are not. As British historian of ancient Roman culture A. N. Sherwin-White mourned, "It is astonishing that while Graeco-Roman historians have been growing in confidence, the twentieth-century study of the Gospel narratives, *starting from no less promising material*, has taken so gloomy a turn."[6] Such a conclusion should not surprise us, of course, since much scholarship is itself rooted in agendas, usually secular or anti-religious ones.

## Matthew, Mark, Luke, and John

In his incomparable book on the New Testament, N. T. Wright contends that each Gospel, in its own unique way, depicts the life of Jesus as the climax to Israel's story. Matthew, likely written second of the Gospels, presents Jesus as the fulfillment of an earlier story. It begins with a genealogy, which positions it as a reshaping of Genesis. Matthew's opening words, "*Biblos Geneseos*" (1:1), literally translate as "the book of Genesis." This time, however, the story is not about original creation, but rather new creation. Matthew connected Jesus to the story of Abraham, Isaac, and Jacob, and even casts him as the new and better Moses. It is the story of Israel in exile and slavery, overseen by a foreign, pagan power (now Rome instead of Egypt) awaiting a savior to come and take them to the Promised Land yet again. After giving them a new covenant and a new way to live through the Sermon on the Mountain and the other five major blocks of teaching in Matthew (Matthew 5–7; 13; 10; 18; 23–25), Jesus "goes up a mountain and departs from his people, leaving them with a commission to go in and possess the new promised land, that is, the entire world" (28:16–20).[7]

Luke, likely the third Gospel written (in late AD 50s–early 60s), structures itself around the creation of Israel's monarchy. The story of Elizabeth and Zechariah in Luke 1:5–80 is intended to take the reader's mind back to the story of Hannah and Elkanah in 1 Samuel 1–2. This time the father is in the temple instead of the mother, and he is himself a priest instead of standing before one as Hannah did. "The story has not only the same shape (the couple whose longing for a child is taken up within the divine purpose) but also the same triumphant conclusion (Hannah's song is picked up by both Mary and Zechariah). . . . David's story progresses through his life as an outcast, leading a motley crew of followers in the Judean wilderness, and reaches its initial climax . . . when he is anointed king over Israel. And one of his first acts is to go to Jerusalem to take the city as his capital."[8] The parallels continue: David's anointing is followed, in the narrative of 1 Samuel, by his taking on Goliath single-handedly, as the representative of Israel. Jesus' anointing is followed at once by his battle with Satan—after his anointing by the Spirit at his baptism.

Mark, written first (somewhere between the AD mid 40s and early 60s) presents the new exodus reality, but not according to Exodus directly. Scholars have pointed out that the linguistic connections aren't there, but the fulfillment of Isaiah's presentation of a new exodus is. Every chapter in Mark cites Isaiah, with the beginning of the book arguably telling us that it is giving us the story of Jesus *according to Isaiah* (1:1–3) and the last half presenting Jesus as the Suffering Servant of Isaiah 40–55. Mark presents Jesus as a new Moses as well, feeding the new Israel in the desert, grouping them into groups of "fifties and hundreds" like Moses did, and so on.

John is often referred to as the "other Gospel" or the "Fourth Gospel" because it uses different words, images, ideas, and stories than the previous three, and it presents Jesus in a more mystical way. As the last Gospel written (in the AD 90s) by the last surviving disciple, John likely knew of the other Gospels and wanted to offer a different presentation of Jesus. Similar to the others, John reflected on an earlier story, closely mirroring Genesis in both theme and structure. When John finally recorded Pilate declaring to the crowd, "Behold the man!" (John 19:5), John intended his readers to hear echoes that had been present since the very beginning of his book. Jesus, as the *Word* having become flesh, is the truly human being.[9] While the historical trustworthiness of John has come under scrutiny in the past, it has become increasingly clear over the last century that he is a trustworthy guide. John consistently gives *more* references to chronology, geography, topography than the other gospel writers. Blomberg notes, "These have been demonstrated to be highly accurate, particularly in light of modern archeological discoveries: the five porticoes of the pool of Bethesda by the Sheep Gate (5:2), the pool of Siloam (9:1–7),

Jacob's well at Sychar (4:5), the "Pavement" where Pilate pronounced judgment on Jesus (19:13), Solomon's porch (10:22–23), and so on . . . [and] it is only because of John that we know Jesus had at least a three-year ministry; most harmonies of the gospels wind up using John's chronological framework."[10]

Contrary to what skeptics espouse, once we grasp what the Gospels actually are and how they work, we see in them an astounding record of the life and teachings of Jesus that cared for both history and theology without ever compromising on either. Each had their own authorial intent in describing Jesus one way or another, but all of them captured both the reality and the spirit of Jesus' life in a powerful and truthful way. But can they really be trusted? To this we now turn.

# CHAPTER 4

## Can We Trust
# THE GOSPELS?

As we consider the legitimacy of what material in the Gospels actually comes from the historical Jesus, it's helpful to frame our analysis around four criteria outlined by one of the most exhaustive and respected studies on the historical Jesus of the last century, John P. Meier's, *A Marginal Jew*: apostolicity, embarrassment, discontinuity, and multiple attestations.[1]

## The Criterion of Apostolicity

The criterion of apostolicity refers to authorship during the apostolic age before the last of the twelve apostles (most likely John) died. This requirement ensures that no book is more than one person removed from an authoritative eyewitness of the life of Jesus. Accounts from the early church fathers (AD 100–AD 300) uniformly support the belief that Matthew, Mark, and Luke, for instance, wrote the Gospels attributed to them. The oldest and most significant testimony is that of Papias, who wrote in AD 125, "Mark, in his capacity as Peter's interpreter, wrote down accurately as many things as he recalled from memory . . . of the things either said or done by the Lord. For he neither heard the Lord nor accompanied him, but later, Peter, who used to give his teachings in the form of *chreiai* [short and useful]. Consequently, Mark . . . wrote down some individual items just as he related them from memory. For he made it his one concern not to omit anything he had heard or to falsify anything." Papias also affirmed Matthew as the author of the Gospel with his name attached. Other early church writers, such as Eusebius and Irenaeus, are consistent in their accounts. Irenaeus wrote, "Matthew published his own Gospel among the Hebrews . . . when Peter and Paul were preaching in Rome and founding the church there. . . . Luke, the follower of Paul, set down in a book the Gospel preached by his teacher. Then John, the disciple of the Lord, himself produced his Gospel while he was living at Ephesus in Asia."[2]

## The Criterion of Embarrassment

The criterion of embarrassment is the inclusion of actions or sayings attributed to Jesus that would have created difficulty for the early church. If the early church was writing a mythology of Jesus, then it wouldn't make sense for them to include material that would weaken its positions or embarrass them. Examples of this "embarrassing" material include the baptism of Jesus by John (who was baptizing "for the forgiveness of sins" when Jesus supposedly didn't have any); Jesus not knowing the exact day or hour of the end of all things, despite claiming to know everything (Mark 13:32); and Jesus' attempt to pass off his vocation of saving the world at the last minute (Matthew 26:39–45). It is also interesting to note, as many historians do, that one of the main categories used to describe Jesus became that of "magician" or "sorcerer." This would have been hugely embarrassing and counterproductive if one wanted to gain momentum among conservative Jews!

The criterion of embarrassment similarly offers support for the *authorship* of the Gospels. If we're looking for evidence of authorship that goes beyond the word of early church leaders (who aren't exactly impartial observers), we don't have to go far. In fact, we don't have to go further than an examination of the gospel writers themselves: "Why would Christians as early as the second century ascribe these otherwise anonymous Gospels to three such unlikely candidates if they didn't in fact write them? Mark and Luke, after all, were not among Jesus' twelve apostles. Luke is particularly obscure, being mentioned by name only once in the New Testament, and Mark is best known for his abandoning Paul"[3]—and likely Jesus himself (see Acts 15:36–39)!

Matthew was a tax collector, one of the most hated, despised, untrustworthy types of people in first-century Israel. Mark and Luke weren't even disciples of Jesus. And John? This disciple wrote a book so unlike the other three, its historicity gets challenged seemingly every generation. Technically, the early church had the freedom to ascribe authorship of the Gospels to anyone they wanted. So, if they did in fact falsely attribute them, they couldn't have chosen a less compelling group! Nevertheless, all of the early writers on Christianity in the first three centuries agree that these writers wrote the Gospels, and none of them attempt to challenge their authorship. Furthermore, there are no competing traditions; the early writers on Christianity don't suggest anyone different, and this makes for a strong case for accepting their authorship, according to the discipline of historical research.

Perhaps the strongest argument against the idea that Christians felt free to concoct the teachings and actions of Jesus comes, ironically, from what we *never find in the Gospels*. Numerous Christian controversies surfaced after Jesus' ascension that threatened to tear the early church apart—questions regarding whether believers need to be circumcised, the place of food laws, modes of baptism, speaking in tongues, spiritual gifts, and the role of women in ministry. These are controversies that could have been avoided if the first Christians had retroactively clarified certain points and written them back into the Gospels. One cannot overstate the temptation present for the early church to have fabricated events, stories, and teachings and authoritatively placed them into the mouth and life of Jesus. This absence of clarification supports the argument that early Christians were interested in preserving the distinction between what happened during Jesus' life and what was debated later in the churches.[4]

# The Criterion of Discontinuity

The criterion of discontinuity is the inclusion of words or deeds of Jesus that cannot be derived either from Judaism at the time of Jesus or from the early church after him. Here are some examples:

- His sweeping prohibition of all oaths (Matthew 5:33–34).

    In the Sermon on the Mount, Jesus recalibrated his audience's religious life in a lot of ways that were very unique to him. One of those ways was a kind of "new teaching" wherein he called people never to make an oath. "You have heard it said, . . . 'You must not break your oath,' but I tell you, don't take an oath at all." This was an extreme teaching that is a mutation, or a direct violation of, Old Testament teaching in a sense.

- His rejection of voluntary fasting as a sign of mourning.

    In a similar vein, while Israel had moments of fasting as a way of life in exile and as a symbol of mourning and dependence on YHWH, Jesus rejected voluntary fasting for his disciples (Mark 2:19–20), saying they shouldn't do so because his life and presence and ministry were a time of kingdom celebration not somber anticipation.

- His total prohibition of divorce and remarriage.

    Jesus said, "Whoever divorces his wife and marries another commits adultery against her. Also, if she divorces her husband and marries another, she commits adultery" (Mark 10:2–12). While much time has been spent talking about this teaching and what is meant by it, it was a radical and somewhat novel idea. The Old Testament had given different "outs" to married couples, but Jesus turned the focus from the external act or behavior to the motives of the heart, raising the bar in the era of grace rather than lowering it.

## The Criterion of Multiple Attestations

The criterion of multiple attestations is the inclusion of sayings or deeds of Jesus that are documented in more than one independent literary source and/or in more than one literary genre. Examples include something Jesus said in a Gospel and an epistle of Paul, for instance, like the use of the phrase the "kingdom of God," as well as his words over the bread and wine at the Last Supper—each of which are found in two or three different sources (i.e., Matthew and Mark, and Paul's epistles).

Under this criterion, we move into what scholars call "textual criticism"—an analysis of the number and nature of available manuscripts, copying processes, and thus possible *mistakes* introduced into the Gospels. Two stories in the Gospels initially prove problematic: the longer ending to Mark (16:9–20) and the story of the woman caught in adultery in John (7:53–8:11). Skeptics conclude that these two stories were not original to Mark and John, showing all kinds of linguistic, theological, and "early versus later" manuscript issues, and they cite such examples as if they are new discoveries that should destroy our confidence in the Bible. Biblical scholars, however, concede that these passages likely weren't original to the text—and most are even fine removing them. There is no cover-up conspiracy here. Almost every modern translation of the Bible identifies sections that have been challenged based on manuscript evidence—including John 8 and Mark 16. This includes, as I mentioned earlier, the end of the Lord's Prayer in Matthew.

With over twenty-five thousand ancient manuscripts of the New Testament available for comparison, scholars conclude that no doctrine or ethical practice of Christianity depends on any disputed wording in the Gospels. Another way to say this is that "essential Christian beliefs are not affected by textual variants in the manuscript tradition of the New Testament" at all.[5] As a result—and especially when considered alongside the discovery of the Dead Sea Scrolls in the 1940s—this particular critique of the Gospels has all but faded entirely from academia.

## Just Different, Not Wrong

One of the most striking features of the Gospels is their *similarity*. Ninety-one percent of Mark's information, for instance, appears in Matthew or Luke—and usually in both. Given the wealth of information that could have been relayed, the consistency of their content and order suggests that a fixed manner of telling the gospel originated at an early date in the life of the church—enhancing the case for the Gospels' historical reliability. The gospel writers agree over the most important aspects of the life and teachings of Jesus. That said, a number of *differences* appear within the Gospels. While it may seem odd to highlight disparities when arguing for the legitimacy of the gospel accounts, historians claim such differences bring credibility to them. The subtle differences make a case for texts written with conviction and a theological vision rather than tampering with existing texts to achieve perfect alignment. As one researcher writes, "They display simultaneously, in other words, what one may term *microlevel fluidity* and *macrolevel stability*."[6]

These microlevel discrepancies have perfectly logical explanations. In his book about Jesus' historical setting, *The Shadow of the Galilean*, Gerd Thiessen points out that Jesus was constantly moving around from one place to another, and he, as teachers of the time did, told the same stories many times over, and came up with slightly different variations on those same ideas and stories in those different contexts: "The overwhelming probability is that most of what Jesus said, he said not twice but two hundred times, with (of course) a myriad of local variations."[7]

In his masterful work on Jesus, James D. G. Dunn draws on the work of Kenneth Bailey to show that any of the differences in the gospel accounts, aside from being tellings of different teachings from different times altogether, there is also an aspect of them being a product of oral tradition. Bailey lived in villages in the Middle East for thirty years, and Dunn points out that these villages have retained their identity over many generations and are the closest thing we can get to the culture of first-century Galilee. Bailey puts forward "the idea of *informal controlled tradition*" to distinguish his idea from that of other scholars who propose a "formal controlled tradition." In Bailey's construct, a story can be retold in the setting of a gathering of the village by any member present, but usually the elders, and the community itself exercises the "control." Thus, anyone twenty years and older in the AD 60s could have been "an authentic reciter of that tradition." Bailey points out that poems and proverbs allow no flexibility. Parables and recollections regarding historical people are allowed some, but the central threads cannot be changed, only flexibility in detail is allowed, and then very slight.[8]

A great biblical example of this phenomenon outside the Gospels is Luke's recording of the conversion of Saul, described three times in the book of Acts (9:1–22; 22:1–21; 26:9–23). Here we're dealing with the same author in the same book telling the same story, yet elements of the story differ. What is striking, however, "is the fact that what was evidently seen as the core of the story, the exchange between Saul and the exalted Jesus, is word for word the same in each account, after which each telling of the story goes its own distinctive way."[9] The same could be said about a number of Gospel stories:

The Centurion's Servant (Matthew 8:5–13 // Luke 7:1–10)
The Stilling of the Storm (Mark 4:35–41 // Luke 8:22–25)
The Healing of the Possessed Boy (Mark 9:14–28 // Matthew 17:14–19)
The Widow's Pence (Mark 12:41–44 // Luke 21:1–4)
The Lord's Prayer (Matthew 6:7–15 // Luke 11:1–4)
The Last Supper (Matthew 26:26–29 // Mark14:22–25)

The disparities continue not only in the teachings, parables, and miracles, but also in the central moments of the cross and resurrection accounts themselves. What did Jesus say from the cross? A stunning feature immediately becomes apparent: that only one of the "last words" is attested by more than one author (*"Eloi, Eloi, lema sabachthani"* in Matthew 27:46 // Mark 15:34).[10] Moreover, all the sayings from the cross are unique to their specific Gospels. Rather than deducing they were made up, we can conclude it likely that each one was historical (Jesus hung on the cross for six hours) and that different traditions wanted to emphasize different theological points. If they were making up the story, they would likely have wanted to show agreement and would have been careful to remain in total sync with one another. Instead, they utilized different memories of the cross to make distinct theological points.

The same is true about the differences in the details of Jesus' resurrection. Were there two angels at the tomb, as John tells us (John 20:12), or one, as Matthew says (Matthew 28:2)? How many women were there, and what was the precise location of the appearances of Jesus to his disciples? The Gospels all diverge on some of these details. What implication should be drawn from this? For the historian this is a criterion of extraordinary credibility, for if the Gospels were the fabrication of a congregation, then they would be completely free of discrepancies.[11]

Historian N. T. Wright suggests that one could be forgiven for thinking the writers set out to tell different stories altogether in some respects, and reminds us of the importance of this. He contends that "the fact that they cannot agree over how many women, or angels, were at the tomb, or even on the location of the appearances, does not mean that nothing happened"[12] but that the opposite is the case, namely, that something likely did:

> The surface inconsistencies of which so much is made by those
> eager to see the accounts as careless fiction, is in fact *a strong*

*point in favor of their early character.* The later we imagine them being written up, let alone edited, the more likely it would be that inconsistencies would be ironed out. The stories exhibit exactly the surface tension which we associate, not with tales artfully told by people eager to sustain a fiction and therefore anxious to make everything look right, but with hurried, puzzled accounts of those who have seen with their own eyes something which took them horribly by surprise . . . they were not assimilated either to each other or to develop New Testament theology.[13]

## External Evidence

Rather than spinning legends as skeptics claim, the gospel writers went out of their way to root themselves in external history. As if anticipating the skeptical challenges that lay ahead, Luke began his two-volume work (Luke-Acts) by stating, "Inasmuch as many have undertaken to compile a narrative of the things that have been accomplished among us, just as those who from the beginning were *eyewitnesses* and ministers of the word have delivered them to us, it seemed good to me also, having *followed all things closely* for some time past, to write *an orderly account* for you . . . that *you may have certainty* concerning the things you have been taught" (Luke 1:1–4, italics mine). Luke was a doctor, and from what we can tell, he was a guy who loved facts. "In the fifteenth year of the reign of Tiberius Caesar," he began, "Pontius Pilate being governor of Judea, and Herod being tetrarch of Galilee, and his brother Philip tetrarch of the region of Ituraea and Trachonitis, and Lysanias tetrarch of Abilene, during the high priesthood of Annas and Caiaphas, the word of God came to John the son of Zechariah in the wilderness" (Luke 3:1–2). Sleeping yet? Luke cited *seven* rulers, working from the greatest rulers down, to root his story of Jesus in history—and all of the data Luke laid out is confirmed by secular sources, including Josephus.[14]

At one time some thought that Luke had made a number of factual

errors in his Gospel. Skeptics observed that the birth narrative of
Jesus was filled with historical problems. At that time, they said, there
was no actual census, no requirement for a return to one's ancestral
home, and Quirinius was not governor of Syria. However, archaeological work within the last century has shown that the Romans did,
in fact, make tax payers enroll and participate in a census every fourteen years, with one undertaken around 8 BC (likely the one of which
Luke is speaking). Moreover, two inscriptions found in Antioch have
confirmed that Quirinius *was* governor of Syria around 7 BC. In the
end, between the Gospel of Luke and book of Acts, Luke identified
thirty-two countries, fifty-four cities, and nine islands without error![15]

Skeptics have challenged Mark based on geographical inaccu-
racy. The problem in this instance is that this challenge is based on a
modern approach to mapping. Respected scholar Richard Bauckham
has noted that the geography in Mark is accurate when looked at from
the perspective of a fisherman from Capernaum—which is consistent with Mark relaying the gospel from the perspective of Peter, a
first-century Galilean fisherman. Many scholars use modern maps to
understand Mark, Bauckham says. A Galilean fisherman, however,
would not have had a modern map in mind, but instead a mental map
based on his experiential world.[16]

And then we have the physical evidence of today's archaeological
digs. As Millar Burrows of Yale University asserts, "archeological
work has unquestionably strengthened confidence in the reliability
of the Scriptural record."[17] And modern archaeology continues to
do so. Hundreds of examples of statements the Gospels make about
the geography of the first century have been repeatedly confirmed
by archaeology. Even some that modern scholarship thought were
wrong have since been proven right, such as the 1888 unearthing of
the pool of Bethesda, with its location and details exactly as described
by John 5:2.[18] Even something as small as the coins mentioned in the
Gospels bring legitimacy to what they say. Three coins mentioned—
the "denarius" or tribute penny (Mark 12:13–17), the "thirty pieces of

silver" (Matthew 26:14–15), and the widow's mite (Luke 21:1–4)—have all been identified and verified by archaeology as existing and in usage in the way the New Testament describes.[19]

Over and over again, the Gospels are affirmed by tangible history. As the apostle Peter explained in his second letter, "We did not follow cleverly devised myths when we made known to you the power and coming of our Lord Jesus Christ, but we were eyewitnesses of his majesty" (1:16).

## What about Other Gospels?

Recently I posted online asking what questions people had about Jesus that I could answer for them. What did skeptics believe that kept them from believing in Jesus? Among many interesting questions raised, one of the major themes was why we only categorize the Gospels of Matthew, Mark, Luke, and John as legitimate records. What about the other so-called Gnostic Gospels, such as the Gospel of Thomas and the Dialogue of the Savior? Supposing we were to start over from scratch, are there reasons to include these books now? The answer, somewhat uncontroversial, is *no*, with the reasons well documented by both liberal and conservative scholars alike.

To start, these books lack any significant narratives concerning Jesus' life. In fact, to even call them "Gospels" is misleading. They are more like a collection of proverbs based on Jesus' teachings. One scholar explains, "Most involve long, rambling discourses attributed to Jesus, supposedly given to one or more of his followers secretly after the resurrection, teaching about the nature of creation and the heavenly worlds, with all sorts of esoteric cosmological speculation."[20] In addition to this marked difference in structure when compared to the Gospels of Matthew, Mark, Luke, and John, they lack verifiable facts: statements about specific places, people, and events.

Second, their theology is more in line with Greek dualism and Gnosticism than Judaism. For example, after declaring that the flesh is bad and the spirit is good (a statement that directly opposes the interconnectedness of body and spirit as described in John 5 and first-century Judaism), the Gospel of Thomas credits Jesus with saying that a woman must become a man to enter the kingdom of heaven (Gospel of Thomas, 114). This falls so far outside of what Jesus taught in the Gospels and what Judaism taught at the time that it isn't taken seriously as a legitimate, historical work of the first century by scholars.

## The Dating of the Gospels, and Are They Legends?

Another popular claim about the Gospels made by skeptics is that they were written too long after the events they record to retain truth and history. This claim has almost unanimously been disproved and rejected by scholars. One of the reasons the Gospels have come to be the most trusted documents in antiquity is because of their comparatively quick turn-around time following the events they record.[21] For instance, the most plausible explanation for the abrupt ending of Acts (Paul sitting in house arrest in Rome; see Acts 28:30–31) is that Luke was still writing at the time of the events described. Why else would Acts consist of ten full chapters devoted to the events leading up to Paul's arrest, only to leave us in the dark about the outcome of his appeal to Caesar? We know that Luke was written before Acts, and Mark and Matthew most likely before Luke, with Mark being dated by most every scholar as early AD 60s. This "adds up to a strong case that all three Gospels were composed *within about thirty years of Christ's death* and well within the period of time when people could check up on the accuracy of the facts they contained."[22]

Other nonbiblical writings—which are trusted and drawn upon to construct history by scholars—can't compare to the timeline of the writing of the New Testament in relation to the events they describe. If we compare the gospel accounts to other writings, we find they are the most trustworthy, best-attested, documents in ancient history.[23]

Take the writings of Thucydides, for instance, who lived from 460 BC to 395 BC and wrote extensively about Greco-Roman culture (e.g. *The History of the Peloponnesian War*). . . . We have in existence *eight* copies of his writings, the earliest transcribed 1,300 years after the events of which he wrote. Aristotle's *Poetics* are very trusted ancient documents, of which there are *five* copies dated 1,400 years after the originals. Caesar's *Gallic Wars* describe events that occurred in 58 BC, and the *few* manuscripts scholars have are from 1,000 years after his death. There are two ancient biographies of Alexander the Great . . . the earliest of which was written 400 years after Alexander died. Historians trust all these writings as historically accurate.[24]

So, what about the New Testament? More than twenty-five thousand copies of the New Testament documents are in existence, all of which were composed within thirty years of Jesus' death! This means two things: (1) the documents can be compared to see if there are differences between them that would render them illegitimate, and (2) they were written, read, and passed along by *eyewitnesses* (or by those who knew eyewitnesses) of the recorded events.

Unlike the foundational writings of other religious leaders, the New Testament makes it clear that the spectators of recorded events were still alive at the time it was being written. This means audiences could check up on the accuracy of the facts contained within it. If the Gospels made an inaccurate claim, people could correct the mistake. The documents wouldn't be copied again or continue being distributed because they wouldn't be seen as legitimate. This is somewhat similar to what we face in the early twenty-first century regarding the realities of World War II. My grandfather just celebrated his ninety-eighth birthday, and the last time I saw him, we talked about the war and his part in the air force. How many men and women remain alive today to tell us those stories firsthand? And for how much longer will that be possible? The benefit of having them alive still today is that if I were to claim something had happened historically—that, for example, the Nazis never existed or there was no such thing as an airplane in the 1940s—my grandfather could easily refute these ideas. He was alive at the time. He was there. That is the value of an eyewitness, contemporaneous account, and it is why the Gospels are more verifiable than any other ancient documents. It is almost as if someone knew Jesus' historicity would be challenged in the future and so set out to establish his concrete historical footing with documents that could be trusted for millennia. The dating of the Gospels leaves insufficient time for legendary influences to erase the core historical facts.

Early twentieth-century German critics of the New Testament have claimed that the gospel stories were made up by the early church. Two primary facts dispute this claim. The first is related to the dating of the manuscripts. The publication of these writings would have been too soon after the events themselves to allow any "myths" to gain traction. The second reason is that the New Testament writings don't read like myths or legends at all. C. S. Lewis, an Oxford and Cambridge scholar who studied mythology and literature for a living, said, "I distrust them [German critics] as critics. . . . It sounds a strange charge to bring against men who have been steeped in those books [about the Gospels and the New Testament] all their lives. But that might be just the trouble." A person who has spent his life studying the minutia of biblical scholarship has a lack of literary experiences and thus lacks any standard of comparison.

> If he tells me that something in a Gospel is legend or romance, I want to know how many legends and romances he has read, how well his palate is trained in detecting them; not how many years he has spent on the Gospels. . . . I have been reading poems, romances, vision literature, legends, myths all my life. I know what they are like. I know that not one of them is like this. . . . From first to last the things strike me as records of fact. And, in my opinion, the people who think that any of the episodes in the

Gospels are imaginary are the people who have no imagination themselves and have never understood what imaginative story-telling is.[25]

## Why All This Matters

Ernest W. Saunders once wrote, "Historical inquiry alone cannot give the certainty of faith, but it can prepare the way for it." We have explored the historical and literary case for Jesus of Nazareth and seen that there is an exhaustive amount of evidence to believe in him as a historical figure, and that he was who he claimed to be. We have also seen that the documents describing him are trustworthy, informative, and inspiring. But the decision to believe this, follow it with your heart, and shape your life around it is something else entirely.

As a pastor walking people through their deepest questions of faith, I've discovered over the years that someone can possess all the evidence in the world declaring something to be true and still deny it. Often we have unspoken reasons—what I call *the things behind the thing*. My hope is that you would be courageous enough to face facts rather than twist them, to let them do their work on you rather than taking the easy way out—denying this or that—because you don't want Christianity to be true.

At the start of the last chapter, we looked at John 5. There Jesus gave a warning to his critics at the end of that passage: "You search the scriptures because you think that in them you have *eternal life* . . . yet you refuse to come to me that you may have life" (vv. 39–40, italics mine). I find these to be some of the most haunting words Jesus ever spoke.

We are all seeking "eternal life," not just a *quantity* of life but a *quality* of life—a certain kind of existence in the present world and in the world to come. A kind of life present in God's new creation, a life of joy, meaning, peace, salvation, love, and power. In Greek the phrase is *aionios zoe*. Jesus later called it "life . . . to the full" (John 10:10 NIV). This is good news, for psychologists tell us the motivation that drives most of our decisions is our own pleasure and joy. We want a more meaningful and fulfilling life. This desire drives whom we marry, what we wear, and even what we eat, and yet it is ever elusive.

In fact, our pursuit of the better life will often lead to deeper pain, sadness, and isolation. With the modernist experiment of the last two hundred years, we have tried *human answers* to our deepest longings, and they have all failed. We trusted in secularism to replace traditional religious thought and have found it wanting. "The twentieth century, the most barbaric in history, makes the myth of progress read like a cruel joke: 160 million human beings slaughtered by their own kind; more dying of starvation in a single decade than in all of history combined; the AIDS epidemic; the widening gap between rich and poor; the environmental crisis; the threat of nuclear holocausts—the list goes on."[26]

In John 5 the scholars being addressed by Jesus were looking *to the Bible*—to them the Hebrew Scriptures—for meaning and fulfillment. You'd think if there was one place a person could find eternal life, that would be it! The problem was that they were gaining knowledge *about* God but not *of* God. What a scandal! A person can read and study the Bible and find neither God nor satisfaction because they've never met the One behind the words on the page. We can settle for print instead of Person, rules instead of relationship, letter instead of Spirit. But we must meet the Word *behind* the word.

Why do we do this? The answer is in the story: "How can you believe, when you *receive glory from one another* and do not seek the glory that comes from the only God" (John 5:44, italics mine). We reject that glory because pride keeps us from opening up to Jesus. What will my girlfriend think of me? What will my coworkers say? What will my husband do? What if I start going to church or reading my Bible? Never mind the myriad reasons we cite for pushing Jesus aside. In the end, for many it comes down to *fear*. We care more about what people think than what God thinks. We care more about the finite than the infinite.

This was my experience when I began to explore Christianity. I was in the middle of high school. My family raised me well, though we didn't go to church. We didn't pray. We didn't own a Bible. We didn't believe in God. So I had to stop and consider what it would mean to give my life to Jesus. What would people think? What would happen if I went from being the guy living for himself to the guy following Jesus. I was convinced people would think I was crazy. And they did. I was constantly challenged—mocked by friends and classmates. But there I sat, drawn to the Word, smoking a pack a day while blazing through the New Testament every month. Dating girl after girl while saying Jesus was my all. Going to party after party while telling everyone there what Jesus was doing in my life.

And at some point, after all the reading and praying and fasting, I started to care more about what God was saying and doing than what people said and did. Knowing God became an emotional relationship as well as an intellectual one. And I began to see the blessing and praise of God in my life, though in the most ironic way. The very people I was mocked by, challenged by, and whose opinions kept me from God slowly began wanting what had changed me. The ex-girlfriend of mine, pregnant from her new boyfriend and wondering what to do; the friend who, weeks earlier, had an abortion and was now crying and asking for prayer and needing someone to love her; the close buddy who thought he'd acquired HIV from a girl he'd slept with and was completely terrified. Totally lost and vulnerable, they were all wondering in those moments if there was something bigger.

"Pray for me."

"Help."

"What does God think of me?"

Each saying at some point in the crisis that they wished they had what I had.

"How do I get what you have? Do what you do?"

Looking back, I realize what they were seeking: *aiōnios zōē*. Eternal life, a fuller way, truly human life. Not in heaven one day, but now.

The problem is that the gospel asks us to answer this question by looking at something not of this world and not of ourselves, but to the God behind and within the Gospels. The One who abandoned his own life for our abundant life. We aren't our own saviors. The first problem of Jesus is that he brings a crisis of faith, challenging us to either make him our center or deny him altogether. He gives us only these two options.

# PART III

## The Problem of
# DISCIPLESHIP

*They heard somewhere in that tenantless night
a bell that tolled and ceased where no bell
was and they rode out on the round dais of
the earth which alone was dark and no light
to it and which carried their figures and bore
them up into the swarming stars so that they
rode not under but among them and they rode
at once jaunty and circumspect, like thieves
newly loosed in that dark electric, like young
thieves in a glowing orchard, loosely jacketed
against the cold and ten thousand worlds for
the choosing.*

—CORMAC MCCARTHY, ALL THE PRETTY HORSES

# CHAPTER 5

## More Than a
# TEACHER

Sift through the teachings of some of our most popular religious writers, watch a TED Talk, or ask the couple sitting next to you at Starbucks, and you'll likely encounter this take on Jesus: "He was a really good guy, a great moral teacher, a visionary, a revolutionary, and maybe even a prophet. But let's not believe all this other stuff people say about him being God or rising from the dead." Many people are willing to accept Jesus as an inspiring leader, a friend, or an archetype of a compassionate religious guru, but not as Lord—not as the master and ruler of their lives. The call to follow him is seen as too fanatical, too devoted, and a little naive. I call this the problem, or scandal, of *discipleship.*

In our media-saturated age, we're all used to a good sales pitch. If advertisers want us to buy into a product or if politicians want us to support them, they will sell us on a vision of the good life—a vision of life made easier. We're bombarded with the quickest and simplest solutions to any given problem, with promises of personal benefit and unlimited joy. And we cave to these promises all too easily. Our hearts buy in again and again.

Is Jesus just another advertiser offering us the latest and greatest? No. Jesus does offer us something, but he also asks something of us. To the masses of people in the first century looking for vision and inspiration, for personal and political revolution, Jesus declared, "Whoever wants to be my disciple must deny themselves and take up their cross and follow me. For whoever wants to save their life will lose it, but whoever loses their life for me and for the gospel will save it" (Mark 8:34–35 NIV).

Wait. What? This doesn't sound like a good pitch for winning followers. Over the last two thousand years, this call of discipleship has become infamous, and for good reason.

But before we can grasp *what* it meant—and, by extension, what it means for us—we have to understand *why* this threefold invitation (deny yourself, take up your cross, and follow me), was (and is) something we need. What appears to be the worst strategy for pursuing our personal fulfillment may actually be the best thing for us.

## Temptation and Apocalyptic Romance

So what would motivate a person in the ancient or modern world to take Jesus up on this vision of self-denial? It goes against everything we know about human psychology. Human beings make the majority of their decisions in favor of their *own pleasure*. So why would people want to embrace self-denial and follow someone other than themselves?

The answer lies in an odd place. It is hidden in the stories we are told about Jesus at the beginning of his public life and in the temptations he faced in the wilderness (Matthew 4:1–11). The world Jesus walked into was dying for a leader. Scholars paint a bleak picture when it comes to the lives of first-century Jews. They were discouraged and downtrodden, living in exile in their own land, and pining after someone or something to follow. Their dreams were not all that different from ours today: visions of a preferred future. "Don't bore people with your plans," I read somewhere recently, "inspire them with your dreams." Jewish dreams centered around the One who would end suffering and pain, an *eschatological* (end-time) prophet who would free God's people from the tyranny of the Roman Empire and reestablish God's rule. They longed for a gospel of national prosperity, what they called "the kingdom of God": "Believe this and you can live your best life now; you'll have no more miscarriages, your wives won't die in childbirth, you'll have clothes on your backs and more health and success than you could ever have imagined!"

The promise of a better future played well in first-century Palestine. And this was the tension Jesus faced at the beginning of his ministry. What would he offer people? When Jesus was tempted by Satan, alone in the desert, Satan told him that the way to fame, to accomplish his dreams, was to "command these stones to become loaves of bread" (4:3). In addition to feeding his own hunger, Jesus could have "saved" people in this very practical way. If he were to feed the hunger of a poor and hungry people, they would have made him their king in a moment. *This is the path of least resistance.* To secure their devotion, Jesus would take the ordinary, a dry and dead rock, and transform it into what the people desired.

The second temptation involved a similar ploy: "If you are the Son of God, throw yourself down," off the roof of the temple, "for it is written: 'He will command his angels concerning you,' and 'On their hands they will bear you up, lest you strike your foot against a stone'" (4:6). In other words, show everyone that you are God's prophet, and when they see that you can fly they will follow you.

The third and final temptation was much the same: "The devil . . . showed him all the kingdoms of the world and their glory. And he said to him 'All these I will give you, if you will fall down and worship me.'" (4:8–9). It would all be so easy! But Jesus rejected these three temptations and embraced the long game of obedience, the painful path forward.

Several years ago, my wife and I were sitting in a church listening to Dr. Eric Mason preach on the strongholds we set up in our lives. To this day his message is still one of the best sermons I have ever heard. Mason ended the sermon by reflecting on the temptations of Jesus:

> The devil said, "Listen, if you bow down and worship me, I'll give you all the kingdoms of the"—key word—"*world.*" That was funny. He said, "I'll give you all the kingdoms of the world." But Jesus said, "Be gone from me, Satan." Because Jesus knew that the devil always presents to us on a *temporal* level something that

God has promised on *an eternal* level. . . . Philippians chapter 2 says, "Because Jesus was *obedient to the point of death*, God exalted his name above every name, that at the name of Jesus, every knee shall bow and every tongue shall confess that Jesus Christ is Lord to the glory of God the Father."[1]

In Matthew, Jesus gave his last words to the disciples, saying, "All authority in heaven and on earth has been given to me" (28:18). Dr. Mason pointed out something that had never occurred to me before and has never left me since: "The devil wanted to give Jesus *earthly* kingdoms, but God wanted to give him *all kingdoms.*"

I think this is helpful in understanding how temptation works. *Buy that dress—what's one more? The rush you feel now has no bearing on eternity.* Or, *Sleep with her just this one time; the pleasure you'll experience now is worth the risk of how God deals with you.* In other words, we believe the lie that we can have it all—that we can have the "kingdoms of the world" *and* "authority in heaven." But Jesus makes it clear that this is not an option. Mason concluded his message: "Don't you let the devil make you believe that God doesn't *have better* for you. Don't you believe that the devil has greater passions for you. Christ always has something better to give, because the devil always gives a counterfeit bill, but God owns the treasury."[2]

When we look at Jesus' life, we see that he suffered immensely. He took the hard road, resisting the temptations of the world. But not because he loved suffering. Suffering and pain were not the end for him (following Jesus would be quite depressing if it was). No, he rose again and returned to the glory he had known "before the world existed" (John 17:5). We need the full story to understand why we embrace the difficult path of discipleship. Jesus is our model. Suffering and the hard road are not ends in themselves. Jesus didn't suffer for the sake of suffering; he got through it because he knew there was something better that makes it bearable: the glory and goodness to come. The writer of Hebrews says that Jesus endured the cross for "the joy that was set before him" (12:2).

The invitation to discipleship is more than a call to give up our own comforts and desires. It's about pursuing a better goal, a greater reward. We come to see that the joys, delights, and pleasures God has to offer us is in the next life are *infinitely better* than those of this life. Clinical psychologist Jordan Peterson hints at this in his bestselling book, *12 Rules for Life*: "Long ago in the dim mists of time, we began to realize that reality was structured as if it could be bargained with. We learned that behaving properly now, in the present—regulating our impulses, considering the plight of others—could bring rewards in the future, in a time and place that did not yet exist. . . . *sacrifice now, to gain later . . . sacrifice will improve the future.*"[3]

This tendency runs "absolutely contrary to our ancient, fundamental animal instincts, which demand immediate satisfaction."[4] Yet this is the secret to following Jesus and understanding how Jesus had victory in the face of temptation, how he endured suffering in his life. He had an *apocalyptic perspective*: a future in view that enabled him to face his present trials. Sadly, this is a perspective largely ignored in our modern world, but it is how countless people have endured the pain and tragedy that so often defines human life. We can embrace personal sacrifice, pain, and loss if we experience them in light of future joy. As the apostle Paul put it, "The sufferings of this present time are not worth comparing with the glory that is to be revealed to us" (Romans 8:18).

This paradigm should not surprise us, though it is foreign to our modern, individualistic mindset. It is the basic structure of many religious stories. In his book *The History of Religious Ideas*, Mircea Eliade argues that the concept of suffering followed by a better future is one of the key ideas found in the major world religions.[5] Jordan Peterson powerfully argued for this in one of his lectures:

> I tell my students when they're young, look, don't fool yourself; you're going to develop a serious illness—at least one, maybe two or three, and one of them is likely to be chronic. And if

it isn't you, it's going to be someone you love. It's going to be your husband; your parent; your kids. That's coming, and so is a lot of death and pain. Just exactly what sort of person are you going to be when that shows up? It isn't, how are you going to be happy in your life? That's a stupid ambition because it's too shallow. Happiness comes and goes like the sun coming out from behind a cloud. It's a gift. . . . But a *pursuit*? No. The pursuit is, when the damn flood comes, you want to be the person who built the ark. . . . There's an idea that the end of the world is always at hand, and that you should be prepared to be judged. The thing about that is, it's true. The reason it's true is because the end of your world is at hand. The flood is always coming. . . . Your world is always, in small ways and large ways, coming to an end. So, what do you do? You prepare for it. You prepare for your world to come to an end. And then, maybe, when the end comes, you get another world. That'd be a good deal. So, we're ready for the next week.[6]

All of this answers *how* we in the long run can follow Jesus, deny ourselves, and pick up our crosses daily. How can we live a life of sacrifice in the potentially eighty years we have on this planet. Because we will know a better delight for the next eighty *million* years, precisely because we did. We have calculated the cost-benefit ratio and have concluded that the cost is worth it.

Accepting Jesus' invitation to discipleship is, of course, not our only option. As you read the Gospels, you'll find many people who walked away and rejected Jesus' call—or, at the very least, ignored it. There are many reasons why, but they all come down to one: we don't really believe that the best is yet to come. We lack faith that the future Jesus promises is real and better than what we can experience in the here and now. We are constantly tempted to pursue temporal pleasure over the eternal.

## This Is Water

Discipleship isn't a "Christian thing"—it's a human thing, something we all experience. Whether we like it or not, we are all disciples of something or someone, and we are all *being discipled*. The Greek word for "disciple" is *mathētēs* (from which we get the word *math*), and it literally means *learner*. In Jesus' time, everyone was a disciple in some form or another, often under a local rabbi. Today we may not hitch ourselves to a rabbi, but we are constantly bombarded by messages that teach us how to flourish in life, impressing upon us a vision of the future. We are surrounded by competing voices that shape the way we view politics, sex, money, and the very reason for our existence. Much of this "discipleship" happens passively and unconsciously. It's the water we swim in, and that's why most modern people don't think of themselves as disciples at all! But they are. You and I are disciples. The question is, who—or what—are you following?

Before the brilliant and celebrated writer David Foster Wallace (1962–2008) took his own life after years of battling depression, alcoholism, and drug abuse, he delivered the commencement speech to the 2005 graduating class at Kenyon College in Ohio. He titled his address "This Is Water" and rooted it in the analogy that fish don't know they're in water because it's the environment in which they've always existed. At one moment in his address, he told the graduates,

> In the day-to-day trenches of adult life, there is actually no such thing as atheism. There is no such thing as *not* worshipping. Everybody worships. *The only choice we get is what to worship.* And the compelling reason for maybe choosing some sort of god . . . is that pretty much anything else you worship will eat you alive. If you worship money and things, if they are where you tap real meaning in life, then you will never have enough. . . . Worship your body and beauty and sexual allure and you will always feel

ugly. And when time and age start showing, you will die a million deaths before they finally grieve you. On one level, we all know this stuff already. . . . But the insidious thing about these forms of worship is not that they're evil or sinful, it's that they're *unconscious*. They are default settings. They're the kind of worship you just gradually slip into, day after day, getting more and more selective about what you see and how you measure value *without ever being fully aware that that's what you're doing.*[7]

Wallace was saying that we are all discipled—by the world, by ideas, by a vision of the good life—and this is not something we consciously choose. It is happening all the time and in a thousand ways.

That's one reason why the call to follow Jesus sounds so strange to us. Jesus asks for a conscious choice, that in following him we must die to all other kinds of discipleship. To come into his kingdom, we must come out from every other one. Embracing the spiritual formation of Jesus means rejecting the *de*formation of all the other gods and impulses the world has to offer. That's what makes it so costly—it is exclusive. Consequently, the first step is to *become conscious* of the ideas, philosophies, and people we are following. We need to be discipled out of the matrix and to become aware of the dominant ideologies that shape our lives: materialism, sex as god, allure of status, among others.

At this point, you might say, "All right, I will become conscious of certain ways of thinking, wrestle those to the ground, and consider the call of Jesus over the call of the world." And that would certainly be progress. But I believe a far more difficult and invasive step is needed. It's a step that goes beyond the thinking level to our hearts. We need a change of affection. And this happens, somewhat surprisingly, not by targeting what we *think* about but what we *do*. Not our beliefs but our habits.

This seems contrary to what much of popular Christianity teaches. "Trade in all of that religious ritual," we say, "for a free-flowing, nonreligious, non-rules-oriented relationship with God. God cares solely about what you believe, not your works." And yet what is Jesus' call? "Deny yourself. Pick up your cross. Follow me." Actions. Behavior. Habit. Jesus sets the thinking component aside here and leads with the very shape of our living. Not only are our thoughts discipled by listening to and seeing the narratives daily thrown at us by the world; our lives are molded into these visions by our practices as well. We live out these alternative stories. And every time we do, they root themselves deeper into our desires.

Our actions bubble up from our *loves*. Multiple times in the Gospels we read that Jesus decided to heal someone based on *splanchnizomai*—which literally means "to be moved in the inward parts, or the bowels" (Matthew 9:36; 14:14; Mark 1:41; 6:34). English Bibles tend to translate this as being "moved with compassion" (which has a gentler tone). I can't tell you the number of times I have seen the power of a gut desire win out over reason. I've met future husbands in premarital counseling who tell me, "We don't always get along, and I think she's a little off, to be honest, but man is she hot!" Beauty, in those moments, is more powerful than reason. All the evidence in the world can appeal to our minds without necessarily changing what we do because we aren't primarily rational creatures: we're aesthetically oriented. We get swept up by our desires, often pursuing what glitters and sparkles. To redirect our discipleship away from our previous lords and over to Jesus, it will take more than the reformation of our ideas. We need a reformation of *action and habit*.

If you are a disciple of materialism, your self-worth is defined by how you look and what you buy. But you didn't arrive at that belief through conscious thought. Most of us don't *think* our way into consumerism. Instead, over time we are formed by *practices* that lead us there and influence what we love and desire—what we worship. To put it simply, the mall is a religious experience. "Not because it is theological but because it is liturgical. . . . Its threat isn't found in 'ideas' or 'messages' but in its *rituals*. . . . [It] doesn't care what you think, it is interested in what you love. The mall doesn't try to convince us, it *attracts* us. Its power isn't logic but beauty; a winsome invitation to share in this envisioned good life. . . . The way to the heart is through the body you could say."[8]

The secret power of Jesus' counterdiscipleship is that we *practice* our way out of our plight. This isn't meant to downplay thinking and rational consideration. It's simply admitting that it alone is insufficient. We can't change "with didactic information poured into our intellects. We can't recalibrate the heart from the top down; it happens from the bottom up, through the formation of our *habits*."[9] This is why Jesus didn't simply give us a list of doctrines to believe. His call is more formative and powerful: "Follow me."

We can't just think our way into Christianity; we need to live our way in. And Jesus was and is saying to do that, *our proximity to him is what matters most*. That in the end, most of our preaching and teaching is wrong-headed because it starts in the wrong place, telling people to "be like Jesus" or asking WWJD in this situation or that. But those are downstream calls and questions. Something comes beforehand, namely following Jesus closely and intimately:

> The heart and soul of the Christian existence is not ultimately about being Christlike. It is rather that we would be united with Christ. So much contemporary reflection on the Christian life speaks of discipleship as becoming more and more like Jesus. This is problematic because Christlikeness is derivative of something else, namely, union with Christ. And to pursue it on its own actually distracts us from the true goal of the Christian life.[10]

## How Then Should We Live?

It's the question philosophers have asked for centuries: "How then shall we live?" Every worldview attempts to answer this question, and one of the problems of postmodern philosophy is that it mocks attempts to find a sense of meaning in life. "People seek the meaning of history," the Russian existentialist Lev Shestov (1866–1938), said. "But why must history have meaning? The question is never raised. . . . And yet if someone raised it, he would begin, perhaps, by doubting that history has a meaning, then continue by becoming convinced that history is not at all called to have a meaning, that history is one thing and *meaning* another."[11]

Jesus would say that living without meaning is destructive to the human spirit. And we have seen this devastation play out in recent atheistic regimes, with sixty million dead in China, six million dead in Europe, and twenty million dead in Russia—all driven by secular narratives that empty history of morality and meaning. By contrast, Jesus tells us that history—and human life—has infinite worth and meaning. What you do with your life means *everything*! If we're honest, though, believing something different than your neighbor about the divinity of Christ doesn't cost you much if it doesn't filter down to *a way of being* in the world. A version of Christianity characterized by mere beliefs rarely translates to a different quality of life. You can assent to the fact that Jesus is God and that he forgave you for your sins on the cross. But now what? You spend your money and time no differently than the non-Jesus-believing world around you. You're busy scrolling Instagram while Netflix plays in the background, waiting to cart your kids to yet another soccer game. Jesus addresses us in this moment, reminding us that while there exists a set of beliefs Christians hold and believe, they have a purpose. They are *onto something*, namely, a radical life change. Your life must look different. Anything else isn't real Christianity.

When I was a kid, I attended Christian summer camp, and during one summer I met a girl named Rebecca who had "given her life to Jesus." A few years later, I ran into her again and found out her life was a moral mess. She was sleeping around with different guys and getting hammered every weekend. In other words, nothing about her life had changed from that time at camp. At the time, I was an outsider to Christianity, so I asked her, "Aren't you a Christian?" "I am!"

she responded, laughing. She thought for a moment more, and then added, "I prayed that prayer at camp, and they told me that's all I had to do."

I remember those words surprising me, even though I wasn't a follower of Jesus. *All you had to do?*

A couple of years later, shortly after I myself became a Christian, I was in a car with a friend. He had grown up going to a Christian church, but he wasn't living a life that reflected that upbringing. We were driving along, and as we went through an intersection, a car ran a red light. I swerved out of the way and into oncoming traffic, narrowly avoiding falling into a ditch and barely missing a head-on collision. We pulled over to the side of the road to catch our breath, aware that things could have been much worse.

As we drove home, I asked him, "So what if we had died? I mean, you grew up as a Christian, but it's not translating into your life. What do you do with that?" He looked at me and nonchalantly remarked, "I said a prayer as a kid at church this one time, and that's all they told me I had to do." There it was again: *all they told me I had to do.* Both of these friends had been taught, either consciously or unconsciously, that to be a follower of Jesus, you simply needed to believe something different than those around you. If you did this, you were "going to heaven" when you died. In other words, check the box, do the bare minimum, step over the lowest bar possible, and somehow you will be rewarded with great gain.

By contrast, Jesus' call to discipleship is costly. It is a reprioritization of everything: your relationships, your money, the way you do your job, the way you relate to your spouse, your kids, and your neighbors. You can't compartmentalize Jesus and his demands from the rest of your life. You can't say Jesus is good for "salvation," as your ticket to heaven, and everything else is in another drawer. Yet this way of living is very popular in the modern Western world. People can be a Christianized version of what they already are—without change, cost, or transformation. This is the opposite of biblical Christianity.

And this is precisely why Christianity wasn't for everybody. Jesus met a rich young ruler who couldn't walk away from his wealth, so he walked away from Jesus. The crowds walked away when Jesus told them to eat his flesh and drink his blood. The older brother in one of Jesus' parables wouldn't go into the party to celebrate the radical grace the Father had extended to his prodigal brother. Over and over again we see a consistent theme: people *reject* Jesus and his ways. Not accepting Jesus was the norm—and still is today. The default setting of the human heart is a rejection of Jesus' authority over our lives. And his proposed remedy to this rejection: *Deny yourself. Pick up your cross. Follow me.* Never have there been three more radical—yet life-giving—invitations set before humankind.

# CHAPTER 6

# The Threefold
# INVITATION

## 1. Deny Yourself

The command to deny yourself (Mark 8:34) is counterintuitive to everything our culture, our families, our friends, and our own minds and hearts tell us we need to find "salvation" in life. Our culture tells us to *find ourselves*. Find your inner beauty, your inner person; soul search, because only then will you discover your true self. You—along with your personal enlightenment and inward pleasure—are the highest priority in life. You are the greatest good. And if this is true, it makes sense to spare no expense pampering yourself, loving yourself, worshiping yourself, and setting yourself up for a perfect, pain-free life.

As philosophers have pointed out, if the naturalist story is true and there is no "next life," the logical thing to do is to compile pleasures and wealth, even if those come at the expense of others. This is the one life we will ever have, and there isn't anything more, so we should make the most of it. If I believe this, I should work tirelessly to compile as much money, power, status, and pleasure as possible, even if I have to step on others to get there. "Soul, you have ample goods laid up for many years; relax, eat, drink, be merry," the man in Jesus' parable says (Luke 12:19).

Jesus' call to deny ourselves subverts our most basic impulse. Why? Because he knows that if we look for what we want in a spouse, our kids, our work, or making money, we will never be satisfied. Joy and fulfillment are elusive when we seek them in this world. This is why the richest, most glamorous and powerful people in the world are on their third or fourth marriages, can't stay faithful to their spouse, are addicted to drugs or alcohol, or are obsessed with plastic surgeries. They have massive homes, expensive cars, and all the Botox in the world, and they can't function. They have everything and still search for more.

Nothing in this world can satisfy them. And, to Jesus' point, there is nothing inside that can satisfy them either. N. T. Wright says we answer four fundamental questions to locate meaning: "Who are we? Where are we? What's the problem? What's the solution?"[1] Every worldview is a collection of ideas answering these fundamental questions, especially that last one: what is the solution to our lostness? For many of us, our best working solution is to put ourselves at the center of the narrative. We make ourselves the sun in our own universe, and Jesus says this is the fatal error. If the bedrock of our lives has no transcendent component to it—if this world and its offerings are all we have—then we will hit a ceiling. We will keep wandering.

The human heart asks, *How do I find meaning and joy in my life?* These are the common responses: *Maybe if I just had a better job, a better spouse, better kids, better [fill in the blank], then I would be happy and complete in life.* Our hearts identify the problems of our lives as *external*—out there. That circumstance. That experience. But the biblical story pushes hard against this, knowing it's a doomed approach because we are part of the problem, not the solution. Looking to ourselves keeps us from the one thing that can actually heal us. Welcoming ourselves is the very thing that becomes our undoing, because having the world revolve around us is unbearable in the end.

That's the hint Jesus is giving us in this invitation. "Deny yourself." He's reminding us that we are not the hero of this story, that true saviors come from *outside*. "Whoever would save his life will lose it, but whoever loses his life for my sake and the gospel's will save it," Jesus said (Mark 8:35). Timothy Keller comments on this verse, "The deliberately chosen Greek word for "life" here is *psychē*, from which we get our word *psychology*. It denotes your identity, your personality, your selfhood."[2] Jesus' appeal is not to "lose yourself in order to lose yourself" like Eastern philosophy teaches, but to base your life on him and the gospel—in other words, on Jesus' life, death, and resurrection, not your own life. Jesus says, *"It's not enough just to know me as a teacher or a principle for life. I went to the cross, lost my identity, so you can have one. Base your life on that, not yourself."*[3]

We can be our own worst enemies. Theologian and pastor Richard Baxter (1615–91) put it this way: "Self is the most treacherous enemy, and the most insinuating deceiver in the world. Of all other vices, it is both the hardest to realize, and the hardest to cure," even when the goal is our own joy.

## The Happiness Hypothesis

Jesus' command regarding the denial of self is an invitation to refuse the serpent's promise that we "will be like God" (Genesis 3:5). We're always going to fail at producing true and lasting joy for ourselves because we were not designed for that. Have you ever attempted to do a job you weren't intended or equipped to do? It was probably a disaster. I once showed up to a church service where a large group had gathered, ready to worship, but the drummer didn't show up. I had played drums a few times in my band (don't ask), so I volunteered to help. How hard could it be? I grabbed the drumsticks and started pounding away, and in my little world, I was doing great. But then I looked up. The band members were giving me that awkward, over-the-shoulder glare as they tried to cover my mistakes and errors. The people in the audience had those uncomfortable just-ate-a-lemon faces. In that moment, I realized I was creating a disaster! I was doing more harm than good, so I walked away from the drum set, never to return. My intentions were good, but I was incompetent, unfit for the task. Despite my best efforts, I had an inability to do what was required. Jesus entered our world to save us from ourselves. And the first step is to stop trying to do something you were never designed to do, to let someone who knows what he's doing do it for you. Deny yourself. He who loses his life will find it. Self-emptiness readies us for fullness.

Jesus said that when we finally orient our lives around God, we're like a man finding "treasure hidden in a field." What happens next? In the parable the treasure is "found and covered up. . . . Then in *his joy* [the man] goes and sells all that he has and buys that field" (Matthew 13:44, italics mine). When we find something more valuable than anything else this world has to offer, the wisest course of action is to do whatever it takes to keep it. Self-denial is not a loss; it is the greatest gain, the winning move. And when we face difficulty and trial in this life, we will be able to "rejoice in that day and leap *for joy,* because great is [our] reward in heaven" (Luke 6:23 NIV).

Puritan theologian and preacher Jonathan Edwards (1703–58), recognized by some as "the greatest evangelical mind in American history with no intellectual successor,"[4] preached his first sermon, "Christian Happiness," on this topic. Christians should be happy when they embrace three truths: (1) Our bad things will turn out for good, (2) Our good things can never be taken away from us, and (3) The best things are yet to come. Edwards said such a person "is happy in whatever circumstances he is placed because of the spiritual privileges and advantages, joys and satisfactions, he enjoys. How great a happiness must it be to a man to have all his sins pardoned and to stand guilty of nothing in God's presence: to be washed clean from all his pollutions. God loves him, and He has adopted him and taken him to be His child." He concluded, "The reflection on these things affords such a pleasantness to the mind, as far exceeds and is immensely above all outward delights. How great are the comforts and pleasures of the godly. Their pleasures are of vastly a more refined, higher and more noble kind that no worldly afflictions in the world are able to deprive them of."

Long before self-help philosophy made happiness and joy about our own selfish pursuits, it was a Christian concept of what we could experience, not by searching within ourselves or even for happiness itself, but by being willing to define our lives by our relationship to a loving and all-powerful God. Happiness comes through earnestly seeking the One who created us. "If you go to Jesus to get a new personality . . . you still haven't really gone to Jesus. Your real self will not come out as long as you look for it; it will only emerge when you're looking for him."[5]

## 2. Pick Up Your Cross

The second command is for a disciple to "take up his cross daily" (Luke 9:23). In the first century, crosses were used by the Roman Empire to execute criminals—revolutionaries challenging the agenda of the State. Some commentators identify Jesus' message of the coming kingdom of God as having hidden counter-empire undertones. In his brilliant commentary on the Gospel of Matthew, Warren Carter translates the phrase "kingdom of heaven" as "empire of heaven" through the whole Gospel.[6] "The empire of heaven is like a seed. . . ," and so on. Jesus was inviting those who heard him to join the true and better empire under the rule of the true Lord of the world—not Caesar, but Jesus. In context, we should remember that this was the same Roman Empire that crucified six thousand people on a single day across a one-hundred-mile stretch of road to send a message to insurrectionists that Caesar was Lord. The empire wanted recognition that Rome was the ultimate authority and it had little regard for a young Jewish preacher from Galilee.

Notice that Jesus didn't say, "Pick up my cross." Our discipleship is not just a matter of accepting Jesus' pain and sacrifice for us, though he did suffer for us. No, Jesus instructs his potential disciples to take up our own crosses. In fact, the term *cross* is used twice in reference to a disciple's fate before it is ever made explicit that this is how Jesus would die. Our discipleship, while centered on Jesus' cross and what it did for us, is also about our own cross to bear.

Again, there is a cost to following Jesus. We are to view our lives, desires, agendas, and beliefs as dead and gone. "I have been crucified with Christ," the apostle Paul, said. "It is no longer I who live, but Christ who lives in me" (Galatians 2:20). Why do we have to die for Jesus? Because a seed can't produce a flower or fruit or tree or anything of value unless it goes into the ground and dies first.

In the HBO World War II miniseries *Band of Brothers*, one of the soldiers is scared and finding it hard to fight. He admits that when he first landed in Normandy he saw a dead kid, fell asleep feeling sick, didn't even try to find his unit when he awoke, and had been terrified ever since. That's when a fellow soldier says, "The only hope you have is to accept the fact that you're already dead. The sooner you accept that, the sooner you'll be able to function as a soldier is supposed to function: without mercy, without compassion, without remorse. All war depends upon it."

When Jesus put the image of a cross in front of his disciples, he was saying, "This must be the shape of your life if you want to follow me. You're already dead. The only way you're ever going to be able to get enough courage to sacrifice, to go over and above what you want to do, is to embrace your death. Death to your own desires, to your emotional wants and needs, and even, for some, your lives." If you are building a life in the present world with an eye to success, wealth, and comfort—"civilian pursuits" (2 Timothy 2:4)—then you're not a good fit for Jesus' kingdom. You're holding on to too much.

If you count yourself as already dead, your reputation and your home's square footage will matter far less. These things can be given up at the drop of a hat if the Lord calls you to do so. If you are already dead, you don't have to build an empire. You're freed up to be others-focused, not self-focused. I was reminded of this while reading a story about a group of missionaries sailing to Africa many years ago. The captain of their boat laughed at them, saying, "You'll only die over there!" One of the missionaries responded, "Captain, we died before we started." Those who are already dead have emptied themselves of selfish ambitions. Jesus said that we must decrease so that he will increase.

## Safe for the Whole Family?

Jesus was not trying, as many do today, to fool people into the kingdom by setting a low, comfortable bar. He was front-loading the scandal. When I train church planters, I lead by saying, "What you win people *with*, is what you win them *to*." For many aspiring pastors, the temptation is to grow their churches by making Christianity as easy as possible, and this leads to flimsy theology. They set the bar of faith low: say a quick prayer, raise a hand, and follow a set of ten snappy steps to live a good life (all starting with the letter *S*). This type of evangelism doesn't lead to a faith of any substance, a resilient faith that lasts. If people are drawn to Christianity because it is easy, they will likely remain exactly where they are. And down the line, they'll be surprised to learn that the Christian life is often not about victory but obedience—obedience in the face of trial, suffering, and even death.

I want church planters to understand straight out of the gate that if you want to shepherd a church full of people who have undergone radical life change for the cause of Jesus, people who are ready to go out into the world with you and share the gospel at any cost, you have to lead with that. As Dietrich Bonhoeffer said, "When Christ calls a man, he bids him come and die." Jesus was making this clear to his audience up front.

Everyone dies at some point. And for most disciples throughout history, this "dying" occurs in a figurative way. We "die" to our own plans, egos, and selfish desires. However, there is also an undercurrent of literalism in Jesus' call as well. Luke reported that John the Baptist, the quintessential example of discipleship, was beheaded by Herod because he followed Jesus (Luke 9:9). This was also the fate of many of Jesus' first disciples. I mention this because often modern Christianity is marketed in bookstores, movies, and music as something "safe for the whole family." It isn't meant to be. There's absolutely nothing safe about it. Christianity is a way of life that pushes against the way of the world, and the inevitable clash results in pain and tragedy for the Christian instead of worldly success.

In Revelation 6 the apostle John described a vision God gave him about the spiritual realities of the world: "I saw under the altar the souls of those who had been slain for the word of God and for the witness they had borne" (v. 9). These martyred souls were found "under the altar," the place where the blood of the sacrificial animals ran down and collected in a pool. This haunting picture is a contrast to modern Christianity and the so-called celebrity pastors of the Western church. You may have seen the popular Instagram account called *PreachersNSneakers*, which features pictures of pastors preaching at their churches alongside the retail value of the clothes they are wearing. You'll find a stylish young preacher wearing a $3,000 jacket, or $1,800 sneakers (no joke), or $500 designer T-shirts, and the list goes on. This picture of earthly "success" is far from the paradigm for discipleship that Jesus laid out for us. The New Testament paradigm is akin to the death and suffering that Jesus described as taking up a cross. It's a way of life where those "under the altar," not those on a stage, are the heroes.

The text in Revelation continues with these unsettling words: "They were . . . told to rest a little longer, until the number of their fellow servants and their brothers should be complete, who were to be killed as they themselves had been" (Rev. 6:11). In other words, God has an appointed number of people who will be slaughtered for their faith. There's a number of completeness, and God is not going to bring his vengeance and wrath on the wicked until that number has been reached. The *Oxford Christian World Encyclopedia* estimates that throughout history there have been approximately seventy-five million Christian martyrs (forty-five million of whom were killed in the twentieth century), which means half of the people killed for Jesus over the span of two thousand years met their end in the last one hundred years. And still, that number of "completeness" hasn't been reached. The threat of death is not something from the distant past. It is ever-present, and it is something we must consider when deciding whether to follow Jesus.

A few years ago, I went on a mission trip to Turkey. A week before we left, three Christians were brutally murdered there for hosting a Bible study in their home. A group of men showed up at the meeting with knives, tied the men to chairs, and tortured them before killing them. While on the trip, I was in a park talking to a group of Turkish men about Jesus. I was feeling a little embarrassed that I had come all that way without knowing their language, presuming I had *anything* worthwhile to teach them. They brought up the killing to me as we talked, asking, "Why didn't his family bring revenge on them? How could they forgive people so easily?" I asked the translator to open up the New Testament and read the following: "Jesus said: love your enemies, pray for those who persecute you." The group was dead silent. Then one by one, the young men moved closer to the man with the Bible. They grabbed it from his hand, crowding their heads closer to the page and reading it for themselves. It was as if they were reading the words of an alien. It was an idea extremely counterintuitive to their natural impulses, but they were drawn to it with a sense of awe and wonder.

God used the death of this man to force a cultural conversation and bring these young men to himself. And this is the scandal of Jesus' call to discipleship—he wants to blow our minds and wreck our hearts so he can remake them afresh. In that moment with those men, a terrible thought struck me: Is it more important to God that the gospel advances than that my life continue another day? The answer to that question is clear in the Bible. It is not something Jesus hides from us: "Whoever *loses his life* for my sake will save it" (Luke 9:24, italics mine). That's what John the Baptist's life exemplified. That's what this man in Turkey exemplified. That's what the souls under the altar are all about. God will use our joys to glorify himself and reach people, but he will also use our pain.

## 3. Follow Me

The final exhortation of Jesus' threefold call is "follow me" (Luke 9:23). It's an invitation and arguably the most important invitation of the three.

In his examination of biblical leadership, Jan David Hettinga asserts, "The ultimate issue in the universe is leadership. Who you follow and what directs your life is the single most important thing about you."[7] Jesus asks us to follow him. That is the essence of being a disciple.

The word *disciple* occurs 269 times in the New Testament, while the word *Christian* is found only 3 times. In other words, *the* paradigmatic presentation of Christianity in the Bible is not one who simply believes one set of ideas or doctrines over another, or one who says a prayer one time or comes to the alter, or raises a hand but one who follows Jesus' teachings and way of life as Lord/Teacher/Leader. "Jesus is after followership. He is not merely interested in saving our souls, meeting our needs, and healing our hurts. He intends that we operate under His authority for the rest of our lives and for all eternity."[8]

Most religions work externally, trying to bend a person's behavior through fear or pride. Take honesty, for instance. Timothy Keller says, "People typically try to instill honesty in others this way: 'If you lie, you'll get in trouble with God and other people,' or 'If you lie, you'll be like those terrible people, and you are better than that!'" In other words, the motivation for change is a fear of punishment ("you'll get in trouble") or an appeal to *pride* ("you'll be like a dirty liar"). These are both self-centered motivations, which is why they end up not working. They crush the heart and life of the person under their weight.[9] Modern psychology confirms this is not how people change. They change through what Thomas Chalmers (1780–1847) called "the expulsive power of a new affection." Chalmers used this phrase as the title of a sermon he preached on 1 John 2:15: "Love not the world, neither the things that are in the world. If any man love the world, the love of the Father is not in him" (KJV). Here is his summary of the sermon:

> There are two ways in which a person may attempt to displace from the human heart its love of the world—either by a demonstration of the world's vanity, so as that the heart shall be prevailed upon simply to withdraw its regards from an object that is not

worthy of it; or, by setting forth another object, even God, as *more worthy of its attachment*, so as that the heart shall be prevailed upon not to resign an old affection, which shall have nothing to succeed it, but to exchange an old affection for a new one. My purpose is to show, that from the constitution of our nature, the former method is altogether incompetent and ineffectual and that the latter method will alone suffice for the rescue and recovery of the heart from the wrong affection that domineers over it.[10]

Chalmers was saying that lasting and true change at the heart level, the level of our deepest desires, does not come about through negative motivations but through positive ones. Jesus knows that unless our highest love is God, his other two commands are neither desirable nor possible. Yes, we all need to deny self and die daily to our dreams and visions of the "good life" (which is a pretty depressing and empty message in and of itself), but you can only do this if you are motivated by a new and better desire. We need a new purpose, one that makes the heart soar and enables sacrifice because it is more precious than life itself. The basis of Christianity is not what you don't do; it's a person you walk toward. Christianity is more than accepting Jesus as your *Savior*; he is your *treasure* as well. Many have ceased being Christians because they felt crushed by the weight and burden of the first two calls. They did not follow Jesus as their treasure, the motive enabling the sacrifice.

## Jesus, Gandalf, and Obi-Wan

How do we come to treasure Jesus? We must *learn* from him, taking him on as our Leader, Teacher, and Mentor. We're not called to do this as a one-time assent—through a raised hand at church or summer camp—but through the dozens of decisions we make every day. Jesus challenges us to pick up our crosses *daily*. Christianity is not based solely on a Savior who worked in the past; it is a living and breathing movement. Unlike Islam, Judaism, or Hinduism, we aren't just interested in the ancient teachings recorded in a book. We worship a Savior who is alive, who offers his services to us as our Teacher and Lord daily!

This is the fulfillment of the epic tales. Donald Miller tells us that every great and heroic story is structured in a similar way:

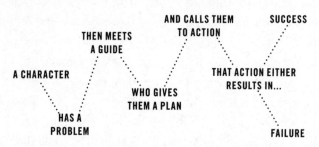

Luke Skywalker has Obi-Wan and Yoda (*Star Wars*); Frodo has Gandalf (*The Lord of the Rings*); Katniss Everdeen has Haymitch Abernathy (*The Hunger Games*), and so on. But all of these are imitations of the true and better story. And Jesus invites us into this true and better story. He is the Hero, and he is also the Guide. He is the Mentor who knows our fears and challenges, who guides us according to his plan. I'm reminded of what Reuven's father says to him in Chaim Potok's brilliant novel *The Chosen*:

> "Reuven, listen to me. The Talmud says that a person should do two things for himself. One is to acquire a teacher. Do you remember the other."
>
> "Choose a friend," I said.
>
> "Yes. You know what a friend is, Reuven? A Greek philosopher said that two people who are true friends are like two bodies with one soul."
>
> I nodded.
>
> "Reuven, if you can, make Danny Saunders your friend."
>
> "I like him a lot, Abba."

"No. Listen to me. I am not talking about only liking him. I am telling you to make him your friend and to let him make you his friend."[11]

When we follow Jesus, we are finding a Savior, but that's just the beginning. He will become a Teacher and a Friend (John 15:14–15), guiding us in every aspect of our lives. His views will shape our views of God, salvation, sex, ethics, money, parenting, and politics. When we allow him to assume these roles, he promises freedom, and we will find the meaning we were always looking for but couldn't find on our own.

## The 10,000-Hour Rule

*How* do we follow Jesus well? How do we walk as Jesus walked (1 John 2:6)? Many of us want to put faith in Jesus as Savior but find it difficult to follow him as Master and Lord. We want to worship and serve Jesus, but we struggle to accept his discipling applied to every aspect of our lives. Jesus called twelve people together, not just to teach them *about* discipleship, but to actually disciple them. He modeled what was expected of disciples and how to achieve it. And it took him some time. The Gospel of John hints that Jesus' discipling of these men took about three and a half years. He called twelve normal men away from their normal lives—lives as fishermen, tax collector, husbands, and fathers. He essentially said, "Drop all of that, and come follow me." And they did just that for three years, until he was killed.

Why did it take three years? Jesus could just as easily have written a systematic theology book, called them together on a retreat weekend, and said, "Here's what I want you to believe and how I want you to live. Now go and tell everybody to do that too." But instead, he befriended them. He did life alongside of them in the hills of Galilee—eating, sleeping, and breathing every moment together—for three years. And that's the point. Discipleship takes time. In his book *Outliers*, journalist Malcolm Gladwell investigates the lives of extraordinary, high-achieving people in an effort to discover what brought their success. What factors put Bill Gates, the Beatles, and Mozart in our history books? Gladwell observes that we often give too much credit to who they are (nature and gifts) and not enough to where they are from and the opportunities they were given or stumbled upon (nurture and environment). He challenges the "they were just born that way" narrative and suggests the story is far more interesting and nuanced. For example, he demonstrates that for someone to become a master of something, he or she needs a minimum of ten thousand hours of practice in it. Drawing from the work of neurologist Daniel Levitin, Gladwell notes that the data received from a number of psychological studies of musicians, artists, and athletes confirms that excellence at a complex task requires a minimum level of practice.

In short, to become great at anything, a person needs time and practice—far more than innate skill, good blood, or intelligence. Experts have settled on ten thousand hours as the magic number for true expertise: "In study after study, of composers, basketball players, fiction writers, ice-skaters, concert pianists, chess players, [and] master criminals. This number comes up again and again. Ten thousand hours is equivalent to roughly three hours a day, or 20 hours a week, of practice over 10 years. . . . No one has yet found a case in which true world-class expertise was accomplished in less time. It seems that it takes the brain this long to assimilate all that it needs to know to achieve true mastery."[12]

To become a true master at anything takes lots of time. I remember using the ten-thousand-hour rule analogy in a sermon once, and when I finished preaching, a young woman walked up to me and said, "If you calculate the time the disciples spent with Jesus, assuming they took a Sabbath but otherwise spent day and night with him for three years, it actually equals just over ten thousand hours!" This is why Jesus didn't simply write a treatise and leave. He wanted his disciples to master what in Judaism was known as a *halakah*, a way of life and being in the world. He wanted them to become experts in his way of living. He wanted them to be the Mozarts of discipleship, and he knew the only way to get there was through practice and lots of failure. This is not about getting it right all the time. As has been noted, grace is opposed to earning, not effort. The only way to become an expert in the ways of Jesus is through time, energy, and effort.

At the end of the Gospel of Matthew, Jesus proclaimed the great mission of the church: "Go therefore and make disciples of all nations, baptizing them in the name of the Father and of the Son and of the Holy Spirit, teaching them to observe all that I have commanded you" (28:19–20). Notice that Jesus doesn't merely say teach them "all I commanded." That would be an easier task. One could teach a parrot all that Jesus commanded. No, he said to teach them "*to observe* all that I have commanded."[13] This teaching includes obedience and is something else entirely. It's one thing to say, "Love your enemies," but a very different thing to actually do it. "Parrots will not repent, and worship Jesus, and lay up treasures in heaven, and love their enemies, and go out like sheep in the midst of wolves to herald the kingdom of God."[14]

## Vampire Christianity

Anything other than a Christianity centered on the final command of Jesus to follow him in all things is not biblical Christianity. Dallas Willard pointed this out years ago, identifying other versions as "vampire Christianity." This is where people take or receive Jesus at *his* cost but not theirs:

> These are people who say to Jesus, "I'd like a little of your blood please. But I don't care to be your student or to have your character. In fact, will you just excuse me while I get on with my life and I'll see you in heaven?" Can we really imagine that this is an approach Jesus finds acceptable? Someone will say, "*Can I not be saved?*"; that is, can I not get to heaven when I die without any discipleship? Perhaps you can. But you might wish to think about what your life amounts to before you die . . . whether you

really would be comfortable for eternity in the presence of one whose company you have not found especially desirable for the few hours and days of your earthly existence.[15]

Willard went on to call such a dichotomy a heresy, and here is why vampire Christianity is dangerous: it means you don't find Jesus all that interesting. He isn't as compelling as Instagram, Twitter, or ordering the latest thing from Amazon. He isn't interesting enough to spend quality time with. Or to read about or learn from. You can't be bothered to listen to him. Forging a relationship is hard work, after all, and Jesus doesn't talk back in any of the usual ways. He isn't physically present in the way we might desire. This is a spiritual relationship, different than our other relationships. But the whole point of discipleship is that it is going to be hard. That's why people walked away from following Jesus and why they still do every day. And these weren't just the "pagan" unbelievers. John tells us that "many of his disciples turned back and no longer walked with him" (John 6:66).

How do we ensure that our relationship with Jesus doesn't meet this same end? The secret is in the passage we have explored in this chapter: "If anyone would come after me, let him . . . take up his cross *daily*" (Luke 9:23, italics mine). Daily commitment is the only way discipleship is going to work. One step at a time. One decision at a time. Theologian and martyr Dietrich Bonhoeffer, who was killed by the Nazis because he wouldn't synchronize the German church with the ideology of the Third Reich, put it this way: "Who is Jesus Christ, for us, today?" This is a question that guides believers in every generation because "the Christian faith is both *faith* in Jesus of Nazareth and also *faithfulness* to him. (This double meaning is in both the Hebrew and Greek words for 'faith' in the Bible.) Christian faith simply is discipleship to Jesus Christ."[16] The call to be faithful to Jesus is a profound call, maybe the most profound in the entire Bible. Who will be found faithful in their hearts, minds, and practices on the last day? It's not about who starts the race but who finishes. Who will put one foot in front of the other daily, empowered by the grace, love, and voice of Jesus? Who among us—until Jesus returns or takes us in death—will wake up each morning and say, "I choose to follow you again today."

## End with Why

Many people in the world have given their lives to Jesus' threefold invitation of discipleship; approximately one billion people on the earth today claim to be Christians. In Mark 10:36 Jesus asked two brothers, James and John, "What do you want me to do for you?" In response, they asked that one sit at Jesus' right hand and the other at his left in his glory (v. 37)—that is, they wanted to be granted power and prestige in his kingdom. Jesus said no.

A profound question is lurking under the surface like some unseen predator: the issue sometimes isn't *if* we are following Jesus but *why*? James and John were doing it to be successful. Why are you following Jesus? What is your motivation? We usually applaud any gesture of intimacy toward Christ; any impulse or attention one gives him is automatically celebrated. But Jesus pushes back with the deeper question: "Why are you interested in me?"

I know people who become Christians for all kinds of reasons: to get more friends, to marry a girl, to absolve guilt over something they regret. I know people who want to plant churches to make up for the lack of love they received growing up, searching for it instead from a devoted congregation. On and on we could go. This is heavy stuff. But the challenge here is as real as the invitation: we have to think through not only *if* we love and follow Jesus but *why*.

Why we ever started to love him. Why we do now.

# PART IV

---

# The Problem of
# LOVING GOD

*Love is life. All, everything that I understand,
I understand only because I love. Everything
is, everything exists, only because I love.
Everything is united by it alone.*

—LEO TOLSTOY, WAR AND PEACE

# CHAPTER 7

## Counterfeit
# GODS

If your house caught on fire, what would you take with you? Your wedding pictures? Maybe the watch your grandfather gave you? Your kids?

I've been in one fire in my life, and I caused it. I was twenty years old, home alone, and I tried to make Kraft Macaroni & Cheese. I poured the dry noodles into a bowl, put the bowl in the microwave, set the time for nine minutes—because that's how you make pasta right?—and went and had a shower.

Dry noodles. In a bowl. In the microwave. No oversight.

Five minutes later the fire alarm went off, echoing all over my neighborhood. I jumped out of the shower, grabbed a towel, threw it around myself, and ran upstairs. A whole section of my kitchen was on fire because the microwave had literally blown up, and fire and smoke were streaming out of it. What did I run out the door with? What in my life rose to the top as a priority? *The towel that was around my waist.* I didn't want to be seen standing buck naked on my front lawn.

Priorities rise to the top at certain moments in life. Every secondary thing fades into the background, and just one thing remains. When the doctor gives a diagnosis or you hear that a family member might be in danger, all of the other problems in the world seem small and insignificant, and your attention singularly focuses.

This is what was happening when Jesus told us all about the most important thing we need to know—what has been called the Great Commandment. A scribe—a smart, educated, and respected man in first-century Israel—walked up to Jesus and asked, "Which

commandment is the most important of all?" We should all be leaning in at this point, paying attention to whatever he said—pens out,
quieting the barking dog, ready to make it the focus of our lives. Jesus'
answer was profound, especially in its application: "The most important is, 'Hear, O Israel: The Lord our God, the Lord is one. And you
shall love the Lord your God with all your heart and with all your soul
and with all your mind and with all your strength. . . .' There is no
other commandment greater" (Mark 12:28–31).

*Boom!*

There are six hundred laws in the Bible. The scribe was saying
to Jesus, "Sum them up and give me the most important one. Give
me the one verse, the one you're going to take with you when the fire
starts." That's a lot of pressure. If someone came to me as a pastor
after a church service and said, "Sum up for me in one verse all of
the sixty-six books of the Bible, with all their thousands of verses and
concepts and commands. What is the most important thing?" I don't
know what I would answer. But Jesus did this without any hesitation.
*Love God* with your whole self.

This may be the most important chapter in this book. Because
contrary to what one might think, the topic of loving God is one of
the most neglected ideas in modern Christianity. Most of the work
done on the historical Jesus or the Christian life ignores this topic. In
my entire library, and among the books owned by my church staff, I
found very few books that explore with any depth the priority of loving
God. Despite being the key focus of Jesus' teaching, little is said about
this in the modern Christian conversation. While I was researching
for this book, I asked my Twitter followers to chime in about the books
on loving God they had read and enjoyed. Surprisingly, I found the
most common responses were books written hundreds of years ago.
The most popular among them was Thomas Vincent's (1634–78) *The
True Christian's Love to the Unseen Christ*. That book proved to be a
treasure, but again, I found it interesting that I had to reach back hundreds of years to find a worthy treatise on the topic. This is my small

attempt to right that wrong, or at least to draw your attention to a topic that Jesus found to be of ultimate importance.

## Heart and Soul

Jesus was not the first person to be asked about the greatest command. Historians tell us it was a common question, often asked of first-century rabbis to help people decide which teacher they wanted to follow. The answer they gave cut to the heart of what a rabbi felt was most important in life. And that makes sense. We want to know what we're getting into before we yoke ourselves to somebody. There's a famous story of a rabbi named Hillel who lived a few decades before Jesus. A Gentile (non-Jewish person) approached him and said, "I'm going to stand on one foot until you tell me what is the greatest commandment." Hillel replied, "Whatever you hate don't do to your neighbor. All the rest of the laws are commentary, go and do likewise."

When we ask Jesus—the greatest rabbi who ever lived—what we should run out of the house with, his answer is *a love for God*, a love that consumes our hearts, souls, minds, and strength. This is the key to everything according to Jesus. It's profound. It's deep. And it is life-changing in ways we could never have imagined. So, what does it really mean?

Loving God first means that the priority in our lives isn't our religious practices, but something inside us, something we possess at the level of heart and soul. It begins where our affections lie. Jesus was affirming that the time had come for people to love God above all things and not just to obey him outwardly, checking boxes off a list. In fact, rightly understood, obedience comes as a result of loving him and not the other way around. The Greek word for "heart" in this passage is *kardia*, from which we get the words *cardio* and *cardiac arrest*. It doesn't refer to the physical organ that pumps blood through our veins. It refers to the center of all physical and spiritual life—your whole self. It's what you value, what you do with your life, and the fountain and seat of your emotions, thoughts, dreams, passions, desires, appetites, purposes, and endeavors. It drives and shapes your will and character. Jesus is saying that everything important and definitive about you needs to be centered around God rather than anything else, including *yourself.*

Your relationship to God must be more than a belief; it must be a *love affair.* Remember when you started dating your spouse? I used to write poems for my wife, Erin. I even wrote a few screenplays and dedicated them to her. I wrote songs about her. I called her. I drove to see her. I thought about her constantly. We would fall asleep on the phone every night chatting. That's what you do with someone you love. And that is a taste of what it means to *know* God. We should have faith in God; after all, we are "justified by faith" (Romans 3:21–28; Galatians 2:16). But our faith (which is really trusting what a person says or promises to us) should be informed by our love for them. Loving God means treasuring the person behind that justification. "Blessed are the pure in heart, for they shall see God" (Matthew 5:8). Our ability to see and understand God is a natural result or outflow of our heart's desire for him.

So what's so scandalous about the command to love God? Today loving God sounds trite and even sentimental, and modern Christianity is definitely no stranger to sentimentalism. But to interpret it as a weak or sentimental thing is to misunderstand the command. What is scandalous about loving God is what it implies. Human beings are hardwired to love, even if that love proves to be self-destructive. Our desires or "loves" drive who we are and what we become. What is scandalous is that Jesus is saying, "Change that thing." He's raising a challenge: What do you already love with all your heart, mind, soul, and strength—and can you transfer that affection to God instead? Are you willing to make that thing you currently love above all else secondary? Will you leave it behind when the house is on fire?

God created each of us with a capacity to love with our whole heart. When he put humankind in the garden, he wired us to love him with all we are. He even gave us a capacity to love something *infinite*—namely, God. But there's a danger in that. If we channel our incredible capacity into loving something other than God, it will consume and destroy us. And not just us; it will harm the people around us too. It's like Dr. Frankenstein endowing the monster with a great capacity for power. The risk is that the power given will be turned against him, against his own creator, as soon as it is invested with energy and life. This is what God did in the garden of Eden. He created potential monsters because he gave humans the infinite desire to love something—even something other than him—with our whole selves.

And then that potential was realized. We turned.

A few passages in the Bible describe this scenario. One of the best is Romans 1, where the writer says that God put us in the garden and gave us the capacity to love, worship, and live with no bounds (but one). We could experience unending joy, pleasure, purpose, meaning in work, love, art, sex, play, marriage, child rearing, and endless discovery. But humankind chose to misdirect that love. God gave us limitless opportunity with one boundary—a test of faith, of our love for and trust in him. He told us not to "eat from the tree," but we couldn't help ourselves, wanting what was not ours to take. And in that moment, we rebelled, we sinned, and we fell: "For although they knew God, they did not honor him as God or give thanks to him, but they became futile in their thinking, and their foolish hearts were darkened" (Romans 1:21).

"Their foolish hearts were darkened." That phrase is important because it points us back to our hearts. Jesus' call to love God with our hearts is his way of reversing that darkening. "Claiming to be wise," Paul continued, "they became fools, and exchanged the glory of the immortal God for images resembling mortal man and birds and animals and creeping things . . . and worshiped and served the creature rather than the Creator" (Romans 1:22–23, 25). The story of the fall is about our enemy Satan tempting humankind to *replace God*: "For

God knows that when you eat of [the tree] your eyes will be opened, and you will be like God, knowing good and evil" (Genesis 3:5).

We exchanged the joy of God for the fruit—for created things (temporal, material, limited things). Another name for this exchange is idolatry. When we give our whole heart, mind, soul, and strength to anything other than God, that thing becomes an idol, an object of worship. The writer of Genesis is telling us that this is the fundamental problem with humanity, the problem beneath all of our problems. We take something finite and temporary—something God has made— and we try to make it satisfy that infinite longing in our lives. We take a good thing and make it a god thing. The finite god replacements range from the familiar bad guys—money, sex, and power—to the more insidious and hidden ones—things like our family, our comfort, or even religion itself. Again, *anything* can become a replacement for God, and sometimes the most difficult idols to identify are the very good things in our lives that keep us from fully loving God.

## Two Modern Idols: Comfort and Family

One of the central scandals of Jesus' ministry was how he called out the idols of people's lives. He identified the idols and called the people to leave behind the things that were competing with God for their allegiance. This took center stage in Luke 9:57–62 when a man approached Jesus and declared, "I will follow you wherever you go." In other words, he was saying, "Sign me up. I want to be a disciple. I want to follow you." Jesus looked with spiritual insight into his heart and saw an idol, so he spoke directly to what that man loved most: "Foxes have holes, and birds of the air have nests, but the Son of Man has nowhere to lay his head" (v. 58). This is a poetic way of saying, "If you are going to follow me, your life may end up like mine: homeless, penniless, suffering, hated." And this is a problem for this man because his idol, like many of ours, is comfort, ease, security, stability, and safety. To follow Jesus means giving up those things up.

## THE GOD OF COMFORT: CITIZENS OF THE EMPIRE

I confess I've never been without a home—a roof over my head, food and water, and clothes in my closet (or in a pile on the floor—sorry, Erin). These are things I depend on and take for granted. More than that, these are things I *love*. But the Son of Man had no place to rest his head. A willingness to give up comfort and ease is central to what it means to follow Jesus. In our culture today, this means we need to be willing to walk away from extravagance and safety to follow Jesus where he leads us, and this is much harder than we'd like to think it is. Where I live, there is a subtle elitism around possessions. People give off the vibe that if you don't own a house or drive an Escalade or dress in the finest clothes, you aren't worthy of their respect. You're not worth leaning into.

I remember a conversation my wife had with someone as we were just starting our church. We were hanging out with a group of people when one of the women looked at Erin and asked, "So how much did you pay for your house?" Erin replied naively, "Oh, we don't own it; we're just renting." From the woman's reaction, you'd think Erin had just admitted to a crime. Her face turned sour, she gave a noncommittal, "Oh," and just walked away. Apparently, as renters we weren't worth the investment of her time or energy. A snobbish focus on possessions as status symbols is one of the inevitable outcomes when a human soul doesn't love God more than reputation and wealth. The heart shrivels from an infinite capacity to love to a very finite capacity—love for a home or a car or a spouse, above all else. We fall for the comfort and ease, safety and status that possessions provide.

I could have taken a number of other jobs in my life, many that would be more lucrative than what I do now. A friend who works in the business world recently told me that if I ever decided to go into business, with my skill set I could make a few million dollars a year. Sometimes when our family is in a tough spot financially, I recall that conversation and begin to daydream. Maybe he shouldn't have told me that—and maybe it's not true—but I am glad he did, because it tests me, forcing me to continually reevaluate why I *choose* to be a pastor. I don't do it for money or attention or comfort. I do it to love God and people and to lead and teach the best I can. Every time I come back to that choice, it reminds me there are more important things, more lasting things, than money.

Was Jesus implying that buying a house is evil? No. Is driving an Escalade inherently bad? No. The problem isn't owning these things; it's when these things become *ultimate* things, things from which we derive our meaning and happiness in life. And these things can easily crowd out any room for God in our hearts. Could you hear God right now if he called you to something else? You're invested in your mortgage, your kids attend a good school, and you have a great friend group. If God called you—as he did Abraham—saying, "I'm directing you to leave and go to a place you've never been, and if you're obedient, I'll meet you there," could you do that right now?

True discipleship is understanding that believing in Jesus isn't just about whether we are going to heaven when we die, but about who we are in the process of becoming for all of eternity. And that means Jesus cares about what we care about, and he wants to change what we love, starting right now in this life. A proper relationship with money is one of many ways Jesus calls his followers to be "in the world but not of it," to live in exile from our true country as "foreigners and exiles" (1 Peter 2:11), citizens of the kingdom of God in the midst of the kingdoms of the world.

"You cannot serve God and mammon," Jesus said (Matthew 6:24 NKJV). Mammon was the Greek god of money worshiped in the ancient world, and worship of Mammon was part and parcel of what was required to live and work in the Roman Empire. To worship Mammon was to show your gratitude to the empire, to show your allegiance to their vision of the "good life" enriched by wealth, politics, sexuality, and power. In saying that one must worship *either* money or God, Jesus wasn't giving much room for people to compromise. There is no out here. We all want to be people who serve both, and as A. W. Tozer said, speaking directly to the modern Christian person regarding money: the man of "pseudo faith, will fight for his verbal creed but refuse to allow himself to get into a predicament where his future must depend upon that creed being true. . . . He always provides himself with secondary ways of escape so he will have a way out if the roof caves in." Tozer concluded, "What we need very badly these days is a company of Christians who are prepared to trust God as completely now as they know they must do at the last day."[1]

Cultural critic Brian Walsh asserts that the church "in all of its piety, serves to give an air of normality to an idolatrously constructed culture, functioning as a polite cover-up for a comfortable life in the empire." The crisis of Christianity, he says, "is that the Christians by and large accept the empire as normal."[2] How do we normalize the ways of the world? Wendell Berry gives us both a good hint and a scathing warning:

> Despite its protests to the contrary, modern Christianity has become willy-nilly the religion of the state and the economic status quo. Because it has been so exclusively dedicated to incanting anemic souls into Heaven, it has been made the tool of much earthly villainy. It has, for the most part, stood silently by while a predatory economy has ravaged the world, destroyed its natural beauty and plundered its human communities and households. It has flown the flag and chanted the slogans of empire. . . . It has admired Caesar and comforted him in his defaults in its de facto alliance with him. . . . [But] Christ's life, from the manger to the cross, was an affront to the established powers of his time, as it is to the established powers of our time.[3]

In other words, as Christians we cannot simply accept the status quo. We must have our hearts and imaginations infused with the kingdom of God and turn a critical eye to the values, loves, and agendas of our modern world, including the way our world worships money and comfort. We will never embrace the ethic of the alternative kingdom life unless we cease to be comfortable in this world. Jesus' point is that "Christians should feel disjointed and out of place in a civilization which divinizes things. . . . The practicing Christian should look like a Martian. He or she will never feel at home in the commodity kingdom. If the Christian does feel at home something is drastically wrong."[4]

A few years ago, I was talking to a guy in our church, a husband and father who was doing quite well in his business. He was awakened by God at 2:00 one morning and felt led to go down to his garage. God spoke to him and asked him to sell all he owned and to drive to the airport with his family in a few weeks. The Lord said he would tell them where to go when they got to the airport. "I woke up my wife," he said, "and asked her what she thought. She said, 'Uh . . . Okay.'" So, believe it or not, they did it. They sold their house, uprooted their kids, and went to the airport. "God told us where to go, so we bought a ticket and went to a third world country and for six months served kids and women who needed a ton of help." When their visas were up, they came back to renew them, but their renewal was denied. They felt God telling them they'd done what they needed to do, and that was it. Before they left for the trip, and even upon their return, their family and friends were unanimously against it. "You know this whole thing is really irresponsible, don't you? You've got kids in school. You've got a mortgage. You've got a career. You don't walk away from all of that."

Maybe you agree with these sentences.

The truth is that modern Christianity no longer has a category for this kind of obedience, this complete detachment from idols. We consider it unwise and reckless. Bumper stickers in Christian bookstores say things like, "The safest place to be is in the center of the will of God." But that's not the biblical story. Most often the center of God's will is a dangerous place to be. Read the life of the apostle Paul, who was right in the center of God's will and was still beaten near to death, shipwrecked, and imprisoned (2 Corinthians 11:23–28). Read about the life of Joseph, Job, or of Jesus himself. God rarely offers us security in the sense that we think he should keep us secure and safe. You are, of course, secure in Christ, and the Bible tells you that no matter what happens to you in this world, Jesus has "sealed [you] for the day of redemption" (Ephesians 4:30). But there is a world of difference between being secure and being *safe*. In Christ, God promises us security. He does not promise us safety.

Years ago, the bridge of Interstate 35W over the Mississippi River in Minneapolis collapsed. It was a bridge a local pastor, John Piper, could see from his church. He recounted what happened that night as he put his eleven-year-old daughter, Talitha, to bed.

> I sang to her the song I always sing:
>
>> Come rest your head and nestle gently
>> And do not fear the dark of night.
>> Almighty God keeps watch intently,
>> And guards your life with all his might.
>> Doubt not his love nor power to keep,
>> He never fails nor does he sleep.
>
> I said, "You know, Talitha, that is true whether you die in a bridge collapse, or in a car accident, or from cancer, or terrorism, or old age. God always keeps you, even when you die. So, you don't need to be afraid, do you?" "No," she shook her head. I leaned down and kissed her. . . .
>
> Usually [God's] people must pass through the deadly currents of suffering and death, not simply ride over them. "When you pass through the waters, I will be with you; and through the rivers, they shall not overwhelm you" (Isaiah 43:2). They may drown you. But I [God] will be with you in life and death.[5]

As I write this, I am in Bali on a family getaway after speaking a number of times in Australia over the last week. Anyone who is close to me knows that I am not a fan of flying, especially long trips. A psychologist once told me it is because of my OCD—fears get trapped in my brain and can't escape like in a normal brain. It's always a challenge for someone who travels as much as I do. Before I got on the plane—a sixteen-hour flight from Vancouver to Melbourne over the Pacific Ocean—I told my church, "Unlike the prosperity gospel, the real gospel doesn't promise me that I will not die flying to Australia later today; what it does promise is that I am safe in dying."

There is a world of difference between those two messages. One promises me comfort and ease—what I consider a false hope and a false gospel. The other promises God's presence and a secure future but no guarantee I'll avoid crashing and dying. In fact, as I continue to study history, I see that while God allows many to escape death for his purpose, he also calls a lot of people to die for his purpose. This shouldn't come as a surprise, for Jesus himself told us, "Whoever wants to save their life will lose it, but whoever loses their life for me and for the gospel will save it" (Mark 8:35 NIV). In God's economy, the advancement of the gospel in the world is more important than our individual lives. God can move the gospel forward by flourishing us or by ending us. Neither is promised and neither should be expected. If you're not being challenged and disrupted in your life on a week-to-week or month-to-month basis, I'm not sure you can hear God over the idols of comfort and security you've built around yourself.

## THE GOD OF FAMILY: DON'T WASTE YOUR LIFE

A second and third idol are hidden under the surface of the story of Jesus interacting with the man in Luke 9. Consider the man's response to Jesus. "Lord, let me first go and bury my father" (v. 59). This seems like a rational request. If you didn't bury your father, you became an outcast in that culture because family was the ultimate love. You didn't neglect your family. And that's why Jesus' response is both unexpected and particularly scandalous. "Leave the dead to bury their own dead. But as for you, go and proclaim the kingdom of God" (v. 60). Yet another man piped in, saying, "I will follow you, Lord, but let me first say farewell to those at my home" (v. 61). Jesus responded similarly to him: "No one who puts his hand to the plow and looks back is fit for the kingdom of God" (v. 62).

*"If you want to follow me, I've got to be more important than your family."*

Wow.

It's easy to nod and affirm this idea. It seems rational and reasonable. Family before ministry. Family before work. Yes and amen. We are told this all the time. But we also need to be wary. When it sounds too good, it probably is. In Tolkien's *The Fellowship of the Ring*, Boromir approaches Frodo as he ponders what he should do next with the ring:

> "Are you sure that you do not suffer needlessly?" he said. "I wish to help you. You need counsel in your hard choice. Will you not take mine?"
>
> "I think I know already what counsel you would give, Boromir," said Frodo. "And it would seem like wisdom but for the warning of my heart."
>
> "Warning? Warning against what?" said Boromir sharply.
>
> "Against the way that seems easier."[6]

Modern Christianity will give a nod to the idea that God must be first, but it sometimes offers us the way of Boromir, a path that is easier and more reasonable. However, those who are paying attention to the ways of Jesus, who have his warning in their hearts, know that it is precisely the subtle, rational realities of idols that make them so insidious to our souls.

The god of family is particularly dangerous for a number of reasons. How often is it that people may be interested in Jesus, but out of allegiance to the worldview of their families, they don't entertain the idea of becoming a Christian. Maybe they are part of a deep religious heritage (Muslim, Buddhist, Hindu) or an irreligious one (atheist, agnostic, new age). They can't dream of denying their own blood. They can't dream of facing the rejection of those they love. Maybe that is you.

We planted Village Church in January 2010. We gathered to plan and pray into its launching for almost a full year beforehand. Yet all throughout the planning process, my stepdad was sick back in Toronto. Three of the sixteen people who planted Village Church saw parents die during the planting stage. My dad died the morning of our second service as a church. I got a phone call from my mother that he had passed, and two hours later I had to be up preaching. I didn't call in sick or ask someone else to preach for me. I preached about Jesus being the hero of the Bible to 110 people in a school gym and then jumped on a plane and flew to Toronto to plan and lead Al's funeral. While I was there, I realized I wasn't going to be able to get back for our third week as a church, and I wasn't keen on having someone preach in my place on week three of our launch, so I called up a friend who had access to a video crew. On a rainy Wednesday in January, I showed up to some guy's beat-up condo in Toronto and filmed a forty-five-minute sermon about facing suffering and pain in our lives. I didn't throw in the towel in the face of my pain, nor did any of the others who lost parents during that launching period (one to a car accident, another to a brain tumor).

Facing the idol of family in another context, Jesus said, "If anyone comes to me and does not hate his own father and mother and wife and children and brothers and sisters, yes, and even his own life, he cannot be my disciple" (Luke 14:26). He didn't mean "hate" in terms of how we often use the word. We don't have to actively dislike our family. Jesus did, however, mean that we should "love them less." This still confounds us, of course, because family is so important to many of us. We wonder why God would want us to be cautious about loving something good, something he has created. But this call is for our own good. Jesus knows what is best for our long-term joy. He knows that if we look to our parents, spouses, or kids to find happiness, we will ultimately be unhappy.

Think of it this way: I have three daughters. I want them to love me, of course, but I want them to love Jesus and the gospel more. Again, I love what John Piper wrote as he thought about his daughter sleeping on the night of the bridge collapse: "Talitha is sleeping now. But *one day she will die.* I teach her this. I will not always be there to bless her. But Jesus is alive and is the same yesterday today and forever. He will be with her because she trusts him. And she will make it through the river."[7]

This makes me pause. At some point, hopefully long after I am gone, my kids will die. And they will face their own judgment: did they know Jesus as Lord and Savior, as the treasure of their hearts? They won't be saved because I was a pastor or through our faith as their parents, so our job as parents is to get them to hold on to Jesus—to love him more than they love us. That's what Jesus was getting at when he called those who would follow him to move their hearts off family and onto him instead.

Everyone who has a good marriage faces a similar danger. I once heard a preacher explain it this way. If a spouse is your "functional savior" in life—the center of your universe who determines your happiness, sense of direction, and self-worth—you are setting yourself up for disaster. Because one day (or, more likely, every day) they are going to fail you. And inevitably, one of you is going to have to bury the other one. You're going to have to plan a funeral, smile as people hug you, eat sandwiches at the reception, and then watch as the room empties, people go back to their lives, and you get in the car and go home. If you put your functional savior in the ground, who is going to comfort you when your heart is breaking? Who is going to pick you up off the ground when you don't feel like moving on? No one. And that's why you have to make your only savior the God who will never die.

John Piper recounted a now-famous story in a sermon he preached in front of a crowd of forty thousand high school and college students years ago. Many in the audience identify this sermon as the one message that changed their lives more than any other:

> Three weeks ago, we got news at our church that Ruby Eliason and Laura Edwards were killed in Cameroon. Ruby Eliason— over 80, single all her life, a nurse. Poured her life out for one thing: to make Jesus Christ known among the sick and the poor in the hardest and most unreached places.
>
> Laura Edwards, a medical doctor in the Twin Cities, and in her retirement, partnering up with Ruby. Also pushing 80, and going from village to village in Cameroon. The brakes gave way, over a cliff they go, and they're dead instantly. And I asked my people, "Is this a tragedy?" Two women, almost in their eighties, a whole life devoted to one idea—Jesus Christ magnified among the poor and the sick in the hardest places. And twenty years after most of their American counterparts had begun to throw their lives away on trivialities in Florida and New Mexico, they fly into eternity with a death in a moment. "Is this a tragedy?" I asked.

The crowd sat in stunned silence waiting for Piper's answer.

> I will tell you what a tragedy is. I will show you how to waste your life. Consider this story from the February 1998 *Reader's Digest*: A couple "took early retirement from their jobs in the Northeast five years ago when he was 59 and she was 51. Now they live in Punta Gorda, Florida, where they cruise on their 30-foot trawler, play softball and collect shells. . . ." Picture them before Christ at the great day of judgment: "Look, Lord. See my shells." *That is a tragedy!*[8]

Sometimes our worst enemy—the person who keeps us from

listening to and following God—is the person who "loves" us the most. They don't want to see us challenged. They don't want to see us shaken up. They don't want to see us in danger. But listening to Jesus sometimes leads us to unsafe places, the places family love would never want us to go. Don't let your identity be so wrapped up in your family and the people who love you that you set aside an identity rooted in the God who loves you more.

Ultimately, if we love God more than our spouse, our kids, and our parents, we are going to be much better spouses, parents, and children. We will be better neighbors, siblings, and colleagues. We will be more sacrificial, more patient, and more compassionate. The best version of ourselves comes when we stop focusing on ourselves.

# CHAPTER 8

## The Expulsive Power
# OF A NEW
# AFFECTION

How do we do what Jesus is asking us to do? How does this extraordinary shift from loving our idols to loving God above all else happen? How do we rid ourselves of the habits and sins that so easily entangle us? All of us have them—the idols that demand time, attention, and sacrifice. For some of you reading this, your highest priority is beauty, and you pay out to keep feeding it. For others it's success or work, and you sacrifice family and personal health to feed your desire to succeed and get ahead. That's the nature of the human heart. So how are you and I going to live free and clear of these idols and avoid their negative effects on us?

Augustine wisely said, "We are what we love." And therein lies the key to understanding the heart. We can't just tell ourselves not to love idols. We can't just stop lusting, being greedy, gossiping, or feeding whatever desire rules over us. I've watched the church approach the people in our culture and demand that they behave "this way" versus "that way" for long enough to know it doesn't work. We can't change by sheer mental determination. Our habits and flaws don't disappear because we tell them to—just ask a drug addict. It all comes down to what we love and how we love it. In his profound sermon *The Expulsive Power of a New Affection*, Scottish preacher Thomas Chalmers (1780–1847) asked how it is even possible for us to hate the things of the world when, in many ways, they are so satisfying. He argued that it is rare for any of our tastes to disappear by mere force of reasoning or determination. However, he explained, we're not quite without hope:

> What cannot be *destroyed* may be *dispossessed*. The heart is such that the only way to dispossess it of an old affection is by the expulsive power of a new one. The youth ceases to idolize pleasure. But it is only because the idol of wealth has become stronger. . . . The love of money ceases to have mastery over the citizen because they're drawn into the world of politics; so now they're lorded over by a love of power. . . . The way to disengage the heart from the love of one great object is to *fasten it to another*. It's not about exposing the worthlessness of the old affection but exposing the worth and excellence of the new one.[1]

More than just saying or believing that your idols are destructive, you must come to believe that God is *better*. Taste and see that the Lord is good! The heart needs to fasten itself to something it loves more than that sin, something that is better than what sin offers and the satisfaction it gives us.

I started smoking when I was in the eighth grade. I stopped shortly after I got married when I was twenty-three years old. I smoked for ten years of my life, and I *loved* it. You could tell me daily I was going to die of cancer—but it didn't matter. You could warn me, you could work on my behavior. The government puts pictures on cigarette packages of bleeding brains and rotting teeth. But that never deterred me. I would just go into the store and say, "Give me one pack of donkey teeth and one dead brain." You know how I quit? I fell in love with a girl who hated smoking. And over time my love for smoking was trumped by something stronger: my love for her. So I quit. That's the expulsive power of a new affection in action. My tendency toward idolatry didn't disappear, but the object of my affection shifted in priority. You can't just tear down idols; you have to replace them with something you love more.

The human heart abhors a vacuum. So when Jesus calls us to love God with our whole hearts, souls, minds, and strength, he is telling us to do something we naturally do, but he is asking us to transfer our deep affection. Not run away from something but toward something that is better. This is the only way to be truly free. There is "no other way by which to keep the love of the world out of the heart [than to] keep in our hearts the love of God."[2] Yes, there are a hundred reasons Jesus invites us to love God with all we are; but this is the one that immediately changes us in profound and life-altering ways.

## Heaven without God?

How is it possible to come to love God in this way—to "taste and see that the LORD is good" (Psalm 34:8) and find our delight in the Lord? First, we must come to see God as our ultimate treasure. This may sound obvious; it is anything but. Here is the subtle challenge we face: the call is not to love him because of the things he produces in our lives. Oftentimes, this is what we do. We relate to God because we want his blessing: health or security or help getting out of financial trouble or just because every good and perfect gift is from him and we want all the gifts we can get. But that is not what the true follower of Jesus wants most of all. The greatest gift we get if we choose to trust Christ is God himself. "For Christ also suffered once for sins, the righteous for the unrighteous," Peter said. And then he explained the *why*—the purpose of that suffering: "that he might *bring us to God*" (1 Peter 3:18, italics mine).

Notice that Peter didn't say the greatest gift we get is going to heaven when we die, seeing our loved ones again, having peace in the face of anxiety, or watching God slay our giants of fear or debt or whatever; it is getting God. We get the greatest treasure in the universe. In this way, "the gospel is not a way to get people to heaven; it is a way to get people to God. It's a way of overcoming every obstacle to everlasting joy in God. If we don't want God above all things, we have not been converted by the gospel."[3] Here is the "critical question for our generation—and for every generation: If you could have heaven with no sickness, with all the friends you ever had on earth and all the food you ever liked, and all the leisure activities you ever enjoyed, and all the natural beauties you ever saw, and all the physical pleasures that you ever tasted, and no human conflict, and no natural disasters, could you be satisfied with heaven even if Christ was not there?"[4]

In other words, do you honestly *feel* the worth of God as an end in and of itself? Or do you elevate gifts above Giver? Our primary motivation for coming to Christ should not be the desire to *go to a place* called "heaven" (as opposed to the punishment of hell). It should be driven by a desire to be with the One we love.

Some versions of Christianity ignore the gift that is God altogether, focusing exclusively on being "forgiven of sin" for instance. But again, why is being forgiven of our sin good news? *Because we get God.* Any other answer doesn't treat God as the final and highest good of the gospel. It treasures the wrong thing. It is why the prosperity gospel is so wrongheaded. Jonathan Edwards pointed out the small but significant distinction when he said, "This is the difference between the joy of the hypocrite and the joy of the true saint. The hypocrite rejoices in himself; self is the foundation of his joy; the true saint rejoices in God, has his mind pleased and delighted in the sweet and glorious things of God. This is the spring of his delights, the dependence of the affections of hypocrites is in reversed order: they first rejoice that they are made so much of by God; and then on that ground, [God] seems in a sort, lovely to them."[5]

In contrast treasuring God as an end in itself is the heart of the Scriptures from beginning to end, summarized well in Psalm 42:1: "As a deer pants for flowing streams, so pants my soul for you, O God." The writer's soul didn't pant for God's "stuff" or the results of knowing him, but for God as a glorious and all satisfying end in itself. "My soul thirsts for God, for the living God," (v. 2).

This should be the goal of life.

## Why Satan Isn't Saved

Recently I was speaking at an apologetics conference, giving a defense of the resurrection. I spoke for forty-five minutes on all the historical and philosophical reasons to believe in the resurrection to a room of three thousand people. Just before I prayed a closing prayer, I looked to the crowd and said, "You know, you could be sitting there agreeing with everything I just said. But that's really not the question, is it? Satan believes everything I just said. In fact, he believes it more than you do, because he was there. He saw it. He knows it happened. And yet it doesn't save him. You know why? Because he doesn't trust it. He doesn't treasure and cherish it above every other truth in the universe."

Jesus calls us to love God with our whole selves, because in the end, this is the kind of faith that saves us. John wrote, "To all who did receive him, who believed in his name, he gave the right to become children of God" (John 1:12). John paired "believed in his name" with "receive him" because they are the same. We are invited to receive Jesus as our treasure, to love him with affection, not just a static "faith." Jonathan Edwards, reflecting on this reality in face of what he feared were thousands of counterfeit conversions in his day, said, "The issue is not just welcoming the truth, but being willing to have the love of the truth in our hearts."[6] Many people presume to have truth and speak truth. But it is all mental, intellectual—notional, Edwards said. They do not love the truth of the gospel. "They say things about Jesus, but they don't love what they say—that is, they don't love the one they speak of."[7]

"Whoever *believes* in him is not condemned, but whoever does *not believe* is condemned already. . . . And this is the judgment: . . . people *loved* the darkness rather than the light" (John 3:18–19, italics mine). So why don't people believe in Jesus? Why don't they receive him? Because they "*love* the darkness" instead. Until the love of darkness has been broken and replaced with love for the light, coming to the light in a way that saves us will be impossible.[8] This distinction between faith and love forced Edwards to draw what is, in my opinion, one of the most profound conclusions and challenges in the history of Christendom: Love is the main thing in saving faith, the life and power of it, by which it produces its great effects.

Behind the question of whether we have "faith in Christ" then is a deeper question: Do we actually *love* Christ? This is why Paul ended his majestic letter to the Corinthians by saying, "If anyone has no love for the Lord, let him be accursed" (1 Corinthians 16:22). Hell is not the result of not having faith in Jesus; hell is for the one who doesn't have love for Jesus.

## Handwashing Doctors

We all tend to do things that benefit us in some way, usually things that make our lives better. And if our motivation isn't strong enough, we don't do it. In their book *SuperFreakonomics*, Stephen Dubner and Steven D. Levitt explore the handwashing practices of doctors at Cedars-Sinai Medical Center, a world-class hospital in Los Angeles. An internal study had discovered that the hand-hygiene rate was dismally low among their doctors (65 percent). They tried to motivate higher rates because dirty hands in the health industry is the number one cause of the spread of disease. Of course the best way to stop that is getting doctors to wash their hands. But simply providing information, sanitizers, even Starbucks gift cards, posters, and emails proved ineffective. Nothing worked.

So how did change come about?

During a lunch meeting of the chief of staff advisory committee—roughly twenty people, most of them top doctors at the hospital—the hospital's epidemiologist handed each of the people there an agar plate, a sterile petri dish loaded with a spongy layer of agar: "'I would like to culture your hand,' she told them. They pressed their palms into the plates. . . . The resulting images were disgusting and striking, with gobs of colonies of bacteria. . . . They then installed one of the handprints as the screen saver on computers throughout the hospital . . . [and] this grisly warning proved more powerful than any other incentive. Hand-hygiene compliance at the hospital went up to 100 percent."[9]

What is the motivation for us to love God above all things? There is both a theological answer (endless in its depth) and a practical one. The theological route revolves around the fact that because God is the most glorious, splendid being in the universe, there really should be no motivation behind our love for him beyond, as I have said, simply *getting him*. Bernard of Clairvaux (1090–1153) said, "Love is sufficient in itself, gives pleasure through itself and because of itself. It is its own merit, its own reward. Love looks for no cause outside itself, no effect beyond itself. . . . When God loves, he desires only to be loved in turn. His love's only purpose is to be loved, as he knows that all who love him are made happy by their love of him."[10] In other words, we should love God because he is extremely lovable and for no reason beyond that. He is the only thing that is an end in itself.

The philosopher David Bentley Hart echoes this sentiment:

The will is, of its nature, teleological [it has an *end goal* that drives it]. . . . What is it that the mind desires, or even that the mind loves, when it is moved? . . . No *finite thing* is desirable simply in itself. . . . Whatever we find desirable about that thing must correspond to some prior and more general disposition of the appetites and the will. . . . I cannot regard that object as its own index of value. . . . The object itself pleases me, perhaps, but only because the appetite it appeases. . . . If not for that rather abstract and exalted orientation of the will . . . I would not desire that object at all. One desires money not in itself but only for what it can purchase.[11]

This is all profound and true, but notice that Hart says all of this about finite things—things we can taste and touch and acquire in this life by working for them, things we can get access to if we make enough money or know the right people. It is not true, however, of the one infinite thing (God). God is fully and completely desirable in and of himself. He is all goodness. He is pure pleasure. He is wholly fulfilling, without remainder.

So that's the theological answer—and it is entirely true. But there is also the practical incentive of loving God, and that's what love for him does, what effect it has. As much as God is an end in himself because he is so good, he goes over and above himself and offers us transcendent things in the afterlife—a state of joy and peace that we cannot here fathom—but also a state of life here and now that takes us to a whole other level of humanness. In his book *The Nature of True Virtue,* Jonathan Edwards explored the difference between genuine gospel-triggered change in our lives versus mere moral compliance with God's law. He called the latter "common virtue" and the former "true virtue." What leads to the difference in our lives? If our highest love is our family, he said, we will choose the good of our own family over the good of other families. If it's our nation, we will choose our nation's good over all others. If our love is for our individual interests, we will serve ourselves over seeking to meet the needs of others. Only if our highest love is God himself will we be freed up to love and serve all people, families, classes, and races, because God's interests are paramount.[12]

As one writer said, while skeptics often claim Christians have their heads in the clouds of heaven and forget about the challenges of this world, the history of the church proves actually the opposite. We see a history of selfless suffering for the good of others, a life of sacrifice that results from a deeper love of God. "If you read history," he said, "you will find that the Christians who did most for the present world were precisely those who thought most of the next. It is since Christians have largely ceased to think of the other world that they have become so ineffective in this."

## The Curious Case of Vance Vanders

Another benefit of loving God that is often not talked about but which Jesus surely knew to be the case is our *mental and emotional flourishing*. Modern neuroscience shows that our brain structure is shaped and affected by our understanding of God. In his book *The God-Shaped Brain*, Dr. Timothy R. Jennings demonstrates this by exploring a number of experiments wherein patients' brains were examined while certain concepts of God were fed to them. He begins the book by giving an account of a man who came to the hospital very sick—days away from death—and the doctors were at a loss as to the cause of his sickness. His name was Vance Vanders. His wife told one of the doctors, Drayton Doherty, that weeks earlier Vance had a run-in with a local witch doctor in a small Alabama cemetery, and the witch doctor told him he had cast a spell on him. So the doctor proceeded to call the family of Vanders into the hospital room and lie to them. He claimed to have tracked down the witch doctor the night before and choked him against a tree until he told him exactly how he had cursed Vanders. The doctor went on to allege that he had the remedy and proceeded to fill a syringe with a powerful emetic (a substance that induces vomiting). Vanders violently threw up, the doctor pronounced that the curse had been lifted, and Vanders awoke the next day hungry and alert. He was discharged a week later.[13] "The brain, and what it believes, is extremely powerful." In Jennings's analysis, "All forms of contemplative meditation were associated with positive brain changes—but the greatest improvements occurred when participants meditated specifically on a God *of love*."[14]

Such reflection causes stimulation in the prefrontal cortex, causing growth in "sharp thinking and memory. . . . In other words, worshiping a God of love actually stimulates the brain to heal and grow. However, when we worship a god other than one of love . . . fear circuits are activated and, if not calmed, will result in chronic inflammation and damage to both brain and body."[15]

In their work on a similar subject, Andrew Newberg and Mark Waldman concluded the same thing. They say that out of what they call "The Four Gods of America" (Authoritarian, Distant, Benevolent, Critical), the human brain works better and is stimulated in a way that produces love and compassion toward others and ourselves, suppressing the impulse to get angry or frightened in life, when it is focused on the Benevolent God. The Critical God activates the limbic system of the brain, creating fear and anger: a brain primed to fight. The Benevolent God, on the other hand, stimulates the anterior cingulate, which produces peace and calm in our lives, a part of our brains these authors call the true "heart" of our neurological soul.[16]

While wrath and anger against sin and injustice is a true reflection of God's character, Jesus' revelation is of a God who forgives sin and invites us back to him with love. And Jesus asks us to return that love with our own love for God in obedience to the greatest commandment. Jesus reveals God to the world as the God who loves and who operates the universe on a principle of love rooted in his very nature, not just in what he does. "God *is* love" (1 John 4:8, italics mine) and can be loving because he has existed in a community since eternity past. He creates human beings, made in his image, who run best on love.

Skeptics often ask not only if Christianity is *true*, but if it *works*: in the real world, does it actually address the challenges we face? My answer is yes, it does. We love God because he alone is worthy of our love but also because it's the best thing for us and for others. It's the best thing for our kids, our friends, our spouses, our enemies, our cities, our churches, and even our physical and emotional health. It is utterly holistic in its effect.

## Death, and Why Einstein Was Wrong

Einstein famously said, "Our time is distinguished by wonderful achievements in the fields of scientific understanding and the technical application of those insights. Who would not be cheered by this? . . . [But] humanity has every reason to place the proclaimers of high moral standards and values above the discoverers of objective truth. What humanity owes to personalities like Buddha, Moses, and Jesus ranks for me higher than all the achievements of the enquiring and constructive mind."[17] Einstein was smart, but here I'm not sure he's right. His point in this statement was to make sure we hold on to a moral vision of humanity and not simply rely on science to provide all the answers. So often we play these two off against one another as if they can't be the same, when in reality, the one feeds the other. Jesus tells us to love, and science and psychological discoveries confirm why this needs to be the case. In truth, however, God doesn't see a difference between "the high moral standards and values" and "discoveries of truth"; they unite together in the person and work of Jesus. Nothing Jesus commands from us would ever be without our best interests in mind. While we think in a temporal framework, Jesus envisions and directs our lives from an eternal framework.

Consider how this relates to a topic none of us likes to talk about: our own death. How could Jesus say, "Everyone who lives and believes in me shall never die" (John 11:26)? Obviously, we all die. But Jesus has a different definition of death. The millisecond after we "die" in a worldly sense, we are alive forevermore in the presence of the God we love. So, in that sense, the believer in Jesus never really dies. Once our minds discover that God is love and we set ourselves to loving him above all things in return, we discover that death (identified by psychologists as one of our deepest underlying fears) isn't death at all. Jesus gives us the gift of facing the awful reality that our lives end with courage instead of fear, hope instead of despair. It's the reason the apostle Paul could write that "to die is gain" (Philippians 1:21). It's why men like the great British pastor and preacher Charles Spurgeon (1834–92) declared, "The best moment of a Christian's life is his last one, because it is the one that is nearest heaven. . . . The only people for whom I have felt any envy have been dying members of this very church."

The night before he died, Thomas Vincent (the man who wrote the only treatise on loving God I could find!) spoke words that flowed from a heart deeply committed to loving God: "Hasten, hasten, oh hasten death! Where is your bow, where your arrows? Come, come, come, I am yet in the body, I am yet on earth—but it is heaven, heaven, heaven I would gladly be at! I seek death—but cannot find it. How long, O Lord, holy and true?"

He could scarcely reconcile the thoughts of his recovery, and said to his physician,

Why do you come to keep me out of heaven? . . . Dear Jesus, come and take me away! I have no business here; my work is done, my hour-glass has run out, my strength is gone, why shall I stay behind? Oh, come, come! How long shall I wait and cry? How long shall I be absent from You? Oh, come and take me to Yourself, and give me possession of that happiness which is above—the vision of Yourself, full fruition of Yourself, without any interruption or end! O come, dear Jesus, how long before You send Your chariots? O come down to me—and take me up to You!

## Conclusion: The Fun Part

Do you know how you can tell if your heart is changing and shifting toward really and truly loving God? It's when you sincerely *delight in him*. It's when you start to pray not out of obligation but because you look forward to communicating with somebody you love. It's when you start to read Scripture not from a sense of command but because you are reading the very words of the One you love above all else. You find yourself in Psalm 119: "My eyes shed streams of tears, because people do not keep your law" (v. 136). You care about the things he cares about. What breaks his heart breaks yours.

You come to believe and function with a deep conviction you

didn't have before. Psychologist Dr. George Eman Vaillant, speaking of human relationships, explains it well: "The essence of love is in realizing that someone matters more than you. In the short run, that's the hard part. In the long run, that's the fun part."[18]

Don't just believe *in* God. Don't just nod your head and acknowledge that he exists. Don't focus solely on the amazing truth that by faith you are declared righteous in the law court of God on the last day. Of course these things are true, but there is more! As Edwards said, let the definitive content of that faith be your love for God, not just your belief in him. It's easy to miss this. And for many years, I certainly did—but it was pulsating in front of my face in the words of the Great Commandment the entire time. The answer Jesus gave to the question of what he would hold on to in a fire: his all-encompassing love for God.

# PART V

---

# The Problem of
# MIRACLES

*The genuine realist, if he is an unbeliever, will always find strength and ability to disbelieve in the miraculous, and if he is confronted with a miracle as an irrefutable fact, he would rather disbelieve his own senses than admit the fact. . . . Faith does not, in the realist, spring from the miracle but the miracle from faith. If the realist once believes, then he is bound by his very realism to admit the miraculous also.*

—FYODOR DOSTOYEVSKY, *THE BROTHERS KARAMAZOV*

# CHAPTER 9

# The Odd Probability That
# MIRACLES
# ARE REAL

"Demons?" I asked. It was sort of a question but more of a statement. "Yes," the pastor from Toronto answered. He asked the barista for a piece of paper, pulled a pen from his bag, and began to sketch. "This may sound odd to you," he explained, "but I can see your house in my mind, and I can tell you where they are." He proceeded to draw the upstairs level of my house as accurately as if he'd seen a floor plan. "Your bedroom is here. Your closet is here. The wall for the walk-in closet is shared with your office, isn't it?"

"Yes."

"That's where they are. They were invited," he said. "They are sexual spirits. Violent.

Because they were invited, they are territorial. Legalistic. You are an intruder." This normal, middle-aged pastor I'd just met went on to explain in detail the exact ways they were welcomed into the space and how to get rid of them.

I'm not sharing this as proof for the existence of God. And I am sure a skeptic would find ways to explain all of this away. However, I recount it as just one of many unusual—even supernatural— experiences I've had. What do we do with this, and the many millions of other stories like it, held by rational, credible people, stories that defy all logic? If only one of those stories turns out to be true, then our modern naturalistic and materialistic assumptions about the world and reality fall apart. This is why I believe it takes more faith to be skeptical about miracles than it does to believe in them.

But first, how did a rationalistic skeptic like me—especially regarding the supernatural—ever come to see miracles as something that *made sense?*

## Miracles Just Don't Happen

People reject Jesus for a variety of reasons, and in so doing, reject Christianity. One of the primary reasons is a distrust of the Gospels. And much of this distrust is rooted in the Gospels' claims that Jesus performed miracles. The Smithsonian Museum in Washington, DC, displays a leather-bound version of the Bible, assembled by President Thomas Jefferson, in which the pages of the Gospels are cut and pasted. Why? Jefferson excluded every miraculous event from his Bible. And that represents the kind of Jesus the modern world wants. But it was also something people wanted in Jesus' own day. Rationalists at the time pondered Jesus' teachings and scrutinized his miracles, denied plain evidence, and sought alternative explanations for them (such as the devil or magical powers).

Today the thinking goes like this: we, in the modern era, know miracles don't happen. Therefore, Jesus couldn't have done them, and the claims that he did are simply false. This skepticism is extended to the Bible as a whole, filled as it is with miracles from beginning to end. Belief in miracles is seen as something for the ancient mind—the naive and uninformed—and not for modern, scientific people. The march of science has trampled belief in the supernatural. As German physicist Max Planck predicted in 1937, "Faith in miracles must yield ground. Step by step . . . the steady and firm advance of the forces of science" will plunder it. "Its defeat is indubitably a mere matter of time."[1]

Is this true? I will show in this chapter that it is not. Instead, we find that miracles are actually *probable* given the kind of universe in which we find ourselves, a world that has been opened to us since 1937 in ways Planck couldn't have dreamed of. We are also going to discover, contrary to popular opinion, that there is little conflict between miracles and science. In fact, the deeper science delves into the mysterious workings of the universe, the more that "miracles" are understood to fit.

Before we explore the evidence in favor of miracles, we must settle a philosophical question. Is the naturalist view of reality correct? Are miracles ruled out as impossible, before we even get started? A naturalist is a person who believes his views on nature, reality, and miracles are simply the product of "looking at the evidence" and drawing conclusions based purely on "science," experiment, and observation. And the first thing we must do is point out that this simply is not true. If you are a naturalist, your understanding of what is allowed to happen or not happen in the universe is a *philosophical* approach first, and then a *scientific* one. You approach data and predetermine that your *experience* of nature will dictate what you believe about it (that it has certain "laws" that can't be broken, for instance). But it is dangerous to approach the data with a predetermined understanding of what is possible. In his book *Miracles*, Oxford professor and lifelong skeptic-turned believer C. S. Lewis wrote, "If anything extraordinary seems to have happened, we can always say that we [or they] have been victims of illusion. If we hold a philosophy which excludes the supernatural, this is what we always shall say."[2] In other words, what we learn from *experience* depends on the philosophy we bring to it. If, for instance, we start out with the assumption that miracles are impossible, then no amount of historical evidence about the life of Jesus or anyone else will convince us, so that won't do. That isn't fair to the process of historical inquiry because the matter has already been decided before the adventure has begun!

If miracles are possible, though immensely improbable, then the right evidence could potentially convince us that miracles have occurred. Again, all we must conclude at the outset is that miracles are *not intrinsically improbable* or impossible (even by scientific means of evaluation), and we must be open to the possibility of them occurring. This is why the philosophical question must come first. We begin by asking, Are miracles possible? If they are not possible, we close the discussion and we're done with it. But if they are at least hypothetically possible, we must look at the evidence and decide— rather than dismissing the idea outright because of our preconceived notions. If we are open to the *concept* of miracles instead of deciding the matter beforehand, the way is cleared to examine the evidence and conclude something accurate versus something desired. This is why Lewis said that his "role as a philosopher rather than a historian [was] not to examine the historical evidence for Christian miracles [but] to put readers in a position to do so."[3] I contend that once we are in a position to do so, we will see that "the existing evidence will be sufficient to convince us that quite a number of miracles have occurred."[4]

## The Contradictions of Naturalism

So where do we get this idea that miracles are not possible? As I mentioned, it is rooted in a prior philosophical assumption, that of naturalism, the belief that there is only nature—a material world we can test, see, feel, touch, and smell. There is no "spiritual" or immaterial world. Nature is the "whole show"—a total system in which everything can be explained by hypothesis, observation, and experiment. Nothing exists or happens outside of natural realities or the "laws of nature."

One of the most popular arguments against miracles was advanced by philosopher and skeptic David Hume (1711–76) in his book *Enquiry Concerning Human Understanding*. Hume's arguments are commonly repeated today by the most popular writers and thinkers of the modern "new atheism" (Christopher Hitchens and Richard Dawkins). They typically go as follows:

1. A miracle is a violation of the known laws of nature.
2. Natural laws are immutable (unchanging over time and unable to be changed).
3. It is impossible for immutable laws to be violated.
4. Therefore, miracles are not possible.

This argument against miracles has been cited ad nauseam and is unconsciously in the minds of many people in the modern West. But does it stand up to scrutiny? It appears plausible at the outset and feels obviously true, yet this argument has proved faulty when challenged.

## Science Isn't Static

First, Hume argued that the laws of nature are established by "a firm and unalterable experience" based on the consistent testimony of countless people in different places and times. If one defines natural laws as immutable (*unable* to be changed), then of course miracles are impossible. But who can conclusively say that natural laws are immutable? A number of so-called laws of nature have been overthrown by more recent scientific discoveries: "Consider this dismaying realization. Newton's laws were for nearly two centuries regarded as absolutely true. They worked incredibly well. Indeed, no body of general statements had ever been subjected to so much empirical verification. Every machine incorporated its principles, and the entire Industrial Revolution was based on Newtonian physics and mechanics. Newton was vindicated a million times a day. . . . Yet Einstein's theories of relativity [which came along later] contradicted Newton. Newton's laws were proven in important ways to be wrong or at least inadequate."[5]

In other words, scientific "laws" are not truly immutable. They are not "laws of nature" per se; they are human laws—interpretations that represent our best guess about the world and the way it works. So while Hume insists that miracles violate the known laws of nature, in the end *there are no known laws of nature.*[6]

When it comes to science, so-called laws are always being refuted and rethought. Consider the question of the origins of the universe, where "the steady state theory had triumphed, but then Big Bang cosmology achieved ascendency, but now there are straws in the wind suggesting a reversion to the thought that the universe is without a beginning."[7] The need for humility in regard to conclusions is overwhelming.

Hume built his entire logic on a Newtonian mechanistic view of the universe wherein certain *fixed laws* govern unflinchingly and without aim, but current science has deconstructed this idea. Those who believe in miracles are saying one of two things. Some might say that miracles do not defy natural laws because those laws are just regular ways in which God chooses to work. Others might argue that they are not denying that there are norms or rules that define how things naturally operate. They are only saying that these rules can, at times, be suspended because "a miracle is by definition an exception. . . . How can the discovery of the rule tell you whether, granted a sufficient cause, the rule can be suspended?"[8]

It can't.

## Stacking the Deck

Hume's approach to this topic is set up in such a way that he would never end up with a result with which he didn't already agree. He argued, "A miracle is a violation of the laws of nature; and as firm and unalterable *experience* has established these laws, the proof against miracle, is as entire as any argument from experience can possibly be imagined." When faced with numerous claims of miracles at the tomb of Abbe Paris in France during his lifetime, Hume rejected every one of the claims—not because he undertook a detailed investigation or heard the testimony of eyewitnesses—but based solely on the "absolute impossibility of a miraculous nature of the events."[9] In other words, Hume's denial, and that of many skeptics today, is based on their

experience—or lack of experience with miracles. This is the definition of a circular argument, a self-fulfilling prophecy. A stacked deck.

Hume also failed to recognize he made a category mistake. As
Lewis argued, "When a thing professes from the outset to be a unique
invasion of Nature by something from the outside, increasing knowledge of Nature can never make it either more or less credible."[10] His
point is that when someone believes in miracles, they aren't arguing
that nature, left alone, will produce the event; they assume there is
another Agent acting in the event that transcends the natural order in
some way or other, who tampers with things. In other words, miracles
aren't contradictions of science: they lie outside of the realm of science. But this doesn't make them an odd anomaly. Similarly, things
like ethics, beauty, and morality also cannot be tested and proven in
a scientific way. Rarely, however, does this lead someone to conclude
that they do not exist.

The philosophy of naturalism bases its predictions on the premise
that things like miracles don't happen "if there are no interferences."
But that's the point people who believe in miracles make as well. By
definition, miracles *interrupt* the usual course of nature. And they
must have help to do so. According to the natural order of things,
when one combines oxygen and potassium, they combust. Yet we
have both of these elements in our bodies, so why don't we blow up?
Because *interfering factors* prevent an explosion. Think of it like catching an apple as it falls from a tree. The law of gravity isn't any less real
or effective just because a hand got in the way. Something—in this
case, my hand—has broken the natural process of falling. This is not a
contradiction, merely an interruption of sorts.

But while this way takes us a step closer to the biblical view of
miracles, it's incomplete. The Bible does not see a miracle as something done by an alien outsider, but as the act of an author interjecting
a new element into the story, as we will see. In the biblical accounts
of miracles, we find that the moment a miracle enters reality, it starts
obeying all the laws of the world. "Miraculous wine will intoxicate,

miraculous conception will lead to pregnancy, miraculous bread will be digested. The divine art of miracle is not an art of *suspending* the pattern to which events conform" but of feeding new events into that pattern. "God creates the vine and teaches it to draw up water by its roots and with the aid of the sun, to turn that water into a juice which will ferment and take on certain qualities. Thus, every year from Noah's time to ours God turns water into wine."[11]

In this way, the argument for miracles is an argument for an X-factor that goes over and above nature. This is why a miracle is deemed "supernatural." The view of God as someone "interfering" in the natural world comes from a *deistic* view of God—as a being disconnected or removed from the world—rather than a biblical one. Deism is the belief that God is distant from his creation, the "Big Man up in the sky." It's what I call a "Bette Midler" theology ("*From a distance . . .*"), wherein he watches what we are doing "down here" and once in a while might step in to interfere in the normal course of events. The biblical view of God, however, is far different. The Bible presents God as intimately involved, the sovereign and sustainer of all things, present and active in the universe he created. The writer of Hebrews says, "He upholds the universe by the word of his power" (1:3).

The Christian view is that God is intimately engaged in the processes of his world right down to the minute details. He is not identical with the natural world itself (the view of pantheism); rather, he acts within the natural system in whatever way he desires at a given time. Miracles happen when God does a specialized activity in a particular location. So, for example, the biblical claim is not that nature spit Jesus out of the grave, but that "[God] raised [Jesus] from the dead and seated him at his right hand in the heavenly places" (Ephesians 1:20); "God raised [Jesus] from the dead, freeing him from the agony of death" (Acts 2:24 NIV).

These statements say nothing that contradicts the laws of nature. Saying that God raised Jesus from the dead has zero implausibility with respect to our knowledge of natural processes. "Only if the naturalist has independent reasons to think that *God's existence* is implausible or his intervention in the world implausible could he justifiably regard the resurrection hypothesis as implausible."[12]

This is analogous to what Christians say of the general resurrection of all the dead at the end of time, wherein every person who has ever lived will be raised from death and judged, an event that according to natural laws, cannot really happen. As C. S. Lewis pointed out quite poetically, "For one thing, there would not be enough [units of matter] to go around: we all live in second-hand suits and there are doubtless atoms in my chin which have served many another man, many a dog, many an eel, many a dinosaur. Nor does the unity of our bodies, even in this present life, consist in retaining the same particles. My form remains one, though the matter in it changes continually. I am in that respect, like a curve in a waterfall."[13]

Lewis said it is a foolish fancy (one not justified by the words of Scripture) to believe that "each spirit should recover those particular units of matter which he ruled before."[14] In other words, according to nature a general resurrection from the dead can't actually happen. But Christianity doesn't argue this will happen according to nature; it posits God and his supernatural power to do something beyond what nature could or would ever produce left to itself.

The mistake skeptics make regarding miracles is first assuming that nature is a closed system that defines the entirety of reality. They have mistaken a part of the system that defines reality (what we call nature) for the whole. Miracles are not contradictions of nature; rather, we believe that nature cannot produce these effects when left to its own resources. When a miracle happens, it's not "abnormal" in the sense that it is a violation but only in the sense that it is rare. Skeptics' objections to miracles are similar to the way we might feel about the plot of a good novel. You don't introduce something completely foreign to the plot just to resolve an issue. You don't bring a ghost into your story to solve a plot point you are having trouble resolving. The modern objection to miracles is along these lines: miracles are "marvels of the wrong sort"; a story of a *certain kind* (nature) is being interfered with. Events are happening that don't really "belong" to the story. But all of this is simply missing the point, and if I thought the story of nature was a complete story, I would likely not believe in miracles either. But that's the point—nature isn't the full story. Again, Lewis pointed this out: "If [miracles] have occurred, they have because they are the very thing this universal story *is* about. They are not exceptions. . . . Death and Resurrections are what the story is." If to this point you have disbelieved in miracles, is it "chiefly because you thought you had discovered what the story was really about?—atoms, and time and space and economics and politics were the main plot? And is it certain you were right? It is easy to make mistakes in such matters."[15]

## No Divine Foot in the Door!

The modern skeptical, atheistic view that says "miracles can't happen because we know the laws of nature and they can't be violated" isn't necessarily the true version of reality. We think it is such only because it has felt so pervasive, so convincing. After all, it has been the underlying worldview behind much of our education, science, media, politics, and art. But there are growing cracks in the facade. We now see it as simply *one construct of thinking* in a vast and ever-expanding marketplace of ideas. And just because an idea is popular doesn't make it true.

The reality is that naturalism is a philosophical pre-conviction, not a scientific one. It is a "faith commitment" that ignores evidence to the contrary instead of facing it and weighing in. Harvard University biologist Richard Lewontin wrote an article published in the *New York Review of Books* in which he admits that he and the scientists with whom he works prefer naturalistic and atheistic explanations for what they study because the scientific community "has a *prior* commitment. . . to materialism [naturalism]." He continues, "It is not that the methods and institutions of science somehow compel us to accept a material explanation of the phenomenal world but, on the contrary, that we are forced by our *a priori* adherence to material causes. . . . We cannot allow a divine foot in the door."[16]

This quote is telling: it is an admission that what drives his science is not *facts* but *philosophy*.[17] His faith position predetermines his science and not the other way around. And this is the often unexamined point every skeptic must face: to conclude that miracles *can't* happen is an assumption, not a proven fact. It comes from *prior* conclusions. This is why many modern philosophers regard Hume's conclusions as rather trivial: "All that Hume accomplished was to show that if we do not already believe in supernatural agencies, no miracles can prove their existence."[18]

There are also many things that naturalism just can't explain. For example, take the problem of *consciousness*. By this I mean a kind of awareness, morality, and way of thinking that human beings have that transcends what nature by itself would ever have produced in us. It is arguably, as David Skeel says, "the single most complex and mysterious feature of our existence."[19] It has always been a problem for a naturalist, so much so that when Richard Dawkins was asked in a recent debate where it ever would have come from in the human psyche, he simply said he didn't know but that computers would one day solve the mystery (a faith position if there was ever was one!).

In other words, one must believe in a kind of thinking that transcends nature, something deeper and more expansive than the chemical reactions in our brains. All the evidence seems to point to consciousness as something trans-natural or supernatural, which is why Dawkins doesn't deny it but simply defers the explanation to a future generation, one that will (he hopes) explain the "ghost in the machine." Anthropologist Marilyn Schlitz explains, "The data I see tells me that there are ways in which people's experiences refute the [naturalist] position that the mind is the brain and nothing more. There are solid, concrete data that suggest that our consciousness, our mind, may surpass the boundaries of the brain."[20] This is why

Cambridge professor John Polkinghorne concludes, "The fundamental problem is not about miracles but transcendence."[21]

If we have a consciousness that makes up our personhood, it couldn't evolve from our brain because the brain is pure matter. "No matter how many atoms you line up . . . you cannot get a wholly different thing—thought, consciousness, reason, self-awareness—from mere bits of matter. *Awareness of the material universe is not one more part of that universe.* The knowledge of a thing is not one of the thing's parts, it is an addition from without."[22]

## Science and Miracles: Is There a Conflict?

Some readers may be surprised to learn that naturalism as a philosophy is now seen by many people as an outdated philosophy, a product of eighteenth-century, post-Enlightenment ideas. The *mechanistic* portrait of nature given by the science of that day exerted widespread influence on scientific conclusions, but many of those conclusions are now viewed as out-of-date and irrelevant. Often the perspective of this time is referred to as "classic" science or "the old picture."[23] The new picture and the latest science do not conflict with miracles at all. Ironically, as in the fields of biology and cosmology, the more deeply science has delved into the complexity of the universe, the more legitimate miracles have become. Even though miracles don't need to fit into any scientific framework to be true, over time they have been recognized as "completely consistent with modern science."[24] To give an example, the older, modernistic way of thinking held that no event could be *uncaused* in any way. But the entire field of quantum theory today is founded on the very notion of uncaused events. Quantum theory is counterintuitive to a mind trained in older, classic, Enlightenment scientific paradigms—to the point where it seems wrong to many people. This isn't a license to throw up our hands and say anything goes, however; it is, as the former professor of mathematical physics at Cambridge Dr. John Polkinghorne says, "a cautionary tale to warn us of our intellectual short-sightedness about the range of possibility."[25]

Ironically, Hume himself recognized the limitations of science. While arguing that miracles defy scientific laws, he admitted that those laws are technically "empirically unverifiable," since "no finite number of observations, however large, can be used to derive a . . . general conclusion that is defensible."[26] If one asserts, for instance, that all swans are white, how would this assertion be verified? By observing ten thousand swans? A million? All it would take is one black swan to make that hypothesis false. And this is exactly what happened when Europeans landed in Australia. Until that point, Western civilization had believed all swans were white.[27] It was an irrefutable, scientific fact—until our awareness of our limited perspective changed and a black swan was found. Similarly, the idea that an occurrence is impossible simply because we've never experienced or observed it is a weak argument. Before we can decide on a thing having happened or not, we must discover whether a thing is *possible*—and, if possible, how probable.

By Hume's own set of rules, one cannot dismiss miracles absolutely, since it's impossible to investigate every potential miracle. In fact, out of the millions of claims of miraculous events throughout history, it would take only one of those events being true to overthrow the entire naturalistic worldview. In his thoroughly researched and celebrated work on the subject (released in 2011), Dr. Craig Keener investigated miracle claims on all seven continents and found that over two hundred million people alive today have personally experienced or witnessed what they deem an extraordinary event, unaccounted for by current scientific understanding, in direct response to prayer— that's one in every thirty-five people on the planet![28]

Many people I meet have stories that demand some kind of explanation that cannot be simply explained by natural means. And this is not a rare occurrence; it is something I encounter regularly, perhaps because I work in the realm of the spiritual as a pastor. I've witnessed

completely rational and "normal" women—women I know personally—
suddenly thrashing around on my office couch with eyes not their own,
shouting threats at me in a male voice that stops instantly as I pray over
them in the name of Jesus. I've seen people healed of once-thought-
incurable diseases. I've had times when I am praying and find I have
knowledge of things about people in the context of prayer that I did not
know just a few minutes before, knowledge that is confirmed when I
talk with them. While these are not everyday occurrences, they happen
often enough to make me sit up and take notice.

Maybe there is something behind the veil.

The "new picture" of the universe unfolding before scientists every
day makes miracles more probable than ever before, certainly more
so than the old picture of reality. Quantum mechanics, for instance,
has blown the roof off any theory that posits a closed and mechanistic system of nature. Dr. John Earman, philosopher of physics and
professor in the History and Philosophy of Science Department at
the University of Pittsburgh, explains, "If we try to define a miracle
as an event that is incompatible with laws of nature, then it seems
that water changing into wine, a dead man coming back to life, etc.,
are not miracles because they are not incompatible with Quantum
Mechanics."[29] Classic science presented things like the "periodic
table of the elements" as immutable, but today not even something
as dependable as the elemental table is safe in light of quantum theory: "Its nether regions have for some time been filling up with new
elements that physicists have forged from smaller atoms. Now even its
more mundane areas, populated by familiar, everyday elements, are
undergoing a fundamental change: elements are losing their precisely
defined atomic weights."[30] To put it simply, the universe is far more
complicated than previously thought, and the so-called laws of nature
are being rewritten every day. In the "new picture":

> special divine action, including miracles, is by no means incom-
> patible with QM [quantum mechanics] . . . because QM doesn't

determine a specific outcome for a given set of initial conditions, but instead merely assigns probabilities to the possible outcomes. . . . [It] doesn't constrain special divine action in anything like the way classical deterministic mechanics does. . . . There is no question that special divine action is consistent with science; and even the most stunning miracles are not clearly inconsistent with the laws now promulgated by science."[31]

Today's best thinkers at the intersection of science and faith are exploring the tension of God's action in the world as a "violation" by pointing out that such action, when seen as working on a quantum level, never suspends natural laws at all, and that the state of affairs of the universe, and the atoms therein, "might very well have a *non-physical* cause. It's wholly in accord with these theories."[32]

The Bible's presentation of God as a loving Creator who is involved continuously in his world, which includes the routine, natural ways the world works, designed at the dawn of time, could very well fit with the current scientific theory. Miracles would, as theologian Herman Bavinck said, be "nothing but a special revelation of the same divine power which works in all things. . . . So God has the power to make this created world serviceable to the carrying out of his counsel. What the miracles prove is that it is not the world but the Lord that is *God*."[33]

G. K. Chesterton observed the normal rhythms of the world and cautioned us against taking them for granted because, in a way, an unimaginative take on how things work is a reflection more on us than on how God runs the universe:

Because children have abounding vitality, because they are in spirit fierce and free, they want things repeated and unchanged. They always say, "Do it again"; and the grown-up person does it again until he is nearly dead. For grown-up people are not strong enough to exult in monotony. But perhaps God is strong enough to exult in monotony. It is possible that God says every morning,

"Do it again" to the sun; and every evening, "Do it again" to the moon. It may not be automatic necessity that makes all daisies alike; it may be that God makes every daisy separately, but has never got tired of making them. It may be that He has the eternal appetite of infancy; for we have sinned and grown old, and our Father is younger than we.[34]

Indeed.

My point here is similar to what Oxford philosopher Richard Swinburne argues when he says, "If there is no God, then the laws of nature are the ultimate determinants of what happens. But if there is a God, then whether and for how long and under what circumstances laws of nature operate depend on God."[35] To deny the reality of miracles, one must prove God doesn't exist. And this is a much harder task than the atheist will acknowledge. Evidence from history, science, philosophy, and even sociology seems to repeatedly point us toward a theistic reality behind the universe, even if one believes in the popular theories of the Big Bang and evolution.[36]

## Sweet Baby Jesus: The Trouble with Probability

The mistake many skeptics make is to equate *evidence* with *probability*, but this is a failed experiment in logic. It's like arguing a lottery winner is lying because the chances of winning the lottery are so minuscule (76 million to 1), or that because the odds of getting dealt the perfect hand in bridge are 1,635,013,559,600 to 1, it has never happened (yet we know it has). If it is true that we cannot believe in one-time events that are unwitnessed and mathematically improbable, then by the same logic the naturalist cannot believe in the Big Bang or the idea that organic life originated through unguided evolution.[37] In the end, the skeptic fails to fully consider the evidence of rare events, instead focusing on the evidence for regular events and suggesting this somehow makes all rare events unworthy of belief. Philosopher William

Lane Craig illustrates this point using one of the greatest miracles ever recorded—the resurrection of Jesus Christ. "The opposite of the statement that Jesus rose from the dead is not that all other men remain in their graves; it's that Jesus of Nazareth remained in *his* grave. In order to argue against the evidence for the Resurrection, you have to present evidence against the Resurrection itself, not evidence that everybody else has always remained in their grave."[38]

Allow me to illustrate the weakness in the probability argument, the argument that a miracle like the resurrection of Jesus is impossible because it is improbable. A few years ago, some friends and I went golfing in Phoenix. Since there were only three of us, we were paired up with a guy named Ethan. He was a great golfer and was trying to get his card on the PGA Tour. Ethan asked what I did for a living, and it wasn't long before I was giving him a pretty passionate sell on Jesus. Ethan laughed and said he didn't care much for "religion" or church—there wasn't enough evidence for him to believe in God. We kept the conversation light and had some good laughs as I did my best to convince him otherwise.

On hole twelve or thirteen I drove my ball deep into the desert (a rare occurrence, of course). When hunting for my ball, I came across another ball stuck in a bush. I picked it up, and on it, to my surprise, someone had written, "Sweet Baby Jesus." I laughed and put it in my pocket. We finished up the hole, and then I told our group about the ball. Catching the irony of it in light of our previous conversation, they all wanted to take a look. I decided to play the ball on the next tee. I drove it out of bounds again (it wasn't my best driving day). To our amazement, however, the ball bounced off something way up in the cliffs and right back into play in the middle of the fairway. We were all blown away. *Sweet Baby Jesus!* But that was just the beginning.

I mishit the next shot terribly again, and it went sailing into the desert thirty yards off the fairway. But, yet again, the ball came shooting back from the abyss onto the middle of the fairway just a few yards from the green!

*Sweet Baby Jesus.*

We were in total awe. Never in our lives had we seen such a thing. But there it was. The very next hole was a challenging shot downhill with water on one side. My friend, Lu, not the greatest golfer on the planet (but definitely the most fun to play with) hit a shot that was less than stellar, and it found the water. He was disappointed. To cheer him up, I dug into my pocket and grabbed the Sweet Baby Jesus ball. I threw it to him, and as he opened his hand and read the inscription, he looked at me in astonishment and said, "I can't possibly."

"I believe in you," I retorted.

The group of us watched him tee it up, and Ethan said, "If this goes in the hole, like a hole-in-one right now, I have no choice but to believe in Jesus—if I don't believe already from the last hole. Miracles do seem to exist."

We collectively held our breath as Lu pulled his club back and drove it down on the ball. As if in slow motion, the ball flew into the air and almost hovered, fighting the breeze, the water, and the trees. Finally, it came down. Not only did it land on the green—something that had eluded Lu all day—but it started rolling toward the hole. Eight feet. Seven feet. Six. The ball was on a slope that moved it toward the hole with every turn. Four feet. Three. Two.

At this moment, it felt like Ethan's salvation was in the balance. The ball stopped a foot short. It had still been an amazing shot, though, and we were celebrating Lu like he had just won the Masters. I looked over at Ethan and saw a little bit of relief. But I sensed also a little bit of disappointment.

Maybe it was just me.

Amazingly, this is not the end of the story. Years later I recounted this story in a sermon to illustrate how good God is—he will use anything or anybody to hunt us down, to draw us to himself. Months after that we were eating lunch at a restaurant when a young woman from our church approached our table. "I need to tell you something," she said. "A few months ago, I met a guy in a pub in Vancouver. He was from New York City and was visiting on business. We got to talking, and I told him about Jesus and our church, and he said he had never gone to church or thought much about God. I told him he should listen to your sermons, since they had helped me when I was skeptical about Christianity. I literally went to the Village Church website, copied the URLs for three random sermons from ten years of material, and sent them to him. Weeks went by, and then I got a crazy text message from him."

This guy, a lifelong New Yorker, had recently gone to Phoenix on a golf trip. On one of the days he was golfing, his group was one man short, so another random guy was called off the driving range and thrown into their foursome. His name was Ethan, a member of the course, who was fighting hard to get his PGA Tour card. He was the best golfer this guy had ever seen. And then a few months later, he found himself talking to the girl from our church in a pub. She sent him some random sermons. The *first one* he listened to included a story about golfing in Phoenix with a guy name Ethan, and how God will use *anything* to hunt us down. He said he almost threw the phone away from him as he listened to my sermon, as if it were magic. As if it were unexplainable.

In a sense it was.

*Sweet Baby Jesus.*

I know this story sounds far-fetched. But it's true. All of it. I am not saying that any of this *proves* God. I am saying simply that the skeptics are wrong to simply add up the evidence for all the regular events we experience each day and suggest this somehow makes all rare events unworthy of belief. The issue is not whether an event is regular or rare but whether we have good evidence for it. When we speak of miracles, we are referencing events that are admittedly rare. But that doesn't make them impossible.

Hume's argument against miracles is based on the idea that "the evidence for the regular is always greater than that for the rare."[39] When this is applied to the claim of a miracle, it seems reasonable, but upon reflection it is not true. The evidence for the regular is not always greater than for the rare. Take the two foundational ideas for the entire naturalistic worldview: the origin of the universe and the origin of life. Both of these events are rare, unrepeatable, and non-testable—events without witnesses at all! As Keener concludes, "Hume's arguments are now shown to be simply a product of his time. . . . Had he lived in our day, an argument based on the nonexperience of miracles would have proved much more difficult and less persuasive. For these and many other reasons, scholars are no longer entitled to simply dismiss the possibility of supernatural causation outright without proving why they are doing so."[40]

As we have seen, *rarity* is not the same as implausibility. It is the case that all medical attempts to revive the dead have failed so far. Can anyone say for certain that in the future, medical advances will not reach a point at which clinically dead people can be restored to life? Of course not. So: it "is a *practical* truth—useful for everyday purposes—but it is not a *necessary* truth."[41] And if it might happen one day, there is at least the logical possibility that it could have happened before. Not necessarily because nature's laws are overthrown, but because we lack complete and full knowledge of what those laws are! Furthermore, today's modern physics concede that beyond the natural world the laws of nature do not apply.[42]

So examining how often an event happens or doesn't happen has its limitations. It is unfair to say a miracle is a rare event by definition and then punish it for being a rare event! The theist agrees that a miracle is a rare event. Depending on how one counts, throughout the entire Bible approximately 250 miracles are recorded. When we speak of miracles, it can mean an extremely rare event that is nevertheless scientifically possible, or it can be an event that would not have occurred by natural means alone. Either way, it remains a possibility.

We've seen that the "laws of nature" are not as "solid" as we once thought. It is possible that these laws—the regular ways in which reality seems to operate—could be manipulated by God, the One who designed them, if he wanted to. To take this one step further, we should understand that the biblical view is that these laws were put in place by God himself not just to *run* things but to *reveal* things to the world—namely, and most importantly, truth about God himself. They are part of his revelation. They exist *under* God, to be sure, but more importantly they exist *unto* God—to draw us to him. Bavinck commented on Isaiah 28:26, "We read that God instructs the plowman, teaching him how he is to do his work. But this instruction does not come to the plowman in writing . . . nor in the form of lessons at school; it is teaching, rather, which is contained and expressed in all the laws of nature, in the character of air and of soil, of time and place, of grain and corn. What the plowman must do is conscientiously *get to know all those laws of nature*, and in this way to learn the lesson which God teaches in them."[43]

The reasons we struggle to believe in miracles say less about their probability, I think, and more about us. We struggle with the limitations of thinking and perceiving something of a higher order than what we can grasp with our natural senses. It has been said, and rightfully so, "For the stone it is a wonder that the plant can grow, for the plant it is a wonder that the animal can move about, for the animal it is a wonder that man can think, and for man it is a wonder that God can raise the dead."[44] We should recognize this and adopt a posture of humility when we try to address the "problem" of miracles.

We also struggle because most of us have an unconscious commitment to secular, materialist explanations for things. We are the fish in the water that David Foster Wallace speaks of, who, when asked how the water is, respond, "What the hell is water?" In other words, we are limited and finite. We don't know what we don't know, and this leads to a blind confidence. Consider the claim that miracles do not defy science. It likely surprises you in some way, and this is because naturalism dominates the lives of us westerners.

The real scandal in all of this is that these beliefs are not pervasive in our modern consciousness because they are the most accurate ideas, but because they are carried along to the "empires of our minds" by very powerful forces (media, education, politics) operating with an agenda. This is what sociologists call the influence of "soft power." A government may make laws or rules around this or that, and science may conclude A or B, but if a phone or social media company decides how you get (or don't get) said information, then you simply won't get it. In this way, soft power is a commanding influence on our day-to-day thinking. My fear is that our modern world and its constructs are more influenced by these vehicles of soft power—vehicles that are rarely theistic and are often consumeristic—than by any pursuit of truth. Their goal is to make you think a certain way and live a certain way for many different reasons, but more often than not so that you buy a particular product and spend your money in a certain way. That's a topic for another day. For now, it is enough to be aware of this worldview and cognizant of the agenda behind the sources of information we assume to be valid. This is especially true when they are speaking to the most foundational questions of our lives—questions of our origins, of life's meaning, of morality, and of our ultimate destiny. The question of miracles, and by inference of God, sits at the crossroads with each of these key questions of life.

All of the discussion in this chapter has been for a purpose. Our objective has been to clear the way scientifically, philosophically, and experientially to explore the idea that miracles are, at least, possible. Now we turn to what is arguably a more exciting task. We will explore miracles as they relate to Jesus' life and ministry and see what they *meant* to his world and to our own world today.

## CHAPTER 10

# Jesus' Miracles: Signs and the
# DAWNING OF
# A NEW WORLD

In no other major religion besides Christianity do miracles occupy so central a role, nor do the founders of any other major religion outside of Christianity have miracles attributed to them in their earliest and most fundamental documents.[1] Two major questions need to be addressed when we consider Jesus and miracles: (1) Were miracles a part of Jesus' life and ministry? (2) If they were, what did they mean? What was their purpose, or aim, for his audience, and beyond, for us today?

The first question has been hotly debated. There is little doubt that the Gospels and the historians at the time of Jesus, such as Josephus (a Jewish historian working for the Roman Empire during the first century), claim that miracles were a part of Jesus' ministry. In the Gospel of Mark alone, 31 percent of the material deals directly or indirectly with miracles.[2] In addition, a dozen or more references to Jesus that appear in *non-Christian* sources of the time speak of Jesus' miracles. The Talmud, a source that is not friendly to the theological claims of Christianity, repeatedly acknowledges that Jesus "practiced magic and led Israel astray" (*Sanhedrin* 43a; cf. *Shabbat* 11.15). Josephus, writing in the late first century, called Jesus "a worker of amazing deeds" (*Antiquities of the Jews* 18.3.3). In his exhaustive study on the historical Jesus, James D. G. Dunn surveys the most recent historical research and the first-century documents about Jesus and concludes, "One of the most compelling features of the whole sweep of ancient opinion regarding Jesus is his reputation as an exorcist and healer. It is no exaggeration to claim that it is one of the most widely attested and firmly established of the historical facts with which we have to deal."[3]

From the perspective of the skeptic, the most popular alternative explanation for these miracle stories is that they were *made up* by the early church and the writers of the Gospels. Some of them, skeptics allege, are modeled on older archetypes of pagan gods (Egyptian, or Greco-Roman) who visited earth, healed people, walked on water, and raised the dead. Other parts of Jesus' life, they assert, are just mythological stories meant to be allegories or parables designed to teach principles. Yet however popular these explanations may be among skeptics at the street level, scholars of all stripes firmly reject them. Even the most skeptical of biblical scholars agrees it is highly likely that the historical Jesus performed miracles. Take, for instance, Rudolf Bultmann (1884–1976), who became popular for arguing that historical analysis of the New Testament is both futile and unnecessary and is well known for his work on *demythologizing* Jesus and the New Testament (saying Jesus lived, preached, and died by crucifixion, but the rest of the details aren't necessary). Bultmann concluded, "The Christian fellowship was convinced that Jesus had done miracles. . . . Most of these stories contained in the gospels are legendary or at least dressed up with legend. But there can be no doubt that Jesus did such deeds. . . . Doubtless he healed the sick and cast out demons."[4]

Similarly, historian N. T. Wright points out,

> More thoroughgoing recent history has been concluding that we can only explain the evidence for Jesus before us if we reckon that Jesus did indeed perform deeds for which there was at the time no "naturalistic" explanation. . . . We must be clear that Jesus' contemporaries, both those who became his followers and those who were determined *not* to become his followers, certainly regarded him as possessed of remarkable powers. The church did not invent the charge that Jesus was in league

with Beelzebub, but charges like that are not advanced unless they are needed as an explanation for some quite remarkable phenomena.[5]

John Dominic Crossan, the most famous scholar within the Jesus Seminar (a group made famous through the 1990s, sometimes deemed demonic by conservative Christians) notes as a powerful indication of the probability of Jesus' miracles that they were actually not all that helpful in moving the Jesus tradition along. So why include them if they were problematic? "I hold," he says, "that Jesus, as a magician and miracle worker, was a very problematic and controversial phenomenon not only for his enemies but even for his friends."[6] It is noteworthy that the gospel writers repeatedly admit that the response to Jesus and his miracles was not awe and wonder but the opposite. His exorcisms often led to the charge that he was in league with Satan and led some observers to plot his death (Matthew 12:14; Mark 3:6). If the early church was creating a narrative and trying to present a white-washed apologetic for Jesus, which is what many skeptics claim, they could easily have avoided controversy by downplaying or ignoring his miraculous works.

It is also telling that the gospel stories are remarkably *free from the sort of embellishment* that appeals to a bought-in audience, which would have been tempting for them to include. The stories of miracles are somewhat short and to the point, without a lot of unnecessary information or extrapolation. In this they are quite different from other legends and myths of the time. C. S. Lewis, a scholar of medieval literature at Oxford, noted that this was one of the things that stood out to him as he read the Gospels: "I have been reading poems, romances, vision literature, legends, and myths all my life," he said. "I know what they are like. I know none of them are like this."[7]

It could even be argued that the Gospels *downplay* the miracles. Often Jesus warned witnesses not to tell anyone about them (Matthew 8:1–4; Mark 1:40–44), and they were rarely presented as the reason why one should believe in Jesus' claims. Jesus often only performed miracles in front of his closest disciples, and he turned down requests for a demonstration to amaze the crowds and impress people with his power. In a sense, Jesus' ministry was actually quite subdued if he was in fact able to perform miracles: The Gospels portray him as having performed just over *thirty miracles* in thirty years of life, three of which were public ministry. That averages to only ten miracles a year! John, one of Jesus' disciples, tells us that Jesus did more miracles than we have recorded (John 20:30), and the other gospel writers allude to the fact that he healed many more people than they recorded (Matthew 12:15; 15:30; Mark 3:10; Luke 4:40). And yet the gospel writers recorded the details of only these thirty miracles. Why only these? They were showing rather amazing restraint in their presentation of Jesus, which speaks to their trustworthiness. They could have easily exaggerated or embellished, but instead they stuck to plainly stating the details of these thirty.

Furthermore, the mention of the *specific names* of those involved in the miracles is a marker of historical legitimacy. The writers name the subjects of the miracles to allow for verification among their first-century communities, rooting the events in eyewitness testimony. It is one thing to claim Jesus healed a faceless, nameless person, but to identify the location and subject of the healing makes it possible to verify what they wrote. It is a compelling case for the historicity and trustworthiness of the accounts. A document containing fake stories about real people (or fake stories about made-up people!) would not be taken seriously and would tend to go out of print quickly.

In his celebrated work on the historical Jesus and a massive volume dedicated almost exclusively to the miracles of Jesus, John P. Meier contends that from a historical perspective, the miracle stories are respected and accepted among most scholars because they meet two very important criteria: *multiple legitimate sources* and *coherence* between those sources. Studying these twin pillars of historical analysis, Meier concludes,

The tradition of Jesus' miracles is more firmly supported by the criteria of historicity than are a number of other well-known and often readily accepted traditions about his life and ministry (e.g., his status as a carpenter). . . . If the miracle tradition from Jesus' public ministry were to be rejected as un-historical, so should every other Gospel tradition about him. For if the criteria of historicity do not work in the case of the miracle tradition, where *multiple attestation* is so massive and *coherence* so impressive, there is no reason to expect them to work elsewhere.[8]

## Jesus the Sorcerer?

But what exactly do the Gospels present of Jesus' miracles? We must first wrestle with what we mean by "miracle." It is a word we have been using repeatedly, but it is not a word the gospel writers use. Instead, they use a few different terms, "words like *paradoxa*, things one would not normally expect; *dynameis*, displays of power or authority; *terata* or *semeia*, signs or portents. . . . The closest we come to 'miracle' is the single occurrence of *thaumasia*, 'marvels,' in Matthew 21:15."[9]

James D. G. Dunn argues, "It is preferable to use the less loaded definition 'remarkable occurrences,' the common New Testament term, 'deeds of power' (*dynameis*), or Josephus' description of Jesus as a 'doer of extraordinary deeds.'"[10] The fact that non-Christians used these words about Jesus makes our inquiry into his life all the more intriguing. All of these different words are simply describing what is happening, rather than attempting to interpret the meaning of the events.

One other term does require a bit more discussion. Dunn points to it when he says, "It will not be possible to avoid some discussion [also] of the term 'magic.'"[11] This does not occur to modern readers, but for a first-century audience, "magician" was a common category for labeling people, and a category people put Jesus into. But was it justified? Much has been written about this topic, but the best scholarship draws a few consistent conclusions.

Arguably, one of the most consistent attacks directed against Jesus by the early opponents of Christianity was the charge that he was practicing *sorcery* (see John 18:30). However, the grounds for such a charge are weak. While Jesus did things that seem to be "magician-like" when analyzed in a vacuum, they fade away when viewed in their historical-cultural context. Using spittle in his healings, for instance: "spittle was a popular folk remedy [and] highly regarded by professional physicians" and was popular in Jewish circles.[12] When understood in this light, the act is hardly surprising or scandalous at all. The same is true of what is perhaps the most "magical" of all Jesus' healings: the woman healed by the power that flowed through Jesus' garment (Mark 5:24–34). Was this evidence that Jesus was a sorcerer, leading Israel astray into the dark arts, as some claim? Remember that Luke, himself a doctor, saw no difficulty in attributing cures to the power of Peter's shadow and the power of handkerchiefs touched by Paul (Acts 5:15; 19:12), while at the same time depicting Peter and Paul as distancing themselves from and as triumphing over magical practices. Jesus also never healed or did exorcisms the way magicians of the time did, calling upon an external power. Rather, Jesus performed miracles in *his own power*, which was unique and was not the practice of anyone at that time. In the end, "Josephus may have characterized him as a "doer of extraordinary deeds" but he avoided terms like *magos* ("magician") and *goés* ("sorcerer"), which he did not hesitate to use of the sign prophets and others of the period.[13] Jesus could not be dismissed as a magician. Even his critics knew there was something else going on.

Meier explores the charge of "magician" by examining several objections skeptics raise, including Mark's use of Aramaic in the healing of the little girl (5:41, *talitha koum*) and in the healing of the deaf and mute man (7:34, *ephphatha*). These phrases have been interpreted by some people as incantations or as magical foreign words. But Meier points out that this charge makes no sense, for Aramaic would have been a language Jesus spoke on a regular basis. It was the common language of Jesus' audience and the furthest thing from a secret language. In Mark's own storytelling, he translated what the Aramaic meant for readers not familiar with the language, which further dispels any suggestion that Jesus was using esoteric knowledge or secrecy.

Mark provided Aramaic words on two other occasions as well: when Jesus prayed during the passion narratives (*Abba* in 14:36; and *Eloi, Eloi, lema sabachthani* in 15:34). "These are examples of intense prayer, not magic," Meier says, and "indicate a high point of emotion and drama in the narrative, not magical practices."[14] Meier also agrees that the spittle was in line with practices of the day, but recognizes that according to the Torah (Leviticus 15:8), spittle was seen to defile a person. So Jesus may have been healing in this manner as a way of challenging the Jewish purity laws. Perhaps he was seeking to redefine covenant participation, challenging head-on the ritual purity laws of the Pharisees.

These contentions that Jesus practiced magic do make an important point. This is the category a first-century audience had to understand what Jesus was doing. Whatever he did, they used this category to describe and explain his actions. In this sense, they indirectly supported the historical case that Jesus was actually doing miracles.

## What Miracles Did Jesus Do?

If it is true that Jesus did miracles, whatever that might mean, our second major question is, what do the miracles mean? Why did he do them? To understand that, we need to take a closer look at the kinds of miracles Jesus actually did. Thirty-one separate miracles of Jesus are recorded in the gospel accounts, and generally speaking they can be divided into three kinds: (1) healings, (2) exorcisms, and (3) nature miracles. Herman Bavinck pointed out that these categories also highlight the enemy Jesus was exercising power over: sin, Satan, and nature.[15] The total miracle count breaks down into six exorcisms, seventeen healings (including three stories of raising the dead), and eight nature miracles.[16] Along with these are fifteen texts that refer to

Jesus' miracle-working activity and include allusions to a number of miracles he did that we simply aren't told about, wherein the writers say he healed "all the sick that the crowds brought him."[17] This consistent activity condensed into three years of ministry is what led the crowds to constantly ask, "Who is this man who is master of nature, disease and even death?" Many have suggested that traveling healers were a dime a dozen in Jesus' day, but the historical data says otherwise. Craig Keener explains, "Most people sought divine help at healing sanctuaries; public individual miracle workers were not nearly so common in this period, and those who did perform wonders rarely specialized in healings."[18]

All four of the Gospels present Jesus as having done miracles. Yet only one miracle, other than his resurrection from death, makes it into all four Gospels: the feeding of the five thousand. The most extraordinary deeds attributed to Jesus are the "nature miracles"—the stilling of the storm (Mark 4:35–41), the feeding of the five thousand (Mark 6:31–44), turning water into wine (John 2:1–11), and walking on water (Mark 6:45–52). Skeptics present these accounts as untrustworthy partly because they so closely resemble earlier miracle stories in the history of Israel. The stilling of the storm has clear echoes of the Jonah story. The feeding of the five thousand has echoes of 2 Kings 4:42–44 and seems to have shaped the account of the miracle itself, wherein Elisha told a man with a small amount of bread to feed a hundred people, and it multiplied out exactly as needed with "some left." The turning of water into wine echoes the water of Egypt turning to blood. Once free from Egypt, Moses selected leaders over groups of "thousands, of hundreds, of fifties, and of tens" (Exodus 18:21). In Mark's account of the feeding of the five thousand, "Jesus directed [his disciples] to have all the people sit down in groups on the green grass. So they sat down in groups of hundreds and fifties" (Mark 6:39–40 NIV).

Noting the parallels with the Old Testament is correct. There are many. But this is not a reason to doubt their historicity. In fact, the parallels should be expected because Jesus' actions were intentionally revelatory. He was fully aware of an earlier story that was now reaching its climax in his life. As we already saw: Jesus wanted people to see that he was reconstituting Israel around himself by choosing twelve disciples and by going into the wilderness for forty days to symbolize Israel's wilderness wanderings of forty years. Jesus saw himself as the climactic, final prophet. We don't need to conclude that the early church created these symbolic stories. It is far more probable that Jesus himself intentionally crafted and performed the miracles to reflect and allude to these earlier events.

Note that I am not saying the gospel writers didn't intentionally shape the stories they wrote to make a theological point. I believe they did. But that does not mean they are fabricated scenarios. The elements were there in the events and the activity of Jesus, and the disciples needed to see and understand their significance and then report them in light of how they fit the unfolding story of God's work.

## What Did the Miracles Mean?

All of this leads us to our final, and arguably most important, question regarding the miracles of Jesus. What did they mean?

When I was growing up, there were these big green electrical boxes all over my town. Each box had a large sticker showing a guy being electrocuted with a big line through him. These were warnings: *Don't climb on this or you could be electrocuted.* It was a sign, a picture that pointed to a deeper reality than the sign itself. The same is true when Jesus does a miracle. It is never an end in itself. It always has another layer of meaning, a deeper something it is pointing to. So, what was Jesus trying to say through his miracles?

The terminology used by the first-century writers points us in the right direction to understand the why and what. The gospel writers and Josephus employed three sets of terms: (1) a *sign*, something that points to or indicates something else; (2) a *wonder*, an event that causes people to be amazed or astonished, and (3) a *mighty work* or *marvel*, an act displaying great power, especially divine power.[19] These terms all point to the fact that the miracles were more than an attempt to better the world for a handful of people who lived two thousand years ago.

Of course, healing lepers and raising the dead were good and beautiful things that did improve the world in different ways. This good shouldn't be underestimated. If you were Jairus getting your little girl back after she had died, that would mean everything to you. If you had leprosy and hadn't been touched in years, being healed and back in the world of people again would be life-giving in ways most of us can't imagine.

Jesus' intentions, however, went beyond meeting these immediate, individual, temporal needs. His actions were pointers to deeper revelation about God and salvation, and how humankind can connect to the former and experience the latter. They had a *theological purpose* and aim, not just a practical one. "The Messiah was not going to save the world by miraculous, Band-Aid interventions: a storm calmed here, a crowd fed there. . . . It was going to be saved by means of a deeper, darker, left-handed mystery."[20] The miracles weren't an end in themselves; they relayed important messages—teachings about life, love, God, humankind, the way all these things interacted with one another, and how Jesus was bringing about a new way that pointed beyond the miracles. They were about the redemption of a broken world and broken people. "But for one exception, namely, the cursing of the fig tree, all the miracles of Jesus are redemptive in kind. He did not come to condemn the world, but to save it."[21]

When grappling to identify the "why" behind God's work through miracles, German theologian Jürgen Moltmann pointed out that God was doing something *restorative*. According to the Bible, death, decay, entropy, and destruction are the true suspensions of God's laws—his created intentions—and miracles are our early glimpses of restoration. Biblically speaking, we can say they are "not supernatural miracles in a natural world, [but rather] they are the only truly 'natural' things in a world that is unnatural, demonized, and wounded."[22] Consider the account of the man Jesus healed from blindness in John 9, for instance. The disciples asked, "Rabbi, who sinned, this man or his parents, that he was born blind?" (v. 2 NIV). Jesus healed the man, and then the story pivots and becomes about something else:

> "I have come into this world, so that the blind will see and those who see will become blind."
>
> Some Pharisees who were with him heard him say this and asked, "What? Are we blind too?"
>
> Jesus said, "now that you claim you can see, your guilt remains." (vv. 39–41 NIV)

The disciples—as well as the readers of John's Gospel—were looking backward to find out the answer to the question "Why?" "Jesus redirect[ed] their attention forward, answering a different question: 'To what end?' The miracle in this sense was making a theological point not about the one man's blindness but about everyone else's blindness."[23]

Craig Evans points out that miracles are an intrinsic part of Jesus' "proclamation of the kingdom of God. The mighty deeds and the proclamation must go together; neither can be understood without the other."[24] Jesus' words are accompanied and confirmed by his works. They are the physical evidence to the world of the reality of what Jesus claimed was happening through his life: the restoring of all things. This is why John repeatedly used the word "sign" (*semeion*) for Jesus' miracles (John 2:11; 4:54; 6:14). A "sign" of what? A sign of the new creation breaking into the world. Philip Yancey writes,

> Why miracles? Did they make any difference? I readily concede that Jesus, with a few dozen healings and a handful of resurrections from the dead, did little to solve the problem of pain on this planet. That is not why he came. Nevertheless, it was in

Jesus' nature to counteract the effects of the fallen world during his time on earth. As he strode through life Jesus used supernatural power to set right what was wrong. The miracles give me a glimpse of what the world was meant to be and instill hope that one day God will right its wrongs. To put it mildly, God is no more satisfied with this earth than we are; Jesus' miracles offer a hint of what God intends to do about it.[25]

The purpose of miracles was to authenticate the message of the gospel (John 3:2) and to bear witness to the fact that the reign of God was dawning in a new and special way. God's rule was now breaking through the clouds of sin and death and birthing a new world, right there and then in the presence of Jesus (Matthew 12:28), all to bring glory to God (Matthew 9:8; John 9:3).

Another aspect of Jesus' miracles is often overlooked, however. As signs, they not only work to show the world the redemptive *plan* of God, but they help us better know and understand the redemptive *person* of God. They work not only as redemption but as *revelation*. Bavinck suggested that in the Old Testament, miracles function as both judgment and redemption by God. The flood during Noah's time, the miracles grouped at the time of Moses and Joshua, including the plagues and conquest of Canaan—all of these were miracles, but they were also judgments on God's enemies as well as a restorative work of establishing a secure home for his people. The miracles in Elijah's day occurred at a time when paganism was threatening to suppress the worship of God, and they achieved their purpose by proclaiming the God of Israel as the one true God.

They also serve as revelation of God to the world (Matthew 11:27; John 1:18).[26] This is YHWH in person. He is the One who controls the wind and waves. The One who walks on water, for he created water.

Jesus *shows us something about God* in each miracle. Take the story of changing water into wine. Jesus wasn't just helping people at a wedding; he was hinting at who he is. This is the reason for the controversy between Jesus and his mother about whether "his time had come" (see John 2:4). Was it time yet for him to reveal his identity? Miracles were another way for Jesus to say, "I am God in person." That's why miracles have the flavor and shape they do.

In this context, miracles also reveal a new way of salvation. "The end and object of all revelation," Bavinck said, "and of the miracles in that revelation, is the restoration of fallen mankind, the re-creation of the world, and the acknowledgment of God as God."[27] This is, I think, the main purpose of Jesus' miracles. They were about the people of God—and how to become one of them—almost more so than about God himself.

In his first-century Jewish context, Jesus' healings and exorcisms would have been clearly understood as acts done to bring about the restoration of a person to membership in Israel. They would have been a welcome of those who, through sickness or sin, had been excluded as ritually unclean. Evidence from the first century suggests that in some Jewish circles a maimed Jew could not be a full member of the community, so Jesus' healings brought shalom (peace) in several profound ways. They restored many people to wholeness physically, yes, but they also brought social and relational restoration, allowing for a renewed membership in the people of God. Many of the people Jesus healed belonged to the "banned" categories: the blind, the deaf and dumb, lepers, and the crippled. The miracles of Jesus weren't simply about Christology but ecclesiology, answering the question, Who belongs to the people of God? Who is welcome in the new work that God is bringing about in the world?

The miracles of Jesus make sense in this context. Israel always believed themselves to be the linchpin of what YHWH, the creator God, was doing and would do for the world as a whole: "When Israel was restored, the whole creation would be restored. Thus, it is not surprising that we find echoes in the gospels of strange events in which Jesus exercises power over the natural order, bringing it into new harmony with itself . . . the restoration of creation, which Israel had expected to happen when her god became her king and she was vindicated by him."[28]

Understood in this context, Jesus' miracles tell us that God's people were no longer to be defined by a particular ethnic group, not by blood or geography or holy lands as they once were, but by Jesus and the Spirit. This is what the rest of the New Testament teaches (see Galatians 3–4; Romans 1–8) and, I believe, one reason why a disproportionately large number of healing miracles occur on the Sabbath. Jesus was in effect saying, "I am bringing in a new era of salvation history that breaks the old mold."

The older prophecies of God's people returning from exile, of God's return to Zion, of the restoration of Israel, and of a new creation itself had now focused in on the work of Jesus as he healed the sick, performed nature miracles, and included the outcast among God's covenant people. Jesus was redefining all of these end-time expectations and redrawing them so that "the expectation of restored land [had] become focused on restored human beings."[29] This required a new paradigm for Israel going forward, minus the concerns that were once the top priority—the physical land (Canaan) and their physical demarcation (circumcision and food laws). What once defined the people of God was passing as the kingdom of God became a transnational people of all races. The traditional symbol of sacred land was "swallowed up in the eschatological promise [as] YHWH was now to be king of all the earth."[30]

## What about Miracles Today?

One of the great purposes behind this miracle-as-revelation was *to stir up faith among people.* We see this over and over again in the gospel accounts. John tells us, "Many people saw the signs [Jesus] was performing and believed in his name" (John 2:23 NIV). And we read that later, after Jesus rose from the dead, John "who had reached the tomb first . . . saw and believed" (John 20:8 NIV). The book of Acts tells us, "Simon himself believed and was baptized. And he followed Philip everywhere, astonished by the great signs and miracles he saw" (8:13 NIV).

Some scholars, like D. A. Carson in his examination of signs and wonders, as well as others who react strongly against the extreme charismatic movement, argue that Jesus rebuked requests for miracles and that miracles do not produce lasting faith. They cite Matthew 12, where Jesus says, "A wicked and adulterous generation asks for a sign!" (v. 39 NIV). But this view is mistaken when treated as normative or prescriptive (rather than descriptive) for our own perspective on miracles. It is not intended to discourage us from seeking signs today.[31] Some, like John Woodhouse, even went as far as saying that "a desire for further signs and wonders is sinful and unbelieving."[32] Yet this interpretation ignores the fact that these examples of rebuke were given to hostile unbelievers who sought miracles, not sincere followers of Jesus who longed for his kingdom to come. Interpretations that view miracles negatively also ignore the fact that miracles do not always lead to shallow faith in the Gospels, but sometimes produce true and lasting faith in God (see John 2:23–25; 4:48; 20:29–31). Hear also the writer of the book of Hebrews: "This salvation, which was first announced by the Lord, was confirmed to us by those who heard him. God also testified to it by signs, wonders and various miracles, and by gifts of the Holy Spirit distributed according to his will" (2:3–4 NIV).

Bringing about revelation of God that leads to saving faith is one of the stated purposes of miracles the gospel writers tell us about. Jesus did miracles to reveal to the world what he came to do. Again, we see this in the miracle mentioned earlier, the turning of water into wine. John 2:6 tells us that there were six stone jars filled with water and then gives their purpose, which is the key to uncovering the meaning of the miracle: they were "for the Jewish rites of purification." Why did John include this detail? Because John's larger purpose was to show us through this miracle that the Jewish observance and ritual of purification was being upstaged and superseded by Jesus. This phase of history, where humankind connected with God through religious observance of rituals, was coming to an end. It was being fulfilled by Jesus and what he was doing in the world. Jesus was doing something new, and he was saying, "I'm the new wine." Religion was giving way to relationship.

Here we find the scandal of Jesus' miracles, the real problem Jesus was creating. What he was saying was like a cultural hand grenade, upending centuries of tradition and belief. This would have been extremely offensive and controversial to John's audience. How do I know? When I was in Israel a few years ago, I had the unique privilege of preaching in front of one of these big stone water jars at Cana in Galilee, where this miracle took place historically. The jar was up to my waist and must have been two or three feet wide at the mouth. My audience was a collection of tourists standing around as well as our Jewish tour guide, Abraham. I explained what the story of the water being turned to wine was about, and later Abraham pulled me aside and asked, "Are you serious about what you said back there?" I said, "Yes, of course." He said, "I've done this tour with two hundred Christian groups, and I've never heard any of them get up and say what you just said. Do you really think that that's what Jesus was trying to say?"

Here was a man who was religiously living under the idea that purification jars were still necessary in relating to God, and I was able to clarify what Jesus was saying. He began to grasp the idea that one phase of God's work was over and a new had begun, and it hit him hard. As it should hit all of us. You can see why the miracles Jesus did were powerful, not only for the activity itself, but for what it meant about God and God's work in the world. Jesus was not just healing people or doing marvelous things. He was more than a doctor or a magician. In every miracle, he was reinforcing what he taught: "I'm replacing everything the temple and all of the purification rituals ever meant or were used for. I'm here—and I'm shutting it all down."

You can understand why Jesus' audience often got angry with

him. Jesus claimed to be bringing about a new era, or as John said, "The law was given through Moses; grace and truth came through Jesus Christ" (John 1:17). With Jesus came a cosmic shift in how God related to the world, for Jesus was bringing creation back to what it was intended to be before sin and death.

What does this mean for you and me? It means that miracles are an invitation to all of us, God's invitation to enter in and experience restoration at a personal level.

## Transformation: The Point of It All

The final offense of Jesus' miracles is that Jesus was not just the true way of relating to God, he was the *better* way. Better than all other ways. This is the meaning behind Jesus' turning water into wine. The master of the feast said, "Everyone serves the good wine first, and when people have drunk freely, then the poor wine. But you have kept the good wine until now" (John 2:10). In communicating this miracle story, John hoped that his readers would see the broader context of *salvation history* as the deeper meaning. In other words, God has kept the good way—the far better, more fulfilling, satisfying way—of relating to God and the world and ourselves as the second phase of his work. Jesus was showing us a new way, and in light of it, the old ways are like poor wine.

Why? Because religious observance is external, and while it changes what we do, it is less effective in transforming what we *want* to do. And Jesus doesn't want us to miss the fact that this miracle is all about that latter kind of transformation. He isn't a magician doing tricks. He came to set free and transform people from normal, everyday, stale, water-in-a-pot existences to something sweet and colorful—something that affects the senses and stimulates the soul. The real transformation of water into wine is about *us*. That's what John wants us to see. It's about your anger problem, the guilt you still live with because you did that thing you can't forget, the materialism you can't shake, or that addiction that makes you feel worthless. It is the story that promises to take the bland ruins of our tasteless lives and make them sweet again. Jesus is creating something new, something so good that the world when it tastes it will forever be unsatisfied with anything else.

Ten years ago the team of people that planted Village Church where I pastor were dreaming up a mission statement, and we landed on this: *to see people transformed into fully devoted followers of Jesus.* We intentionally focused in on the word *transformed.* We knew our church wasn't about just telling people what the Bible said or who God was. We were striving toward the singular goal of seeing practical and real transformation in people's lives, and we got that from the ministry of Jesus.

The biblical story is about what God has done and is doing to take us from who we were and transform us into the image of his Son (Romans 8:29). And that's good because people today are not just asking whether Christianity is true but whether it *works. Can it turn my marriage around? Can it help me overcome an addiction? Will it change the way I feel and what I want in life?* Yes! In their book *The Experience Economy,* B. Joseph Pine II and James H. Gilmore outline the different ways eras within civilization have been built. First there was an economy built on trading commodities. Agrarian societies were built on farming and hunting, and then trading or selling the commodities to someone (a market). The next phase was the goods of the industrial age, where a manufacturer would make something and a user would buy it. This phase gave way to the modern service industry, wherein services were provided to clients, and then to the modern experience economy, wherein a stager provides something for guests; it's the difference between sitting in a Starbucks and sitting in a Dunkin' Donuts.[33] We long to experience a type of life that a product and environment gives versus simply consuming it.

*The Experience Economy* is celebrated among business leaders as a brilliant exposition of past and present business realities, and the final chapter of the book predicts the next major phase of activity among consumers and companies: the *transformation economy*.[34] That, arguably, is where we find ourselves today. People desire at the deepest level more than goods, services, or experiences. Their desire is that those things will actually transform their lives, and this is where Christianity has something the world does not. Christianity is more than a set of teachings or a philosophy of life. It is an offer of a living, breathing relationship with God himself, a relationship that transforms one's life. "My son, who was dead, is alive!" says the father in the prodigal son story. The apostle Paul made it clear that what is truly amazing about the salvation he had just described for five chapters in Galatians is what it actually *does* in a person's life: "The acts of the flesh are obvious: sexual immorality, impurity and debauchery; idolatry and witchcraft; hatred, discord, jealousy, fits of rage, selfish ambition, dissensions, factions and envy; drunkenness, orgies, and the like. . . . But the fruit of the Spirit is love, joy, peace, forbearance, kindness, goodness, faithfulness, gentleness and self-control" (5:19– 23 NIV).

Jesus is still doing miracles. He transforms us from the selfish, idol-driven, sinful, hopeless people that we were into something entirely different, so that we spend money differently, treat our spouses and friends (and even strangers) differently; raise our children and do our jobs differently. Everything changes when it's put into the hands of Jesus. And it changes for the better. That's why John tells us what these jars were used for "purification" (John 2:6). The Christian word for this is *sanctification*, a word that speaks to the purifying work of Christ in our lives. And John was saying, "Transformation happens through purification." Jesus changes our minds, souls, and bodies from what we used to value and celebrate and take joy and pleasure in into something else entirely. People who give their lives to Jesus become different people if they follow Jesus where he takes them. We cannot simply add Jesus into our existing lives; we must reorient everything around him.

In his famous children's book, *The Voyage of the Dawn Treader*, C. S. Lewis captured this tension pointedly. One of the characters, Eustace, is selfish and mean and desires power above all else. He wakes up one morning to find, with horror, that he is a dragon. He has gotten what he wanted, and yet he hates it. He meets the lion Aslan (the Christ figure of the story) who offers him a way out—salvation from his existing state—but there is one catch: it will hurt immensely. Eustace agrees to what Aslan will do, and later explains, "I was afraid of his claws, but I was pretty desperate now. So, I just lay down on my back to let him do it. The very first tear he made was so deep that I thought it had gone right into my heart. When he began to pull the skin off, it hurt worse than anything I've ever felt. . . . He ripped it off, and there was I as smooth and soft as a peeled orange and smaller than I had been. I'd turned into a boy again."[35]

Real transformation is scary, and it hurts. It's *humbling*. "*I was smaller than I had been*," Eustace says. Transformation begins as we humble ourselves, coming under the guidance and leadership of Jesus. And while it can be painful, like surgery, it is also exciting. When one becomes smaller, the world becomes larger, and as many who have made this decision will testify, the universe opens up in a new way that they did not see before. Moments are more meaningful than they once were. Memories carry a kind of weight that they didn't when they were just a collection of things that happened, discarded into the cold universe without remainder. Once we meet God, we see that everything that happens is part of the story that he is writing in the world. We become smaller, yes, but in a good way—in a way that makes life larger, *more* significant than it was, not less.

From the raising of Lazarus to the feeding of the five thousand and walking on water, Jesus' miracles help us see the world in a new way. They enlarge things and show us that there really is something behind the veil. Could it be that the two hundred million modern cases of healings and miracles recorded on all the continents of the planet aren't just psychosomatic or wishful thinking? Could they point to something else? Could it be that God actually exists and is living and moving and inviting us all to believe still today?

Miracles are the flashes of true reality breaking through, like a blade of grass through a crack in concrete. We catch a glimpse of the world to come in the midst of the shadow of pain, depression, sickness, disease, suicide, divorce, poverty, and discouragement. Jesus' miracles are early arrivals of the New World. Outside of the Bible, I have not read a better description of this reality than Tolkien's description at the end of *The Return of the King*, as he described Frodo's experience on the Elven-ship as it transports him to the Undying Lands: "And the ship went out into the High Sea and passed into the West, until at last on a night of rain Frodo smelled a sweet fragrance on the air and heard the sound of singing that came over the water. And then it seemed to him that as in his dream . . . the grey rain-curtain turned all to silver glass and was rolled back, and he beheld white shores and beyond them a far green country under a swift sunrise."[36]

## When the Miracle Doesn't Happen

We all have different backgrounds. If you, like me, grew up not going to church, you probably weren't exposed to conversations about miracles very often. We didn't sit around the dinner table at my house and talk that about this stuff; it just wasn't part of my experience. But if you did grow up in church, then miracles may have been a regular part of your conversation. And they probably weren't about spectacular healings or people rising from the dead. People testify to parking spaces opening up in busy malls or that house the Joneses wanted to buy becoming available and affordable because of prayer. Of course there are also the more serious answers to prayer: the cancer that was cured or the church floor that collapsed during a concert without killing anyone (which happened in our city a few years ago).

But then there are the times when miracles *don't happen*. We pray and the tumor keeps growing. *Where is God then?* I stood over my stepdad's casket a short time ago. He had struggled with a lung disease for a year and a half, and I had prayed for him every day, but he still succumbed to the disease and died. And in moments like that, the question of miracles is raised afresh. Every time we celebrate a miracle, the backside to that celebration is a question: Why not that one miracle I needed? Why not just one more in the life of that family, or mother, or child . . . or me?

This crucial tension is present in the story of water being turned into wine as well. It shows us that *we can't control God.* That we don't get to tell God when he's going to heal somebody. And we don't get to tell God how he's going to heal somebody. Mary came to Jesus and said, "We're at a wedding. They're out of wine. Do something about it." And his response was, "Woman, it's not my time" (John 2:3–4, author's paraphrase). Jesus was saying, "You can't control me." You don't get to tell God how or when or if he's going to heal somebody. You humbly approach God and ask him, but sometimes his answer is no. Jesus, in the garden of Gethsemane, prayed to God, "Take this cup [of suffering] from me" (Mark 14:36 NIV). And God answered no. In the midst of all the pain, there's stuff happening that we can't see. There's a story going on in which all of this has a place. Jesus promised not one sparrow would fall to the ground apart from the will of his Father. He said that in the midst of a series of dire warnings to the twelve disciples predicting arrest, persecution, and death! It's not that we won't face trials and difficulties in our lives if we follow Jesus, but that we are safe in doing so. Even if his answer to our prayer for a miracle is no.

Again, we shouldn't miss the fact that there aren't more miracles in Jesus' ministry. After all, he could have done as many as he wanted. Why thirty-six when he could have done so many more? Why so few? I think it's because Jesus knows something we know but refuse to embrace: that in life, there are no easy, quick answers. When we face demons in our lives, the answer most often is not deliverance but discipleship. That porn addiction or shopping addiction doesn't just disappear overnight; it takes time and hard work. "Narrow [is] the road that leads to life, and only a few find it" (Matthew 7:14 NIV). The road to transformation is tough. It's not felt in a power encounter or a flashy instant, but hard fought in the dark, when no one is looking, on our knees amid sweat, tears, and confusion.

But don't despair. God is there.

## The Secret Hour

A line in the water-to-wine account helps me to live with this tension. Jesus said to his mother, "My hour has not yet come" (John 2:4). If you keep reading through John, you find that this "hour" Jesus referred to is a theme repeated throughout the book and is mentioned seven times (see also John 7:30; 8:20; 12:23, 27; 13:1; 17:1). And it's not the only thing mentioned seven times throughout John. There are seven "signs" and seven "I Am" statements, all based on the symbolism of seven as the number representing completion to the Jews. As you read through the Gospel of John you realize that the "hour" for Jesus is the hour of his death. "The hour has come for the Son of Man to be glorified," he said as he prepared himself for his arrest (John 12:23). He was going to the cross to die for the sins of the world. That was his "hour," his moment of greatest glory. He was tying the transformation of water into wine to "the hour" to show us that the miracle was pointing to something bigger: the shedding of his blood on the cross.

The purification and transformation of our lives happens by way of the cross. The "hour" of Jesus, when he paid for the sin that entangles our lives, frees those who trust in it from the ongoing power of sin in their day-to-day existence. Jesus' miracles are signs that point to deeper realities that can only be seen with eyes of faith. "This, the first of his signs, Jesus did at Cana in Galilee, and manifested his glory" (John 2:11). And these signs reveal us to be one of two kinds of people. There were people like the *servants* at the wedding who saw the sign but not the future glory. And then there are those like the *disciples* who saw the sign and perceived the glory. "And his disciples believed in him" (John 2:11). Some of us hear about Jesus but it never translates into faith and salvation. Maybe that's you. Jesus says to you, "Do you have eyes that see? Do you have ears that hear? Do you have a heart that perceives the meaning of the signs I did in my life? The miracles that improved people's lives were always about something more profound, which includes something about you."

And then there are those who hear about Jesus and are drawn to him in faith like the disciples were. Those people see, though they still struggle with doubts and sin. They believe in him and have a personal experience. And that makes all the difference.

Have you ever thought about the fact that all of the people who were healed in Jesus' time went on to die? The miracle they experienced didn't end their suffering permanently. But the One the miracles pointed to can. Jesus' miracles aren't signs of what we deserve or how good we are; they are about Jesus and how good *he* is, and thus our relationship to *him*, not his miracles. As Søren Kierkegaard once said, "I am a poor wretch who God took charge of, and for whom he has done so indescribably much more than I ever expected that I can only long for the peace of eternity in order to do nothing but thank him."

My hope is that this is exactly how you feel.

# PART VI

---

# The Problem of
# JESUS' STORIES

*"Stories don't always have happy endings."
This stopped him. Because they didn't, did
they? That's one thing the monster had
definitely taught him. Stories were wild,
wild animals and went off in directions you
couldn't expect. "Stories are the wildest things
of all," the monster rumbled. "Stories chase
and bite and hunt."*

—Patrick Ness, A Monster Calls

# CHAPTER 11

## The Master

# STORYTELLER

The coffee shop was packed full of people. There was a buzz in the air. We had told our church I would be there to answer any questions they had about theology, God, the Bible—whatever (don't ask me why I do these things), and that they could bring their friends to ask their questions too. We were two hours into a night wherein skeptics drilled me about science, sexuality, evil, suffering, and so on, when a hand went up and the person asked a question I had never been asked before: "If Jesus were walking around on earth today, what do you think he would do for a living?" Everyone turned to face the person and then back at me. I thought for a moment and then, to the surprise of all, I said, "A filmmaker, or a writer. I think he would make movies, or television shows."

The crowd looked puzzled and laughed.

"I'm serious," I said. I then sat down, and on a rainy night in Vancouver with a hot coffee in my hand, explained why, based on what we know about Jesus' life and ministry—and what he was trying to accomplish—this makes all the sense in the world. Why Jesus would likely be more a colleague of Spielberg, Nolan, Lucas, and Coppola, than of pastors or priests; rabbis or philosophers; politicians or professors. And why that would be the right thing for him to do. After all, what did Jesus like to do most?

## The Seven Basic Plots

Recent philosophical and psychological studies contend that one of the central ways we make sense of the world is by telling stories. This is how we answer those core questions we all have as human beings: Who are we? Where are we? What's the problem? What's the solution?[1] Stories are more than *entertainment* within reality, they are an *explanation* of reality—a filter through which we experience and understand. Stories construct reality for us. New Testament scholar N. T. Wright says that worldviews are formed and lived out through four basic means in a culture: questions, symbols, stories, and praxis. He goes on to say that "narrative is the *most* characteristic expression of worldview, going deeper than observation, or fragmented remark."[2]

A few years ago, I read a book called *The Seven Basic Plots* by Christopher Booker, and it changed the way I think about Jesus. Not because the book is about him (it isn't), but because it changed the way I think about stories. Early in his seven-hundred-page tome, Booker argues that there are only *seven stories* humankind has ever told, and we tell them over and over again. Here are the seven basic story types:

1. Overcoming the Monster
2. Rags to Riches
3. The Quest
4. Voyage and Return
5. The Comedy
6. The Tragedy
7. The Rebirth

Booker contends that *Jaws* is the same story as *Beowulf* (Overcoming the Monster); *Pretty Woman* is the same story as *Cinderella* (Rages to Riches); *The Wizard of Oz* is the same as *Gone with the Wind* (Voyage and Return), and so on. There is a "small quantity of real fiction in the world," he says, "the same images, with very little variation, have served all the authors who have ever written. . . .There are indeed a small number of plots which are so fundamental to the way we tell stories."[3] These basic archetypal themes are woven through every story we tell and have told for five thousand years, so much so that they feel like they have been programmed into us. These stories connect in profound ways to patterns of human psychology and our deep longings to frame the world and define how we live. "So deep and instinctive is our need [for stories]" Booker says, "that, as small children, we have no sooner learned to speak than we begin demanding to be told stories."[4] He then raises a further question, noting that "what is astonishing is how incurious we are as to *why* we indulge in this strange form of activity. What real purpose does it serve? So much do we take our need to tell stories for granted that such questions scarcely even occur to us."[5]

Booker asks not only *what* stories we tell but more fundamentally *why* we tell the stories we do. His answer, similar to Wright's, is that at both a conscious and unconscious level, stories are meant to *answer our deepest questions* about origins, meaning, morality, and destiny. They frame our experience and give meaning to our lives. Drawing on Freudian and Jungian archetypes, Booker believes these stories explain our basic yearnings as human beings. We have a need to locate reality, or a given event, into a narrative to process and make sense of it. The stories we tell are surface explanations, or conscious 'tellings' of deeper, hidden, unconscious convictions, and fears. "What stories can tell us much more profoundly than we have realized, is how our human nature works, and why we think and behave in this world as we do."[6]

## Jesus as Storyteller

What does all of this have to do with Jesus? One thing we know about Jesus is that he told stories. He was a storyteller, and one-third of his recorded teaching ministry in the Gospels is storytelling, usually parables. Scholars debate why Jesus told the stories he did. What was his aim? Some argue that it was to illustrate theology to people, to tell "earthly stories with heavenly meanings." Others say it was to hide his real message from those seeking to hurt him. I believe these are valid reasons, but I think the reason Jesus told stories is closer to the reason Booker suggests. Quite simply, the stories of Jesus are his answers to the deep questions we have as human beings, helping us frame how we see the world and how we understand ourselves and our lives.

Jesus told parables to challenge the status quo, the commonly accepted understandings of both the ancient and modern world. His stories challenged what people thought about God and salvation, about themselves, about grace and judgment, and about work, sex, marriage, money, and everything that is common to human life. His stories shuffled the furniture of reality, scandalizing the "acceptable" ways humans felt and thought about all of these things. And because of this, his stories demanded a response, summoning those who heard them to a new (and better) way to be human.

In a previous chapter, I mentioned the quest for the historical Jesus, the endless debate about what Jesus really said and did when judged from a critical, historical perspective. Yet even there, nearly every scholar begins with the acknowledgment that Jesus taught through stories. Josephus, a Jew writing for the Roman Empire, said that whoever Jesus was, he was "a teacher of the people."[7] Historical Jesus research acknowledges that this is "the most obvious category for audiences, [even skeptics] and onlookers to 'fit' Jesus into."[8] One of the most prolific modern historical Jesus scholars and a professor of divinity at the University of Durham, James D. G. Dunn, points out that "teacher is the most common title used for Jesus in the Jesus tradition" (the Gospels), and "that a more accurate title for Jesus than 'teacher' would have been *mosel* ('parabolist'), one who characteristically spoke in parables."[9] Or as Kenneth Bailey suggests, a "metaphorical theologian"—one who taught about God, humankind, salvation, and so forth through metaphor and story versus cold logic and reason.

Parables form approximately one third of Jesus' recorded teachings.

Depending on how one counts them, there are 46 separate recorded parables among all four Gospels. The Gospel of Luke contains 24, of which 18 are unique; the Gospel of Matthew contains 23, of which 11 are unique; and the Gospel of Mark contains 8, of which 2 are unique. Here are a sample of some of the parables Jesus:

- New Wine in Old Wineskins (Matthew 9:17; Mark 2:22; Luke 5:37–38)
- The Wise and Foolish Servants (Matthew 24:45–51; Luke 12:42–48)
- The Parable of the Soils (Matthew 13:3–23; Mark 4:1–20; Luke 8:14–15)
- The Mustard Seed (Matthew 13:31–32; Mark 4:30–32; Luke 13:18–19)
- The Good Samaritan (Luke 10:30–37)
- The Lost Sheep (Luke 15:4–7)
- The Lost Coin (Luke 15:8–10)
- The Prodigal Son (Luke 15:11–32)
- The Rich Man and Lazarus (Luke 16:19–31)
- The Pharisee and Tax Collector (Luke 18:10–14)
- The Talents (Matthew 25:14–30)

Notice the amount of times two or more Gospels record the same parable. Skeptics often try to bring doubt to the legitimacy of the Gospels by honing in on these stories, arguing that because the details often differ they can't be trusted. Compare the details of the Wise and Foolish Servants parable (Matthew 24:45–51; Luke 12:42–48), or parable of the Mustard Seed (Matthew 13:31–32; Mark 4:30–32; Luke 13:18–19), for instance, and you will see subtle differences. "Proof that this is all made up!" they say. But any historian knows this is wrong-headed. The fact that Jesus was a traveling prophet meant that he went from village to village, saying essentially the same things wherever he went. We have two versions of these stories and many other teachings (compare Matthew's version of the Sermon on the Mount with Luke's!), not because one is adapted from the other or because they are being made up, but because these are two out of a dozen (or more) possible variations that people in Galilee with a tape recorder might have heard Jesus say.[10]

So what do these researchers believe these parables, or stories, did? What was their purpose? They functioned as an urgent summons "which attempts to *break open the worldview* . . . and replace it with a new one." They tell their audience "that their implicit controlling story has reached its crisis point, threatening some of their cherished symbols, and praxis, and *offering new and startling answers to the underlying worldview questions.* . . . [They are] subversive stories, told to articulate and *bring to birth a new way* of being the people of god."[11] They do not merely give people something to think about. They invite people into the new world that is being created and warn of dire consequences if the invitation is refused.

In other words, stories were the vehicle Jesus used to communicate information in an aesthetic manner for the purpose of bringing about a new reality. He wanted to communicate in a way that went deeper, further than a simple explanation of facts. Klyne Snodgrass, in his exhaustive book on the parables, *Stories with Intent*, defines them this way: "*At its simplest the parable is a metaphor or simile drawn from nature or common life, arresting the hearer by its vividness or strangeness, and leaving the mind in sufficient doubt about its precise application to tease it into active thought.*"[12]

That is the power of stories. They don't spoon-feed us information or allow us to remain passive observers; they invite us, indeed force us, to become active participants and in so doing they capture the one part of us, nothing else can: our imaginations, which, almost above all else, need capturing and re-orientation when shaping our lives. As Andrew Fletcher once said: "Let me make the songs of a nation, and I care not who makes its laws." There is nothing more persuasive than art and stories. Jesus knew it. It's why he told so many.

Hence why I think Jesus would have spent his days today doing exactly that. Capturing the imagination of the world to offer an alternative and challenging vision for their lives through the power of narrative instead of just ideas or straight instruction.

In the Netflix series *The Crown*, there is a definitive scene in which Edward, the Duke of Windsor—a man who may have remained on the British throne had circumstances been otherwise—gazes on a tiny television picture of his niece's coronation. In his house outside of Paris, he is throwing a party to celebrate the day. "Oils and oaths. Orbs and scepters," he says to his guests, as they all stare transfixed: "Symbol upon symbol. An unfathomable web of arcane mystery and liturgy. Blurring so many lines no clergyman or historian or lawyer could ever untangle any of it."

"It's crazy," says his American guest, the voice of reason, of modernity, of everything that is not the Empire.

"On the contrary," says Edward, "it's perfectly sane. Who wants transparency when you can have magic? *Who wants prose when you can have poetry?* Pull away the veil and what are you left with? An ordinary young woman of modest ability and little imagination. But wrap her up like this, anoint her with oil, and hey, presto, what do you have?" The Duke pauses. "A goddess."[13]

Why have prose when you can have poetry? Why flatten something powerful, a reality that cannot be fully captured in words, without an attempt to retain that beauty? Dietrich Bonhoeffer said, "What a mistake to think that it is the task of theology to unravel God's mystery, to bring it down to the flat, ordinary human wisdom of experience and reason! It is the task of theology solely to preserve God's wonder . . . to glorify God's mystery as mystery."[14]

While Jesus sometimes chose to speak plainly, more often he sought to retain the mystery and beauty of God's kingdom through the use of stories. He captured the imaginations of people—and the entire world—with an alternative reality, something altogether different than what is offered by the kingdoms of the world. "Empires maintain their sovereignty not only by establishing a monopoly of markets, political structures and military might, but also by *monopolizing the imagination of their subjects*. Indeed, vanquished peoples are not really subjects of the empire until their imagination has been taken captive . . . as long as [people] harbor dreams of a social reality alternative to the empire . . . their liberated imagination keeps them free. . . . And until that imagination is broken, domesticated and reshaped in the image of the empire, the people are still free."[15]

Jesus told parables to free people by first doing what Walsh says is necessary: freeing their imagination. As J. R. R. Tolkien explained to his skeptical Oxford professor friend C. S. Lewis one evening on a walk, "myth" and "truth" are not all that far removed from one another. It was Tolkien's contention that Lewis's problem (at that time in his life) lay not in his *rational* failure to understand God (since he had already acknowledged his existence), but in his *imaginative* failure to grasp God's significance. "Just as speech is invention about objects and ideas, so myth is invention about truth . . . [they] reflect a splintered fragment of the true light, the eternal truth that is with God. . . . Our myths may be misguided, but they steer however shakily towards the true harbor."[16] Tolkien explained that to a rationalist, a star is a ball of matter moving along a mathematical course, but that the first men to talk of stars saw them quite differently, as "living silver, bursting into flame in answer to eternal music."[17] They saw the sky as a "jeweled tent and the earth as the womb where all living beings have come into existence." To them the whole of creation is "myth-woven" because the stories invest life with *meaning*.[18]

For Tolkien, and later for Lewis, and for countless believers for the past two thousand years, Christianity is fairy story incarnate, the intersection of legend and history. Christianity was the only place where *transcendence*—the joy that myths create inside us—and the *reality* of history, collide. The nexus of romanticism and rationalism was the path on which Lewis eventually came to Christ, but more importantly, this is what holds together every parable Jesus told. His stories spoke to the deep hunger and longing of his audience—no matter how old. As Lewis would later write to his goddaughter in the dedication of his most famous story, *The Lion, the Witch, and the Wardrobe*, stories are not just for children. They are adult things:

> My Dear Lucy,
>
> I wrote this story for you, but when I began it I had not realised that girls grow quicker than books. As a result, you are already too old for fairy tales, and by the time it is printed and bound you will be older still. But some day you will be old enough to start reading fairy tales again.

Jesus told stories because, if his audience had ears to hear, their "old souls" would hear a call from a land they had not visited, but one they somehow *knew*. It was as if Jesus were singing the words to a song they hadn't heard but which they could somehow hum. Jesus was uniquely able to reach beneath their reason to their passions and desires. This made them powerful, and that power, when unleashed, was anything but safe for him or his audience. People ask why Jesus hid the message of the kingdom in stories like this but that is to misunderstand. As one of the great authors of the twentieth century, Chaim Potok said in his brilliant novel *The Gift of Asher Lev*: "Truth has to be given in riddles. People can't take truth if it comes charging at them like a bull. The bull is always killed. You have to give people the truth in a riddle, hide it so they go looking for it and find it piece by piece; that way they learn to live with it."

If you read some of the bestselling spiritual authors in the modern world—people like Deepak Chopra or Eckhart Tolle—you might get the impression that Jesus told stories because he was a "good" guy. He was a peacemaking spiritual Teacher telling us how to be better people—how to live our best life now. But that's not why Jesus told stories. His parables did far more than teach; they subverted and re-envisioned life, calling us to the life God intended.

# The Ultimate Story?

In Booker's analysis of storytelling, he writes, "There are many stories which are shaped by more than one 'basic plot' at a time. . . . There are even a very small number of stories, including *The Lord of the Rings*, which include all seven of the plots."[19] I've often thought about that line—that there are a small number of stories throughout time that stand out because they contain all seven basic plots. Then, one day in my office, I was replying to some emails between meetings and I thought about Jesus' best-known story, the prodigal son—found in Luke 15:11–32. It dawned on me: this is true about that parable! I walked over to the eight-foot-wide whiteboard that hangs behind my desk. I wrote the different plot categories along the top, and under each heading, I recorded if and how the parable of the prodigal son contained these fundamental plots. Staff members came in and out of my office, asking me questions, and when I told them what I was doing, they sat down to see for themselves if my thesis was true. As I finished sketching on the board, there was no doubt. This short parable contains *all* the plots of every great story we have told ourselves since the dawn of civilization! Let's take a closer look at this parable as we unpack several of the types in more detail.

## 1. OVERCOMING THE MONSTER (*JAMES BOND, FRANKENSTEIN*)

Booker defines the plot of "overcoming the monster" this way: *Peace and tranquility are disturbed by a power of some sort that needs to be confronted so a community is saved from evil and put back to rights. Characters must overcome a power to reach their goal.* Sometimes that power is supernatural and external (*Nightmare on Elm Street, Jurassic Park*), but sometimes it takes the form of the "monster within" (*Dr. Jekyll and Mr. Hyde*, for instance, or *The Incredible Hulk*). "Above all, and it is the supreme characteristic of every monster who has ever been portrayed in a story, *he or she is egocentric*. The monster is heartless. . . . Although this may sometimes be disguised beneath a deceptively charming exterior, its only real concern is to look after its own interests, at the expense of everyone else in the world."[20]

At the outset, the menace may not look overly problematic, Booker says, but gradually we see its fearsome effects casting a shadow over a family, country, or kingdom (Luke 15:21, 30). Following the introduction of the problem the monster has created, "the hero makes his preparations for the battle to come (i.e., he travels towards the monster or the monster approaches)."[21]

All of these elements are present in the parable of the prodigal son. The monster lies within the egocentric son, who asks his father for money and lives the reckless life until he hits rock bottom. The Father (who is the hero) goes out to meet the son as the son returns home. Booker notes a number of other elements that are also present: the general disruption of peace, family reputation, a reward/kingdom given, a treasure found, and a surprise ending. These are all elements of this kind of story. The haunting curveball within this plot framework is that the surprise ending occasionally involves the *monster remaining in some form* (in my view, this is seen where the older brother never sees the light in the story). Further, the monster remains *inside* for Jesus' listeners, and speaks to all of us, whether we identify with the irreligious, secular person (younger brother) or the religious person (older brother). Both types of people, in different ways, must come to accept the Father's embrace and sacrifice on our behalf (Luke 15:23).

## 2. RAGS TO RICHES (*CINDERELLA, PRETTY WOMAN*)

*The poor protagonist acquires things such as power and wealth, before losing it all and then gaining it back upon personal growth.* Here we find the very shape of the prodigal son story, as it opens with the younger son's acquisition of his inheritance in the form of wealth and property (Luke 15:12), his loss of it all by squandering it in reckless living (v. 13), and his falling to a destitute state, having "spent everything" (v. 14). Hitting rock bottom, he works menial jobs until he is working with pigs. He has received no mercy from anyone and feels as if he is perishing with hunger (v. 17). After he reaches this bleak social position, things turn around through his repentance and the father's mercy. He eventually gains it all back and more (vv. 22–24), being given the father's own robe, a ring, and special sandals, and having a very expensive party thrown for him. He also grows in humility (v. 19), and is described as having been dead spiritually and emotionally but is now alive (v. 24).

## 3. VOYAGE AND RETURN (*THE WIZARD OF OZ, PETER PAN*)

*The protagonist leaves their normal experience to enter an alien world, returning after what often amounts to a thrilling escape.* Clearly this plot is a central motif in the prodigal son story, as the younger son leaves his normal experience, enters a foreign country, and returns home after narrowly escaping death by starvation. He was "dead, and is alive again; he was lost, and is found" (Luke 15:24). Thus, this is the ultimate "there and back again" story.

Booker actually cites The Prodigal Son story when writing about this plot comparing it to *Peter Rabbit*, the Greek myth of Orpheus's journey to the underworld, *The Wizard of Oz* and *The Lion, the Witch and the Wardrobe*. The essence he says is the main character travelling "out of their familiar, everyday, 'normal' surrounding into another world completely cut off from the first where everything seems disconcertingly abnormal." Furthermore, again, as if describing The Prodigal Son story itself, Booker says: "At first the strangeness of this new world, with its freaks and marvel, may seem . . exhilarating. . . But gradually a shadow intrudes [wherein the main character] feels increasingly threatened, even trapped: until eventually they are released from the abnormal world, and can return to the safety of the familiar world where they began."[22]

## 4. REBIRTH (*A CHRISTMAS CAROL, AVATAR*)

*Where the protagonist suddenly finds a new reason for living. During the course of the story, an important event forces the main character to change his ways, often making him a better person.* The younger son, thinking himself smarter than everyone, pining after the Good Life, fails to find himself in the indulgences of life, and finds that the new reason for living revolves around family, not worldly pleasure. He changes his ways because of humbling events, which make him a better person in the end—better even than his judgmental, religious brother. The rebirth narrative is emphasized and explicitly stated twice in the story in dramatic fashion with the declaration that the younger son was "dead, and is alive; he was lost, and is found" (vv. 24, 32).

[To read about the other three types of story, see the endnote.][23]

The fact that thousands of years before a theory was proposed that the greatest and most dominant stories of our lives contain these seven basic elements, Jesus' stories were using them to get people's attention is interesting. The idea that *all seven* are present in this one story—one of the many reasons it has remained one of the greatest stories ever told, and has had maybe the greatest impact on how people think of God, ourselves, and salvation itself—is downright amazing. Now we must turn to a second and just as compelling question: How does the story reframe all of those things for us? In what way does the story represent God and the salvation of all humankind to the world?

To this we now turn.

# CHAPTER 12

## The Meaning of
# JESUS'
# PARABLES

Just after I got my driver's license, I happened to be driving pretty fast when I glanced in the rearview mirror and saw a police car pull up behind me. The officer turned on his sirens, and for some reason, I decided to hit the gas pedal. I quickly turned left onto a random street. And then I turned right. Before I knew it, I was in a full-on police chase in my '88 Grand Am.

At one point, it dawned on me that I should probably stop, but I figured I was in too deep. Still, I needed a way out. I pulled onto a side street, quickly got out of the car, and opened my trunk—all before the officer had made the turn. I had no plan at this point. The police car came ripping around the corner, and he pulled up behind me. I bent down into my trunk and picked up a random cardboard box filled with stuff. The officer got out of his car. "What do you think you're doing?" he asked. "I'm just taking this box and dropping it off at my friend's house," I said, pointing at a random house and hoping he couldn't see the sweat pooling on my brow. He looked at me with doubt. "Okay, go up and do it then," he replied.

As he stood there with his arms crossed, I slowly walked up to the house. I put the box on the porch and knocked on the door. My only hope in the world was that whoever these people were, they wouldn't be home, or they would pretend to know me. Otherwise the jig was up. I waited. No one came. I left the box on the porch and walked back to my car. "Guess they aren't home," I said.

He looked at me, and I'll never forget the look in his eyes. He knew I was lying. Not that it mattered much: he had caught me speeding, so whether I'd seen him following me was irrelevant. I was caught red-handed and now adding insult to my offense by lying. I was cooked.

Then, something happened that I did not expect. Something that turned my universe upside down.

But I am getting ahead of myself.

To understand the multiple layers of what Jesus meant in telling his stories, including his intent in telling them, we need to grasp that the story of the prodigal son is not about one lost son but two. The sons are both lost, but in different ways. The first one is lost because he is completely *irreligious*. He is acting in a way that we would call "secular"—atheistic, or agnostic—perhaps like some of you reading this book. He is living like he doesn't care about God, saying, "I will do my own thing. I'll take gifts from God (like life and breath and sunshine), but I don't care about *relationship* with God." He lives a morally corrupt life, and the story deems him "lost"—disconnected from the Father and his family.

The older brother is someone who is lost because of *religion*. He is conservative, obeying all of God's rules (Luke 15:29). Yet he is self-righteous, comparing himself to others all the time (vv. 29–30), and he ends up outside the party, not accepting the Father's gracious invitation. Jesus' parable is not a nice sentimental message; it is a controversial, scandalous story where he hints that everything we've believed about God has been completely wrong. Salvation is not what we can do for God but about what God does for us, running out to meet us, sacrificing his most prized possession, experiencing shame and mockery himself so that we don't have to. It leads to an amazing celebration for those humble enough to receive grace rather than try-ing to earn a place for themselves. Those who are welcomed in light of this new moment in history are people who do not have a record to stand on. They rely on the "record" of God himself (wearing *his* robe and ring as free and undeserved gifts not rewards). The scandalous generosity of the Father was just as much a problem for Jesus' audience as it remains today.

## Lost: Are We Gods or Animals?

Perhaps the main reason this story remains a scandal to modern people is that it has an underlying assumption—that we are *lost*. Jesus assumes that we are all broken, sinful, and in need of saving. Our culture, however, says it's not nice to say something is wrong with someone—that is viewed as judgmental or old-fashioned. Instead, we should build up one another's self-esteem by being positive and having a softer, more accepting view of humankind and their condition. The modern view runs in a couple different directions, both of which are two sides of the same coin. One side is the belief that human beings are *divine*—we can speak reality into existence and are little gods walking around, part of a "God-consciousness." We will accomplish great things if we just work together and tap into our inherent goodness. The flip side of this is the belief that we're *animals*, here by chance, living by instinct, and hoping to make the best of the world based on tribal and evolutionary motives beyond our conscious control.

These human-centered messages leave us without answers to our deepest needs, crushing us under their expectations, placing large amounts of guilt and shame on us. As cultural anthropologist Ernest Becker (1924–74), winner of the Pulitzer Prize in 1974, argued, "The plight of the modern therapeutic individual is this: that he or she is a sinner with no word for it, or worse, who looks for the word for it in a dictionary of psychology and thus only aggravates the problem of his separateness. . . . All the analysis in the world doesn't allow the person to find out who he is and why he has to die. It is when psychology rather than theology pretends to do this that it becomes a fraud and an impasse from which man cannot escape."[1]

The modern impulse is to say, "It's not nice to talk about people being sinful or lost or broken, because we should try to build up one another's self-esteem, and there is enough negativity in the world." And at first blush, this sounds like the right direction. But it turns out to be dangerous, leaving humankind looking only to itself for solutions. Such a view "can't cope with evil . . . because there's no higher court of appeal when something bad happens. Nobody can come and rescue you."[2] As Becker says, without the category of sin and lostness, the human soul is burdened and depressed.

This is precisely why, in the story of the prodigal son, the brother with the deeper sense of his own sinfulness is the one who is free and filled with joy at the end of the story, while the brother who denies his sin is left lost and alone. Such is the burden of religion (either formal or the secular version), which tells us that we either don't need saving or that we are our own saviors. Jesus challenges both our ancient and modern impulses by reminding us that we're made in the image of God (we're "sons" of God), yet we're lost and disconnected from him.

## Everybody Lies

Human lostness is all around us, a point that needs little proof. If we are honest, we know ourselves to be lost. I only need my experience as a parent to see this. I can remember when my youngest child was about a year old and I took her swimming at our local public pool. When we got out of the water, I carried her into the locker room to get changed. The air was cold, and when I realized that I had only brought one towel, I wrapped it around myself while scanning the room for a towel she could have. I looked down and saw these big eyes looking up at me, lips shivering, her whole body shaking, trying to stay warm. As I dried my legs, I wondered, *Where are the towels in here? She is likely pretty cold.*

As usual, I was looking after number one, thinking of myself first and looking to care for others after. That's a picture of who we all are in the end. It's the reason you lie, cheat at a game when no one's looking, tell stories that make you look better than others, or why no one, even those closest to you, really has a grasp on who you are and what you do when no one is looking.

Seth Stephens-Davidowitz explores this reality in his fascinating book *Everybody Lies*, where he examines Google search data. Private searches give us unfiltered insight into the human psyche. People can search and explore answers to questions, pursue interests, and even express opinions, all while completely alone, unsupervised, anonymously, and without a filter. Stephens-Davidowitz points out that what we as human beings say is vastly different than what we think or do in reality. For example, people say they do not want to stalk their friends, but the popularity of Facebook—today worth billions of dollars—tells us that there is little in this world they want more than to keep up with and judge their friends. People say they don't want to buy products that are produced in sweatshops, but Nike sells enough of these products to be worth twenty-five billion dollars. People say they have no interest in bondage or sadomasochism, but *50 Shades of Grey* has sold over 125 million copies.[3] As one data scientist quipped, "The algorithms know you better than you know yourself."[4]

Jesus understood this long before Google did. We lie to everybody, all the time, and even to ourselves. We are far more lost than we project to the world or will admit to those around us. And because of this, we need saving. We need to be found. We are broken and need to be put back together again.

Luke said there were two groups listening to Jesus' story: "tax collectors and sinners" and "Pharisees and the scribes" (Luke 15:1–2). Jesus' story deconstructs the traditional thinking that concludes that the first group is lost while the second group is found, and scandalously says that both groups are lost but for opposite reasons. The two brothers serve as archetypes for these two groups and, by extension, for every person who has ever lived, whether irreligious or religious, conservative or liberal, good or bad. Jesus' message is that while the younger brother is lost because he is far from God, the older brother is lost because he clings to the traditions of God rather than God himself.

This was a bomb exploding the assumptions of first-century Jewish culture, and it is just as explosive today to modern audiences. By implication Jesus was saying that every person who ever lived is lost, and that includes you! God wants us to be found, but there is only one way for that to happen.

## Lost Like a Rebel

The first way of being lost is represented by the younger brother. In essence he said to his father, "I wish you were dead. I want the inheritance that is coming to me when you die, and I want it now so I can go out and live like you are not part of my life; live how I want rather than how you want." This is the secular person who doesn't think about God, doesn't live like he exists, and doesn't think about any kind of transcendent moral accountability. This is the atheist or the agnostic who lives in rebellion against God, however subtly (maybe living a "good" life in the eyes of Western society); he desires the everyday gifts of God without wanting the Giver.

Maybe that's you. When thoughts of God bubble up inside of you, you push them away. I talk to people in the coffee shops and restaurants in our city who feel obliged to give to certain projects—when there is a natural disaster, for example, and say, "I felt I needed to help." And so they give money. I ask why they feel that impulse.

"Because it's right," they say.

"What do you mean it's right?" I ask. If you don't believe God exists, there is no absolute, ultimate moral reference point; no "right" or "wrong," just one opinion against another.

At this point, they reveal they have not thought about this: "I don't know. I just think it's the right thing to do. I *feel* it."

If the worldview of the younger brother is true and God doesn't exist, not only do we have license to do whatever we want, but in the end there is no *right* thing to do. There are only synapses in your brain firing this way or that, which have been firing for hundreds of thousands of years with the sole goal of survival. You can argue for an evolutionary purpose, but that doesn't explain why we would be moved to altruistic acts or why we have a sense of justice that will often cost us.

Younger brothers don't believe in absolute morals, but rather subjective morals. We do what we feel is right. This has been popularized with Eastern mysticism, but it deconstructs quickly. Francis Schaeffer told the story about a meeting he had at Cambridge University with a young Hindu who suggested that "all is one in the universe." Schaeffer asked him, "Am I not correct in saying that on the basis of your system, *cruelty and non-cruelty* are ultimately equal, that there is no intrinsic difference between them?" The man agreed. Then Schaeffer picked up a kettle of boiling water, lifted it up above the young man's head, and said, "There is no difference between cruelty and non-cruelty"? "Thereupon," wrote Schaeffer, "the man walked out into the night."[5] Ideas have consequences, and if ours can't hold up under philosophical or pragmatic testing, we should consider abandoning them.

We could punch other holes in the younger brother worldview, but in the end this way of life is adopted for *the autonomy it provides.* Social critic Mark Sayers contends with many others that a fundamental shift has taken place in the Western world in the last fifty years. Most significantly, we now believe "the highest good is individual freedom, happiness, self-definition and self-expression. . . . The primary social ethic is tolerance of everyone's self-defined quest for individual freedom and self-expression . . . the journey into self."[6] While most people are just trying to live a life and pay the bills, they are still influenced by the currents of philosophy and history. And the currents of culture—the rise of democratic cultures, developments in technology, among others—have exalted our individual desires and preferences to the point of idolatrous worship of the self. This, Jesus said, was the faith position of the younger brother. We embrace our selfishness and our desire to be our own masters, saying "I want to go out and live my life how I want to live. I don't want to deal with God."

This is functional atheism, and it's the scariest part of the story. This younger brother didn't debate whether his father existed. He knew he did. The reality is that he didn't want him to. He didn't live by what he knew was true because he didn't want to live under the implications of it. The story is a cautionary tale.

This was my faith growing up, though I didn't think of it that way. I never walked into a church building until the age of nineteen, and my father was an ardent atheist. I lived my teenage years like many people: God was not on the radar. I enjoyed partying, girls, using drugs, throwing rocks through windows to steal money to get more drugs, and strolling into 7-Eleven with my friends to pack our coats and pants full of whatever we could get our hands on. If I had been presented with God or invited to follow Jesus, I would not have wanted it. I was satisfied with myself. I did not care if God did or did not exist; I didn't *want* him to exist.

Danish philosopher Søren Kierkegaard observed that humans are born as what he called "aesthetes." His argument was that we do things from the time we are born that *feel* good to us—whatever is thrilling, entertaining, and has a touch of beauty and sparkle to it. We don't ask whether a thing is right or wrong, but only whether it is interesting and pleasing. While this results in some forms of happiness and fulfillment in our lives, Kierkegaard said this is a mistaken idea of freedom. The person living this life "is not master of himself at all; in fact, his temperament, tastes, feelings, and impulses completely drive him. . . . [He] is controlled by circumstance. If a wife loses her beautiful skin and countenance or a husband puts on the pounds, the aesthete begins to look around for someone more beautiful."[7] Such a person is not free but is controlled by external circumstances, a slave to their desires. Lost, but *feeling* deceptively free through the pursuit of pleasure.

If this is not freedom, then what is it? Slavery. Kierkegaard said this is what we must do to be truly free then: *link our feelings to an obligation.* "Only if you commit yourself to loving in action, day in and day out, even when feelings and circumstances are in flux, can you truly be a free individual and not a pawn of outside forces."[8] It is in this—a covenantal relationship with the Father—that the younger son finds the true freedom he has been seeking. Jesus was warning us not to choose this self-inflicted slavery that comes when we run our lives by our own authority. The scandal of Jesus is that he said: Look, friends, whatever you may think or feel about your condition, you're lost. You can't save yourselves. You can only try, and in trying, come to the end of yourselves. I invite you into something better—into the humbling reality that God himself is the only one who can save you, and if you lean into him, you will find the joy you have been looking for in everything but him. Come out of your slavery and be free.

## Lost Like a Church Boy

On the other side are the religious people, who show us there is a second way to be lost. The older brother is lost because he has trusted in spiritual rules and regulations, thinking these can secure his future inheritance, his reward from his father. "Look, these many years I have served you, and I never disobeyed your command," he says to his father, "yet you never gave me a young goat, that I might celebrate with my friends" (Luke 15:29). The tragedy at the end of the story is that it is the religious rule keeper who is left out of the kingdom. The repentant "sinner" receives the love of the Father, the true reward of being in the family, while the obedient son reveals his lack of love. In other words, all of our religious observance cannot earn us a place in the family of God.

Rather than accepting his place by his father's side and celebrating his father's generosity and forgiveness as good things, he sees the blessing of his brother as a loss for himself. In his anger, he points to his moral record, as if this is what has secured him his place in the family. "This is why you need to accept me. All these years I have served you and I never disobeyed your commands. I've taught Sunday school. I've led the worship team. I've got a Bible cover with handles on it. I've listened to Christian music and watched Christian movies my whole life. I am a moral person. You owe me." This posture represents the basic approach of all religious behavior, the ticking of dos and don'ts and attempts to earn the favor of our chosen deity.

Jesus said the people who do this are just as lost as those who pursue a life of indulgence and excess. Author and pastor Darrell Johnson, in his book *Discipleship on the Edge*, explains that on the last day when the books are open, we are going to have two options before God. The first option will be to ask him to judge us on the life we lived. The second option will be to ask him to judge us based on the life Jesus lived for us. He concludes his thoughts by saying, "I shall take the second option. I find no hope in the first."[9] And while the prodigal, who has lived his life in excess and willful disobedience, might humbly admit his failure, doing so can be far more difficult for the older son, who is deceived into thinking his moral record will be his ticket to success. Yet this has been the basic way of dealing with our guilt, shame, and moral failure for all of known human history.

People have always believed that if the gods were going to love and save you, it would be because you earned it. You sacrificed your time, energy, grain, animals, even your children. But in telling the parable of the prodigal son, Jesus was saying we've had it wrong. In John's Gospel there is an account where conservative Jewish society dragged a woman caught in adultery in front of Jesus and asked what should be done with her. Should they be obedient to the law of God and punish her, or be soft on her and unfaithful to God's law? Jesus drew or wrote something on the ground, and when he was eventually left alone with the woman, he asked her, "Has no one condemned you?"

"No one, Lord," she replied.

"Neither do I condemn you; go, and from now on sin no more" (John 8:10–11).

The order here matters. Jesus didn't say, "If you go and stop sinning, I will not condemn you." He said the opposite. "I have done a work that makes it so I won't condemn you. It is that sacrifice for you that will save you. And now that you have known this work on your behalf, go and live a life free of sin."

Jesus saves us from our "pagan secularism," as well as our conservative, family-based, religious lifestyle. Both are characterized by slavery to selfish desires, but for different reasons. The religious person believes their acceptance and salvation hinges on whether they do devotions every morning, go to church/mosque/temple three times a week, and don't swear or watch R-rated movies—or whatever moral rules their particular brand of religion wants to adopt and enforce.

Religious people tend to become coldhearted, drawing bold lines on moral issues and demonizing people. This way of approaching God creates pride rather than humility. I know a man who planted a church several years ago, and a man in the congregation once told him, "Your sermons should only be thirty minutes long, and if they are longer you aren't doing your job right." If this pastor went over that thirty-minute mark, this individual would pick up his chair, turn it around out of protest, and face the rest of the congregation for the remainder of the message.

Most of us recognize this as another level of crazy. But somewhere along the way, this man came to believe this was a righteous act, something necessary for the good of people and obedience to God. And that is what religion tends to do. It channels our energies into perfecting the external, while the inner life that connects us to God rots and dies. Religious lostness can drive a person deeper into the dark of self-deception and hypocrisy than secular lostness. Jesus reserved some of his harshest words for his religious critics. And this is why, at the end of the day, the fifty-year-old man who goes to First Baptist Church, Texas, may be just as lost, or more so, than the addict on the street, the troubled youth, the hardened politician, or the atheist professor.

## The Prodigal God

There's nothing *we* can do to make ourselves whole enough. There's no work we can do to bring us up to the standard God has set. Paul explained salvation in one of his letters with a sentence that sounds like a summary of the prodigal son story: "By grace you have been saved. . . . It is the gift of God, not a result of works, so that no one may boast" (Ephesians 2:8–10). Grace is a gift—it's a beautiful image, but what exactly is grace? According to the Bible it is *undeserved favor*. It's when someone has caught you red-handed and they decide to let you go, not because you are good but because they are good. It's when you are fully deserving of something and grace says, *I'm not going to bring to bear what you fully deserve. In fact, I am going to bring you something good that you don't deserve instead.*

And here is where we pick up the story of the time I tried to outrun a cop. That officer had me dead to rights. Caught red-handed outrunning a police officer for ten minutes, I added insult to it by lying. We both knew I didn't know anybody at that house. But then something happened. Something, as I said, that turned my universe upside down.

The officer looked at me with a twinkle in his eye.

"Okay, just make sure you slow down next time, kid."

And then he winked at me, got back in his car, and drove away.

I deserved a ticket. I had tried to outrun a cop. I had lied. I should have had the book thrown at me. Instead, he chose to give me what I didn't deserve. This is where Christianity opposes karma—wherein we say good things happen to those who do good things. The "universe" brings us good or bad depending on our attitude and output into it. It's what new age thinkers call "the law of attraction." Christianity says the opposite: we get what we don't deserve, but not in a way that subverts justice.

We get what we don't deserve because Jesus got what we deserve. This idea is somewhat unique in the marketplace of ideas. Different religions and worldviews present different ideas about God. Some say that God is an old, *distant* deity disconnected from the world. Others say God is an *angry* God who just wants to throw lightning bolts and destroy people for every bad decision. Jesus blew up both of these ideas of God and introduced us to the true God of the universe. "While [the young son] was still a long way off, his father saw him and felt compassion, and ran and embraced him and kissed him" (Luke 15:20).

In a patriarchal culture, fathers were respected and revered. They did not run. They would never pick up their robes and show their legs to run after a disaster of a son who had deserted the family. In some cultures, even today, a son skipping town with his inheritance would bring about a beating to death by the father.[10] Although the son in Jesus' story had abandoned his obligations and deserted those who loved him, his father threw a party for him, killing the fattened calf and throwing a feast. Author and pastor Timothy Keller suggests this story should be called "the prodigal God" instead of the prodigal son. *Prodigal* means that one has "spent everything" or has been "recklessly extravagant"—an apt description of God's grace.

The older brother hated seeing his father's grace for his youngest son. "Look what you're doing. You're creating a celebration for a son who completely slapped you in the face. He's garbage. You've been reckless, Father!"

I have some friends who were once treated by a wealthy couple to an extravagant, expensive gift: a three-thousand-dollar bottle of wine. The couple said, "Look, this is a gift to you. This is a 'your daughter is getting married' level of gift. It has been aged and kept in the finest barrels." So my friends put it away with velvet gloves in their wine room. Over time, the place where they kept their wine got filled with other bottles they had bought and stored. And one weekend while they were away, they had people staying at their house. These friends were cooking and needed some wine to throw on the pan. So the husband went down to the wine cellar, grabbed a bottle, shot back upstairs, unscrewed the cork, and dumped it into the pan to cook the chicken. It was the three-thousand-dollar bottle of wine! A real tragedy.

That's the older brother's point. All of this cost and effort on the part of the father was a waste, spent on a useless son who had sinned and lost his place. Where was the punishment? Instead, the boy received love and forgiveness. The father paid the price, but the son saw his own future being given away as well. His selfishness rose within. Unacceptable!

The beauty of this story is that God has grace for both sons. The question the story compels you to answer is not which son you are—the indulgent or the religious—but *how you will respond to the Father.* How will you respond to a God of grace? That's the question that will define your life for you from this day forward.

One son sits angrily on the porch digging in his heels, never humble enough to realize he needs a savior. He never joins in the party. The other son recognizes his own sinfulness and repents. "I have sinned against heaven and before you" (Luke 15:21). The old hymn that says, "Nothing in my hand I bring, simply to the cross I cling," gives voice to his condition.

Jesus used stories to create a scandal, a crisis of faith in each listener that demands a response to his new vision of reality. We must ask ourselves, *If the view I've held of myself, God, and the world is wrong, am I brave enough to change my mind?*

# PART VII

# The Problem of
# JESUS AS GOD—
# OR
# GOD AS JESUS

*All that is gold does not glitter, not all those who wander are lost; the old that is strong does not wither, deep roots are not reached by the frost.*

—J. R. R. TOLKIEN, *THE FELLOWSHIP OF THE RING*

# CHAPTER 13

## Rethinking
# GOD

My wife and three daughters have a favorite place. It isn't Disneyland or a beach in Hawaii or a famous hotel in New York City. It is a quiet and forgotten village in Uganda, Africa, called Kibaale. Our friends run a school and hospital there for hundreds of kids orphaned because of AIDS. My family went there without me a few years ago to visit and fell in love with it; more pointedly, they fell in love with all the kids they visited. When they returned home, they begged me to go with them the following year. Yet because of the timing of the trip and my schedule, I couldn't go that time either, so off they went again without me. We frequently talked about the kids they met, the smells, the glorious back roads from which—perched up on the back of a pickup truck—you could see for miles. "And the sunsets. Oh, the sunsets, Dad!"

But there was one thing that diminished the experience for them. I hadn't seen it. I hadn't been there. There's only so much you can understand when you haven't been to a place, haven't touched the dirt or been inside one of the fifteen-by-fifteen-square-foot houses with three kids and grandma living in them. Or seen the faces of children light up as you hand them clothes, beds, and of course, lots of candy.

That all changed this past year. For the first time in my life, I set foot on the continent of Africa and spent two weeks with my family in a small village, where we did our best to bring hope and smiles to kids who, according to everything I knew about life, shouldn't have had either but had both. When my kids talk about Kibaale now, they talk to me in a different way. What changed? Suddenly we had a connection we hadn't had before because now I had been there. I knew what they knew. I'd seen and felt what they had. My presence with them gave my words, thoughts, and opinions a legitimacy and credibility. That one fact made all the difference, opening up the door for deeper relationship.

This experience of presence is not unique to my relationship with my daughters. It is what makes Christianity different from other religions: God himself *came*, Christianity says. He entered our world. He didn't keep his distance from our mess and just tell us how to get to him, or hope we became enlightened enough to reach him on our own through meditating or pilgrimages or living rightly. He came down the mountain to see us. He came to the village, visited our homes, laughed and sang with us, and sat by the fire telling stories. He took in the sunsets for more than thirty years. *"Oh, the sunsets."*

God became human. "The Word became flesh and dwelt among us, and we have seen his glory, glory as of the only Son from the Father" (John 1:14). Stop and think about that for a moment. If this is true, isn't it worth breaking from the busyness of your life to listen to what he has to say, to learn from what he did? Don't your eyes light up? Don't you want to lean into the One who understands what it's like to be human?

I assume you would. In this chapter we're going to explore the legitimacy of Christianity's claim that Jesus of Nazareth—this historical man who lived over two thousand years ago—is in fact God, scandal of all scandals.

## The Supreme Mystery

One of the most controversial aspects of any exploration of Jesus is the question of his divinity. This issue is hotly debated by both secular and religious thinkers. On the *religious* side of the coin is the new age argument, growing in popularity in the Western world thanks to influencers such as Deepak Chopra, Eckhart Tolle, and even celebrities like Oprah Winfrey. They claim Jesus was an enlightened teacher, one in a long line of spiritual gurus who came to teach positive thinking, "spiritual" truths to help us attain a kind of "enlightened state of being," a Christianized moksha or nirvana. A step further from there you have Jehovah's Witnesses and Mormons, who, while believing in Jesus as the only way to salvation, don't believe Jesus was divine, or that he ever claimed to be.

On the secular front, this topic has long been explored in what has been called the "quest for the historical Jesus," which began with Hermann Samuel Reimarus (1694–1768), who suggested that Jesus should primarily be understood as a Jewish revolutionary who failed to achieve his goals. Reimarus was followed by David Strauss (1808–74), who argued that much of what we have in the Gospels likely isn't what Jesus actually taught (and, specifically, should not include miracles). And then in the twentieth century Albert Schweitzer (1875–1965) suggested that Jesus should be seen as an apocalyptic prophet who expected the imminent end of the world, warning of impending judgment and doom, which did not come. This was followed by the demythologization of Jesus by Rudolf Bultmann (1884–1976), seen as the century's most influential New Testament scholar, and then most recently, the infamous Jesus Seminar, which distinguished the "Jesus of history" from the "Christ of faith" and concluded that Jesus didn't say or do most of what we think he did (less than 20 percent).[1] The issue for these thinkers has never been whether Jesus existed—there is no doubt in their minds that he did. Instead, their desire is to show him as a man rooted in history and not mythology. Most of them deny he was God or that he claimed to be God at all.

These visions of Jesus—the religious and the secular—are vastly different from one another, yet they agree in denying that he claimed to be God, at least in the way that Christianity sees that claim. The first group is open to the claim, but only in a new age sense wherein everything and everyone is part of the "divine." The second group dismisses Jesus as divine by rejecting the evidence put forth in the

Gospels. Skeptics belong to either of these groups, and they contend that the idea of Jesus as God was invented by the second or third generation of Christians a hundred or more years after Jesus' original followers: "Until the Council of Nicaea in A.D. 325, Jesus was viewed by His followers as a great and powerful man, but a *man* nonetheless. A mortal. . . . Jesus' establishment as 'the Son of God' was officially proposed and voted on by the Council of Nicaea. . . . By officially endorsing Jesus as the Son of God, Constantine turned Jesus into a deity who existed beyond the scope of the human world and upgraded Jesus' status almost four centuries after Jesus' death."[2]

The question of Christ's divinity may be the ultimate scandal of the Christian faith. It is certainly one of the most definitive and dangerous ideas among the problems associated with Jesus. Theologian J. I. Packer may be right: "The real difficulty, the supreme mystery with which the gospel confronts us [may not lie] in the Good Friday message of atonement, nor in the Easter message of resurrection, but in the Christmas message of incarnation."[3] God becoming human—it has always been the question behind all other questions. If Christianity has this wrong, it has everything wrong. Yet if Christianity has this right, then everyone else is on a very wrong path indeed.

Entire religions—Islam, Judaism, Mormonism, and others—have respect for Jesus while maintaining that he was not God. So, which is it? Let's look at the evidence. Everything hinges on the answer.

## Evidence #1: Jesus as God in the Early Church

The first Christians unquestionably spoke about Jesus as God. In his earliest letters, written prior to the Gospels (dated in the early to mid 50s AD), Paul said that in Jesus "all the fullness of God was pleased to dwell" (Colossians 1:19), and "in him the whole fullness of deity dwells bodily" (Colossians 2:9). He wrote that Jesus "did not count equality with God a thing to be grasped" (Philippians 2:6). And the writer of the letter to the Hebrews said that God has spoken to the world "by his

Son through whom also he created the world. He is the radiance of the glory of God and the exact imprint of his nature, and he upholds the universe by the word of his power" (1:2–3). Paul also claimed that "by him all things were created: things in heaven and on earth" (Colossians 1:16). To a Jew like Paul, creational monotheism was an essential doctrine of God. God was one, and he was the Creator and shared glory with no one. Yet in passage after passage, Paul ascribed the titles of God and his creational acts and essence to Jesus.

For Paul and the early Jewish Christians, the title Lord (*kyrios*) was a title that a Jew would ascribe only to the one God of Israel.[4] This is the title that in Greek is used repeatedly to refer to the God of Israel in the Greek translation of the Hebrew Bible (our Old Testament). For instance, Deuteronomy 6:4, one of the core creedal affirmations of the Jewish faith, reads, "The LORD [*kyrios*] our God, the LORD is one." Fully aware of this background, Paul reworked this claim when he wrote in 1 Corinthians 8:6, "There is one God, the Father, from whom are all things and for whom we exist, and one Lord, Jesus Christ."[5] Paul was intentionally reshaping his Jewish monotheism around Jesus in a way that is without earlier parallels.[6] And the New Testament writers did this over and over again (see, e.g., Philippians 2:10–11; cf. Isaiah 45:23). In truth, there is "no doubt that in the usage of the New Testament writers, the title 'Lord' is regarded as the title used of God in the Old Testament and now applied to Jesus."[7]

For the early Christians, the incarnation was "God plus" (God the Son plus a human nature), not "God minus" (loss of deity, or divine attributes) as some have claimed throughout the centuries. Paul and the rest of the New Testament writers effectively reshape the concept of divinity around Jesus while retaining the earlier commitment to Jewish monotheism (Romans 3:30; 1 Corinthians 8:4–6; Galatians 3:20; Ephesians 4:6; 1 Thessalonians 1:9). The New Testament writers place Jesus in divine roles that related to God's unique identity in the Old Testament. These roles also share and participate in God's creative acts and sovereignty.[8] Most scholars now recognize the clear passages affirming Jesus' divinity as early creeds and hymns the church sang, confirming what they believed as they gathered (e.g., see Philippians 2:5–11). Contrary to skeptical myths, the early church worshiped Jesus as God and came to view him as fully divine and fully human. This was not a heresy (as Judaism and Islam claim) or an impossibility (as Greek and modern thought claim), but a reality around which one should shape one's life.

## Evidence #2: Jesus as God in the Gospels

To understand why the earliest Christians believed that Jesus was fully God and fully man, we must look to the ministry of Jesus in the Gospels. When we dig into the Gospels we see clearly that Jesus made repeated claims to be God, both overtly and subversively, and that his early followers also believed this to be true. As C. S. Lewis wrote,

> I am trying here to prevent anyone saying the really foolish thing that people often say about Him: I'm ready to accept Jesus as a great moral teacher, but I don't accept his claim to be God. That is the one thing we must not say. A man who was merely a man and said the sort of things Jesus said would not be a great moral teacher. He would either be a lunatic—on the level with the man who says he is a poached egg—or else he would be the Devil of Hell. You must make your choice. Either this man was, and is, the Son of God, or else a madman or something worse . . . but let us not come with any patronizing nonsense about his being a great human teacher. He has not left that open to us. He did not intend to.[9]

Lewis said that "a man who was merely a man and said the sort of things Jesus said would not be a great moral teacher [but] a lunatic . . . or . . . the Devil of Hell." So what did Jesus say and do?

Here a word of caution is needed. In this search for Jesus' identity, we must hold our previous assumptions lightly. Our tendency is to understand Jesus based on our own feelings and agendas: "In a foxhole Jesus is a rescue squad; in a dentist's chair a painkiller; on exam day a problem-solver; in an affluent society a clean-shaven middle-of-the-roader; for a Central American [soldier] a bearded revolutionary."[10] We make the mistake of assuming Jesus would reveal things about himself in the same way we would. But that is simply not true.

I am often asked, "Why should you believe Jesus was God if he never said the words 'I am God'?" I respond that the question is based on a mistaken assumption that Jesus would have talked like us and said things in a way that would satisfy our ways of thinking and determining truth. Yet if he had done so, his meaning would have been missed by his immediate audience of first-century Jews. So while it is true that Jesus didn't put those three words in that exact order, it's also irrelevant. In the end, Jesus said even more than that. He made his claim to be God through the words and methods first-century Jews would understand. Furthermore, he did so in a way that ensured his message wouldn't be mistaken for one that was compatible with existing mystical worldviews like pantheism. We might miss Jesus' claims to be God, but that's our problem. The world Jesus lived and breathed in responded right on cue: "For this reason they tried all the more to kill him; not only was he breaking the Sabbath, but he was even calling God his own Father, *making himself equal with God*" (John 5:18, italics mine).

So if you are ready to lay down what you think Jesus should have said to satisfy your personal standards and demands for claiming to be God, then you are ready to look at what he did and said to make this crystal clear to his audience.

## What He Said

- He claimed that he invented the Sabbath and had the authority to update the rules about observing it (Mark 2:23–28).
- He put his own knowledge on par with God's (Matthew 11:27).

- He claimed to be equal with God (John 5:18).
- He claimed that whoever saw him saw the Father (John 14:9).
- When he was given the opportunity to correct people treating him as if he were God, he didn't (Matthew 26:63–65; John 19:7–10).
- He claimed to have preexistence: having descended from heaven (John 3:13) and being older than Abraham (John 8:56).
- He claimed to be replacing the temple (John 2:19–21), which was the place where God's presence resided and where forgiveness of sins occurred.
- He claimed to have shared "glory" with God before the world existed (John 17:5).
- No less than thirty-nine times he claimed to be a missionary from heaven.
- He claimed he would send "his angels" (Matthew 13:41; elsewhere in the Bible, angels are always referred to as "angels of God" (Luke 12:8–9).
- He claimed the authority to forgive sins (Mark 2:5).
- He assumed the authority to judge the world (Mark 14:62), and that one's attitude toward him would define the judgment they received at the end of their lives (Matthew 10:32–33).
- He claimed to be perfectly sinless (John 8:46).
- He claimed to have the power to raise himself from the dead (John 2:19; 10:17–18).
- He claimed that to know him was to know God (John 8:19), to see him was to see God (John 12:45), and to receive him was to receive God (Mark 9:37).
- He took the divine name "I Am" for himself (John 8:58, from Exodus 3:14).
- He said he was the only way to heaven (John 14:1–7).
- He claimed, "I and the Father are one" (John 10:29–33), which, while modern audiences may miss it, was not lost on his first-century Jewish listeners, who responded, "You, a mere man, claim to be God" (John 10:33).

- He consistently upstaged the Law, or Torah, in his teachings, most notably in the Sermon on the Mount (Matthew 5–7), which indicated he regarded himself as authoritative over the Torah. And he issued a new version of it in a way that made him not a new Moses but a new YHWH.[11] Jewish scholar Jacob Neusner acknowledged this when he described why he as a Jew would not have followed Jesus if he were alive in the first century:

Here is a Torah-teacher who says in his own name what the Torah says in God's name. . . . Sages say things in their own names, but without claiming to improve upon the Torah. The prophet Moses, speaks not in his own name but in God's name, saying what God has told him to say, Jesus speaks not as a sage nor as a prophet . . . so we find ourselves . . . with the difficulty of making sense, within the framework of the Torah, of a teacher who stands apart from, perhaps above, the Torah. . . . We now recognize that at issue is the figure of Jesus, not the teachings at all.[12]

## What He Did

- He taught people to pray to him (John 14:13–14; 15:16; 16:24), and subsequently people like Stephen (Acts 7:59–60), Paul (1 Corinthians 1:2; 2 Corinthians 12:7–9; Ephesians 5:19) and John (Revelation 22:20) did so.
- He did nature miracles, including walking on water and turning water into wine, to communicate that he was God over nature. "Who is this? Even the wind and the waves obey him!" his disciples exclaimed (Mark 4:41).
- He claimed a number of titles that were used in the Old Testament for YHWH: Shepherd of Israel (John 10:11–14), I Am (John 8:58), Alpha and Omega (Revelation 1:8; 22:13), Almighty (Revelation 1:8), Light (John 8:12), First and Last (Revelation 1:17), judge of all nations (Matthew 25:31–46), and Bridegroom (Matthew 25:1).

- He received worship from people (John 20:28; see also 5:23; 9:38; Luke 5:8), which not even angels would accept (Acts 14:11–15; Revelation 22:8–9).
- He lived into his name Immanuel, meaning "God with us" (Matthew 1:23).
- He received declarations of his divinity and did not correct people; for instance, when Thomas declared, "My Lord and my God!" (John 20:28).
- He spoke as one whose mission already enacted God's reign in the present.
- He spoke as one who transcended the typical roles of prophet, saying, "I say to you" instead of "Thus says the Lord," and "I came" rather than "I was sent." The same authority is seen in his exorcisms, wherein he said, "I command" rather than "I adjure you by. . . ."
- He called a reconstituted Israel around himself (Mark 3:13–14)—twelve disciples replacing, or fulfilling, the twelve tribes of Israel.
- He demonstrated that he had the power that can destroy death itself (John 11:25–26).
- He assumed authority to forgive sins, which only God can do (Mark 2:7–10).
- He claimed to be the means by which YHWH was returning to Zion (Matthew 25:14–30; Luke 19:28–44).
- This last idea is probably the most neglected. Christians have understood the many parables of a master returning to a field or a to house and asking for the tenant to give an account for their life to be about the second coming of Jesus versus what they are arguably about: his first coming as the embodiment of YHWH back to his people, the "visitation" of God to Jerusalem (Luke 19:44). Historian Ben Witherington III is right in saying that in the end, when the evidence is studied, there is no doubt "Jesus saw himself not merely as a great king but in a higher and more transcendent category."[13]

- He claimed to determine people's eternal destiny before God (Luke 12:8–9).

As you can see, Jesus claimed to be God through both word and deed and did it in a way that upended everyone's ideas.

In my experience there are generally two reasons people reject the idea that Jesus claimed to be God. Either people (1) already have an idea of who God is and can't fit Jesus into that, or (2) they already have an idea of who Jesus is and can't fit God into that. When we study the life and teachings of Jesus and the New Testament letters that followed from those teachings, we see that he challenges both of these streams of thought and presents to his listeners a radical, alternate picture of both himself and God.

The Gospels paint a pretty clear picture that Jesus understood that he possessed divine authority. This claim was not just wishful or even the later thinking of the early church. Instead of claiming he was God in a more direct and obvious sense that we as modern people prefer, Jesus cast himself as God in a very specific way. He aligned himself with the story of God, the one known and taught for generations by the Jewish people. Jesus wasn't making an abstract claim to be God. He positioned himself as the center of Israel's concept of the one true God and said, "I'm *that* God!" Jesus claimed divinity in every way that mattered and made sense to the first-century Jewish world. "Jesus offered membership in the renewed people of the covenant God *on his own authority* and *by his own process.*"[14] This claim to be God incarnate is not made by the founder of any other world religion. The closest thing we have to it is the assertion by some Hindus that the Buddha is an avatar of Vishnu. But the Buddha himself never made such a claim.[15]

## "God" and 9/11

Now that we have established Jesus within his context, we are ready to come to terms with the second (and equally scandalous) reality that

Jesus forces upon us: the need to rethink our understanding of "God" in light of Jesus (rather than just the other way around). There is no doubt that one of Jesus' central aims was to teach the world about God. "Jesus' primary and ultimate idea, the thought with which he began and conducted all his thinking, was the idea of God."[16] That was the essential content of his life and ministry: who was God; what was the kingdom of God; how did God relate to the world, love the world, and judge the world; and what did God want the world to believe and do? This is why in his extensive work on the historical Jesus, T. W. Manson concluded, "The fact with which we have to reckon at all times is that in the teaching of Jesus his conception of God determines everything."[17]

Jesus was inviting his listeners to think of God—or rather to rethink what they knew about God—in relation to everything he was saying and doing. When Jesus told the story of the prodigal son, listeners were prompted to rethink God's posture toward sinners (Luke 15:20–24). When he talked about the mathematics of grace—when the workers who showed up last and worked only an hour got the same payment as those who were working hard from the beginning of the day (Matthew 20:1–16)—listeners were challenged to rethink the position of Gentiles as second-class citizens in the kingdom of God. Through his Sermon on the Mount, Jesus' hearers were moved to rethink what actually matters to God when hearing that it will be the persecuted, poor, meek, and hungry who will see him in the end, not the successful, proud, and rich (Matthew 5:1–12). When we read about and study Jesus, we need to see this fundamental truth about him: he wants us to reconsider our understanding of "God" in light of who he is and what he said about God.

Jesus' life pulled back the curtain about the nature of God and specifically his relationship to human beings. How far is God really removed, or *other*, from the world? How much does God *care* about our situation and the pain we face in life? Jesus causes us to rethink all of this.

On the Sunday following the September 11, 2001, attacks on the World Trade Center, attendance was at an all-time high at Redeemer

Presbyterian Church in downtown Manhattan. In one week the church grew from two thousand people on a Sunday to over five thousand. My friend is a pastor there, and he told me they had to add additional services on the spot because there were so many people trying to get through the doors. One day more than a decade later I decided to look up what their pastor, Timothy Keller, had preached that Sunday. As a young preacher, I was interested to know what you could say to a roomful of people who had just lost loved ones, coworkers, parents, and kids in a horrific tragedy like that.

I listened to the sermon and was weeping by the end, and I don't weep. Two things he said in that message I have repeated in every funeral I have done since. Keller was preaching from John 11 where Jesus came to the tomb of his friend Lazarus. The text says that when he reached the tomb of Lazarus, Jesus was "deeply moved" (v. 38). Keller explained, "The translators are afraid. The Greek word here means 'to roar or snort with anger like an animal,' like a lion, like a bull. So, the best translation would be, 'Bellowing with anger, he came to the tomb.' That must at least mean nostrils flared with fury. It might mean he was yelling."[18]

What a powerful picture of strong emotions in the presence of death. Jesus was yelling in anger at death, which is fascinating if you believe he was God in the flesh. He, like us, *hates* death and sees it as his enemy. Death angers him like it angers us when we lose a loved one. And there is comfort in that, knowing that God shares our anger—our grief over loss and death. I am not sure I can entirely explain why, but I know it brings me comfort.

The second idea Keller shared was when Jesus came to the tomb itself. John said, "Jesus wept" (v. 35). It had never occurred to me that this would be an odd thing for Jesus to do, as Keller pointed out.

To five thousand people in that 9/11 crowd, people in deep pain and looking to God for maybe the first time in their lives:

Jesus knows that in just 10 minutes or so, they're all going to be rejoicing. You and I, when we go into these tragic situations, have no idea. We go into these situations. We can't do a thing to undo it. Now here's what's so interesting. We say, "Boy, if we had that. . . ." If you went into this knowing what you're about to do, knowing how you were going to turn everybody's weeping into joy in about 10 minutes, *why would you weep?* Why would he do that?

Does it make psychological sense to you that if you knew you were about to turn everything around, you would be *drawn down into the grief,* you would enter into the trauma and the pain of their hearts? Why would he do that? The answer is because he is perfect love. He will not close his heart, even for 10 minutes. He will not refuse to *enter in.* He doesn't say, "Well, there's not much use in entering into all this grief. After all, we're going to be putting it away in a minute." *He goes in.*[19]

Indeed, Jesus goes in, and he enters into the pain of the world to fully identify with our lives in every way. When we ask the question of *why* God suffered on the cross, the traditional theological answer sometimes misses the fullness of what his suffering meant. We understand the beauty of why and how he suffered to save us from our sins, but we neglect the rest of the story. Christianity goes even further: it says the suffering of the cross was not only about God's *will* or his *plan* to save us, but it also says something about his *nature,* about who God is. The suffering of Jesus for our sake is not just something he *did;* it tells us who God *is.* "If the incarnation of the Son," Jürgen Moltmann said, is viewed merely as something functionally necessary to make an atoning sacrifice for sin possible, "then it is only an expression of the saving will of God . . . [and] only affects God's relationship with the world."[20] It has little to do with who he himself is in his nature. But the New Testament writers said the cross is more than merely a means to an end. It says that our need was the *occasion* for the suffering, but not its only *reason.*[21] Jesus suffered not in spite of his identity but because of it (Philippians 2:5–11), revealing to the world a God who is utterly unique among the gods on offer.

Jesus also helps us to look back at the story of God's dealings with his people through the Old Testament and see them with fresh insight and vision. We see a God with *pathos*, who hears the cries of his people and enters into their story in the form of a burning bush, a cloud by day and a pillar of fire by night, in a tabernacle, in a temple, all to be *with them*, to save them. When Moses asked what God's name was at the burning bush, God replied, "I AM WHO I AM" (Exodus 3:14). Many have wrestled with what this phrase means, but I think Hebrew scholar Everett Fox has it right: "I will be-there howsoever I will be-there."[22] The rest of the Bible tells us this is true. It's what the rest of the story from this point forward is really all about.

Christianity isn't about a temporary experience of a man becoming God or God becoming a man. The incarnation was not for *a* time, but for *all* time. Jesus' humiliation and sacrifice, his taking on of human form and giving up the glory he knew, was not just a thirty-year experience in the distant past. It was a moment when the eternal entered history in a way that will never be changed. Jesus will forever be human. This is why all the visions of him in heaven in the New Testament are in human form (Acts 7:56; 9:5; Revelation 1:13). Yes, it is a glorified version of humanity, but he is still human. And again, we should pause here, because if this is the true reality, it should cause the world to stop. What did God mean in Genesis when he said he had made humans in his image? Perhaps, as Christianity teaches, God knew from the very beginning that he would one day come and show us the fullness of what it meant to be human, stepping into the story as one of us. Could it be that this was the plan from eternity past—that in some ironic way a human being would be at the control center of the universe, not as an extraordinary being, but in a form we could never have anticipated, as a suffering servant, pouring himself out for the sake of others (see John 1:14; Philippians 2:5–10)?

Jesus is presented not just as any man, but as a *suffering* man. He is like "a lamb, slain" (Revelation 5:6), and when he appeared to his disciples after his resurrection, he still bore the wounds of the cross (John 20:27), marks of suffering along with signs of his glory J. R. R. Tolkien was likely alluding to at the end of *The Lord of the Rings*. Two years after the ring is destroyed, Frodo is granted a special grace by the Elves: to go to the Undying Lands and be rewarded for his sacrifice. He was, after all, the Ring Bearer who went through extreme pain and suffering, both physical and emotional, to bring evil to its end in Middle Earth. And the story makes it very clear that those wounds—from the Morgul-knife of the Nazgul on Weathertop and the Ring itself, hung round his neck for all that time—were never healed. Frodo's sacrifice was the reason he was given a white jewel on a silver chain that he wore around his neck before he left from the Grey Havens—something to replace the evil ring that once rested there. Tolkien wrote: Frodo "wore it always, a white gem like a star, that he often would finger."[23] Jesus will forevermore bear the scars of his mission and his sacrifice, even as he enters his final glory and receives his reward.

## What, or Who Is "God" Exactly?

Again, if all this is true about Jesus, it should cause all of us to sit up and take notice. This is at the heart of what Christianity teaches, that God is not a distant and aloof being, but rather one who cares so much that he suffers with us and for us. And this is who God has always been, a suffering servant. Christianity is the only faith that says God became one of us to face pain, poverty, trial, temptation, suffering, and the loss of friends and family to death. What Jesus taught about God and demonstrated through his actions forces us to entirely rethink what we assume is true of God. The early disciples (and authors of the New Testament) "had discovered the crucified, risen and enthroned Jesus, the Lord of the world" and, in so doing, had filled the meaning of the word *God* with new content—or, rather, "discovered what its true content always was."[24]

New Testament professor G. B. Caird agreed, arguing, "It is the contention of [the New Testament writers] that with the coming of Jesus the whole situation of mankind has so altered as to change the semantic content of the word 'God.'"[25] N. T. Wright contends it's one of the central purposes of Jesus' whole life. That the New Testament is doing far more than has been often felt "in that it is not just recounting a story of a person . . . but articulates and invites its hearers to share a new worldview which carries at its heart a new view of 'god,' and even a proposal for a way of saying 'God.'" Judaism claimed that Christianity, by putting Jesus in the middle of its doctrine of God, had damaged that doctrine. Christianity claimed that Judaism, in clinging to the national privilege and not recognizing the saving act of their own God in Jesus, had stepped aside from the covenant. "Both religions claimed that they were giving the true meaning of the word 'god,' in line with prior scriptural revelation, and that the other was not."[26] Jews looked toward an event, a great act of liberation, in which their God "would reveal to all the world that he was not just a local, tribal deity, but the creator and sovereign of all. . . . The early Christians looked back to an event in and through which they claimed Israel's god had done exactly that . . . [they] repeated the Jewish claim: this story concerns not just *a* god but God. It revised the Jewish evidence: the claim is made good, not in national liberation, but in the events concerning Jesus."[27] In other words, when the New Testament writers spoke of Jesus as Israel's God, they were redefining what "god" (or "God") meant as much as they were defining who Jesus was. And thus "those who have desired to explore and understand the incarnation itself have regularly missed what is arguably the most central, shocking and dramatic source material on that subject, which if taken seriously would ensure that the meaning of the word 'god' be again and again rethought around the actual history of Jesus himself."[28]

Christianity presents us with the craziest of notions: what we deduce about God is what we can deduce from what we know about Jesus. He exegeted God for the world in a way that it never knew before.[29] Only Buddha and Jesus so impressed their contemporaries that they were asked not just "Who are you?" but also "What are you?" What order of being do you belong to? What species do you represent? Buddha asserted that he was not a god or even some angelic, divine being, "while Jesus took an approach that could not be more different. He repeatedly and continually claimed to be *the* God, the creator of the universe."[30] In this way we see that Jesus' life was a way of revealing God to the world. Theologian Cornelius Van Til wrote that Jesus was not just revealing a part of God, he is the way in which we know God: "There is much in the Scriptures about Christ. He is the only way through whom God can be known. . . . Christ's work is a means to an end. Even if we think of the fact that Christ is the second person of the Trinity, we ought still to remember that it is the full Godhead with whom we ultimately have to do and about whom, in the last analysis, we wish to know. Hence, theology is primarily God centered rather than Christ centered."[31]

In other words, when Jesus stepped into the story of Israel and told us he was God, he was speaking of God as a unified whole. He taught that God is one but also a plurality: Father, Son, and Holy Spirit eternally one yet eternally distinct (Matthew 3:17; 28:19). Until Jesus came, all of this was a shadow of something we did not yet see. Now in Christ that shadow is gone and the light shines with clarity and color. The news from the far country has finally been delivered, and we understand what it means.

Today we are living in a time when philosophically you can believe anything so long as you do not claim it to be true. Morally, you can practice anything so long as you do not claim it is a "better" way. We are fixed in a particular cultural mood, and "a mood can be a dangerous state of mind, because it can crush reason under the weight of feeling."[32] Our feelings are defining reality for us, and even where "religions" are making a comeback, they are often just "a hybrid of western marketing techniques and eastern mythology. . . . The first casualty in such a mix is truth, and, *the person of God*."[33]

This is why the claim of Jesus—that God not only exists and is knowable, but is knowable exclusively through Jesus himself, is such a scandal still today. Jesus claimed that he is the way to God and that he is the person of God. He challenges atheism by claiming that God exists and challenges Hinduism by saying that there is only one God. He challenges Islam and Judaism by claiming that he, a mere man, is divine; and agnosticism by saying that God is knowable. No matter what our religious views or life philosophies, Jesus won't let us fit him into our ways of thinking. He confronts us with his claims and won't let us off the hook until we've made a decision about him.

Yet oddly enough, his claims are also the answer to our deepest longings. And in this we find hope: that not only does God exist, but he is for us and he is after us—so much so that he became one of us to bring us home.

## What Do You Get the Man Who Has Everything?

So, we've talked about what it means that Jesus is "God with us" (Matthew 1:23). But this begs an important follow-up question: *Why* did God become one of us? Why did he do what one writer has described as something comparable to you or I becoming a slug or a crab? Everything in life has some motivation or incentive, from people to animals to cells. There is always a *why* behind the *what*. We marry who we marry because there is enough joy or pleasure or practical positive impact on our lives. It's the same reason we eat what we do, spend money on what we do, and live where we live. We want to become happier, richer, and more fulfilled, so we make a hundred decisions a day driven by those motives. So what do you get the man who has everything? In other words, how do you motivate God to do something? After all, he owns everything. He's sovereign over everything. He has fullness of joy, perfect fulfillment, and is always at peace. What would motivate Him on a trajectory of downward mobility to suffer and die?

The answer is hiding in what is perhaps the most famous passage in the Bible, John 3:16: "For God so loved the world, that he gave his only Son, that whoever believes in him should not perish but have eternal life." John tells us that God was motivated by his love. And God's love was made manifest in a very particular way: God gave—because this is the nature of love, not to get, but to give. God is not motivated by something he lacks, because he lacks nothing. Instead, God is motivated by who he is, to give generously out of the overflow of his boundless love.

That was his incentive.

Human beings are disconnected from God. In our selfishness we think much like Adam and Eve—what can I get that will make my life better? But what does God do? He moves in the opposite direction with the opposite motives. He isn't motivated by what he can get but by what he can give. He becomes one of us in order to save us and to give us the best gift of all, himself. Because what we needed in the end was not just a sacrifice in our place: we also needed someone. Someone to live righteously for us, a perfect life applied to us. If Jesus had only earned forgiveness of sins, then we would still be stuck in our sinful selfishness, not fit for heaven, because our guilt would be removed but we would lack a heart filled with holy love. We would be forgiven but not truly saved. And for this reason, Christ had to live a life of perfect obedience to God in order to earn a righteousness for us that could be applied to us. And best of all, his work secured the greatest gift of all, the gift of God's Holy Spirit, who was poured out upon his followers following his death, resurrection, and ascension. This is the mystery hidden for all time but revealed in Jesus Christ—that God would live in each of us, making his home with us, and filling us with the same love that he has so that we might love one another.

God's motive was love. And while this may sound sentimental and cliché, I have come to learn that God's love is anything but those things. It is the heartbeat of the universe, the mystery that weaves the fabric of reality. "The world moves for love, it bows before it in awe."[34] Not only in poetry, but in real life.

## A Philosopher in My Office

What are the implications of rethinking God? A. W. Tozer said, "What comes into our minds when we think about God is the most important thing about us." What we think about God filters down to every other thing about us, from our identity to our desires, to what we value in life and what makes us happy. The rethinking of God that Jesus forces upon us affects not just what we think about God but how we understand ourselves. In his remarkable study on the book of Revelation, Richard Bauckham concludes,

> One of the functions of Revelation was to purge and to re-furbish the Christian imagination. It tackles people's imaginative response to the world, which is at least as deep and influential as their intellectual convictions. It recognizes the way a dominant culture, with its images and ideals, constructs the world for us, so that we perceive and respond to the world on its terms. . . . In its place Revelation offers *a different way of perceiving the world* which leads people to resist and to challenge the effects of the dominant ideology . . . to open it to transcendence.[35]

This is precisely what Jesus has done. In re-visioning how we see God, he is pushing back against pagan and religious views, purging and refurbishing the human imagination about God. He leads us to a transcendent reality that is deeper and more meaningful than anything the cultures of the world can offer. As Emil Brunner argued, "There is only one question which is really serious, and that is the question concerning the being and nature of God. From this all other questions derive their significance."[36]

Whether we will admit it or not, we relentlessly seek that which brings us joy and pleasure. Could it be that by redefining our understanding of God in light of Jesus, we can somehow fulfill that longing in a way that has eluded us otherwise? Everyone wants to be happy.

We all want to live a life of meaning. Could the way of Jesus lead us there? Could what he revealed about God hold the secret to what we've been missing in life?

Recently I met with a young man at my office. His mother had reached out to me, telling me she was desperate for her son to meet with me. He had grown up in church, and he knew the details of the gospel but had fallen away from his faith. He arrived that morning, eyes half open and dressed in workout gear. This visit was just another thing to check off his list on his way to the gym. We sat down, and I asked him how I could help. He laughed, "I don't know why I am here, to be honest. A number of years ago, I became very interested in philosophy and rethought my faith. I'm not aggressively anti-Christian or anything; I'm just an existentialist [one who believes there is no real point to anything or everything]." He hesitated before continuing, "Lately I've been having these debilitating anxiety attacks. I'll be in my bed at night, staring up at my ceiling, and the world seems to close in on me. I can't move and my throat starts to close up—all at the real-ization of the universe's emptiness and lack of meaning."

He continued, "One night a few months ago, I was outside, star-ing into the dark. I felt one of these attacks coming on, and then out of nowhere, for a fleeting moment, I could sense something like a presence on the other side of the veil. This calm came over my entire body. I had total peace, unlike anything I had experienced in my life, and then it was gone."

I asked him why that was, and his answer didn't surprise me. "Weakness," he said. It's what an existentialist would say.

"I started to wonder whether God was real again. But then I reminded myself I was only thinking that as a crutch, as a hopeful fan-tasy, because I was scared—not because it actually made any sense."

"You are an existentialist, though," I said. "You don't wholly trust reason either. So why would it have to make sense to you?"

He laughed. "I know."

"So, you think you entertained the concept of God out of fear and wishful thinking?"

"Maybe, yes."

"But even if it *was* fear and wishful thinking that drove you to rethink your doubts about God, is that necessarily wrong? We aren't blank slates, as much as we'd like to think we are. There are reasons we adopt the beliefs that we do. You didn't come to believe in existentialism just because. You were driven by your upbringing, things you read, teachers, friends, and all the feelings that came with them. If that's a legitimate way to reach your belief in existentialism, it should be an equally legitimate way to explain a faith in God."

"I guess that is true."

"In your case, fear is leading you to the question of God's existence. Our rational minds say fear must be the opposite of fact, but the Bible says fear is sometimes a great guide: 'the beginning of wisdom.' The Bible identifies fear as a guide *toward* truth, not away from it. Which was certainly the case with our ancestors. I mean, fear is part of what's kept us alive as a species: it's told us to stay away from lions and stick close to camp. So why *not* trust it, even a little bit in this case?"

He stared at me, thinking.

"I have a theory about your moments of fear and anxiety," I said.

He asked, "And what is it?"

I pointed over his head to a book on my shelf and explained, "A medical doctor, Timothy R. Jennings, wrote a book a few years ago called *The God-Shaped Brain*. In it he demonstrates through detailed clinical tests that a person's brain literally functions differently depending on his or her view of God—that neural pathways are carved out over time in one shape if the predominant understanding of God is that he is, for example, an angry judge—"

"That's me," he interrupted. "That's how I think of him."

I continued, "If he is wrathful, vengeful, and simply waiting for you to make a mistake so he can hold you accountable for it, your brain lights up in one area. But it lights up in a different area if your predominant understand of him is as . . . a God of love." I hesitated a bit at the end, because if this philosopher was anything like me, he'd roll his eyes at what seemed like sentimental church speak. I wanted to make sure he understood the meaning I was actually pouring into that word.

He kept staring at me, so I kept going.

"Jennings says that when we conceptualize God as love, our brains literally function in a less anxious way; chemicals are released and pathways are carved out that create joy and happiness and feelings of hope and anticipation for good things to come."

He leaned forward in his chair and put his face into his hands for a few minutes.

When he looked up, he said. "What you are saying right now is blowing my mind. And I have to tell you, when you were talking, the same feeling—that one I had looking out into the sky, that feeling of peace and love—just flooded over me again. It's like this affirmation from the other side of a door. For the second time in my life, it all just rushed over me, right here."

For the next half hour or so we just talked. We talked about the implications of this shift—this rethinking of God—and what it means for our lives. We talked about how Jesus showed us a God who *is* love by definition.

He said, "I think I need to come back to church. I need to pursue God again. What else should I do?" I told him to go home and read the Gospel of John, which illuminates how Jesus' whole ministry was saying, "You thought God was like this, but I am here to show you who he really is."

As this young man stood up to leave, I handed him Dr. Jennings's book. And as he walked out the door, he said, "You know, I thought I was going to come here and just kill an hour chatting and then go home none the wiser. I mean I'm a philosopher, so what do I have to learn from a pastor? But this changed me today. I can't explain it.

Funny, isn't it? To think that after all this time, what I really needed to hear was the most basic thing that I had been told in church my whole life. That God is love and that he loves me rather than being against me. Crazy. Thank you. You have no idea." And he walked away.

Whether you're running to God or from him, it's essential for you to understand the nature of God. If Jesus is right—that happiness and contentment are only experienced if we find him—and God is who we see in the human face of Jesus himself, then anything we believe about God that is not explicitly centered on Christ is misguided and will lead us astray one way or another. Will you look to him as the One who brought this mystery into the light?

# CHAPTER 14

# The Only
# WAY

The only thing even more scandalous to a modern skeptic than the idea that Jesus is God is the idea that he is the *only way* for someone to experience salvation. The claim of exclusivity, that Jesus is the *right* way and every other way of trying to find God is *wrong*, repels our culture. To a culture that insists all religions and spiritual views are true, it is deemed judgmental, bigoted, and narrow-minded. That's because people misunderstand what Christianity is proposing. Often the question of exclusivity is presented as a separate question than that of Jesus' divinity. But if what we have said so far is true, the two ideas are directly connected; exclusivity is a natural corollary to the fact of Jesus being God. And, of course, he would then be the only way.

There a couple of questions to explore in this context before we can accept this claim: (1) Did Jesus really claim to be the only way to God? (2) If so, does the claim even make sense, is it morally right for Jesus to have claimed this, and what does it mean for other worldviews?

## Did Jesus Claim to Be the Only Way?

Surveying the data of the Gospels, it is clear that Jesus saw himself as the only way to God (and consequently salvation). It is implicit on almost every page of the Gospels, but he addresses it more specifically too. In what has become one of the most scandalous verses of our time, Jesus clearly laid out a stark exclusivity: "You know the way to where I am going." Thomas responded, "Lord, we do not know where you are going. How can we know the way?" Jesus said to him. "I am the way, and the truth, and the life. *No one comes to the Father except through me*" (John 14:4–6, italics mine).

This is why Christianity says it's not that Jesus of Nazareth is blazing a trail or giving us right teaching or pointing us along the true path; rather, he is saying that he *is* the path. Jesus isn't saying, "Listen to me and you will get on the right bus." He's saying, "I am the bus."

And he's the only bus.

Similarly, in the Gospel of Matthew, Jesus said, "Enter by the narrow gate. For the gate is wide and the way is easy that leads to destruction, and those who enter by it are many. *For the gate is narrow and the way is hard that leads to life, and those who find it are few*" (7:13–14, italics mine).

This is the exact opposite of our cultural idea that there is a gate that leads to life and the way through it is easy (whatever you want and feel at a particular moment). Or, to paraphrase Jesus' words, "The gate is wide and everyone finds it."

Consider also the Gospel of Luke. The disciples came to Jesus and asked, "Lord, will those who are saved be few?" Everything he was saying seemed to point in that direction, so now they asked him outright. And he answered them, "Strive to enter through the narrow door. For many . . . will seek to enter and *will not be able*" (13: 23–24). Why? Precisely because they're trying through different ways. Jesus continued, "When once the master of the house has risen and shut the door, and you begin to stand outside and to knock at the door, saying, 'Lord open to us,' then he will answer you, 'I do not know where you come from'" (v. 25). Jesus was not saying that all the different ways of the world lead to heaven; he was saying that they all lead to destruction. They lead to a place where "there will be weeping and gnashing of teeth" (v. 28). Every road ends there except one—and very few find it.

## The Gospel of Self-Fulfillment

Why do so many people find the narrow road? Often it is because we aren't willing to get over the hurdle of our own pride and ideology. We will not surrender to God and repent of our self-sufficiency. It's just too high a price to pay.

Over fifty years ago, Jewish philosopher Martin Buber discerned an emerging and destructive trajectory within society. He warned that a new religion was being accepted in the West: "This new religion could be detected in an increasing obsession with the self, with personal development and the preference of spirituality over religion, and with therapy over communion with a transcendent God. It was the elevation of self above God."[1] It wasn't a new religion per se, but rather the return of an older strain of thought: Gnosticism—an ancient belief in a private, mysterious knowledge/spirituality that was about being made "full" and "complete" as an individual—the gospel of self. This belief was now becoming the norm for the western mind: "Truth was not found in class struggle or political consciousness [anymore], but rather in the journey into the self. Politics had been superseded by psychology. The countercultural revolution had morphed into a therapeutic quest to discover individual fulfillment."[2]

This is where the claims of Jesus to be God and to be the *only* way to know God collide and challenge us. We are not God; Jesus is. We can't save ourselves—no religion, worldview, or behavior can—only Jesus can. Salvation is not about what we do for God; it's about what he did for us. All of this counters our self-love philosophy and rejects outright the way of Jesus, a way that necessitates "the most countercultural act one can commit in our culture: to commit *self-disobedience*."[3] Jesus urges us, "Deny yourself, pick up your cross, and follow me." In today's world it is not popular to give up what we want to follow the will of another, but Jesus was clear. And his followers doubled down on this clarity. Peter began to preach shortly after Jesus arose from the dead and ascended into heaven, and his message was this: "There is no other name under heaven given among men by which we must be saved" (Acts 4:12). Only Jesus.

Whatever one might say about whether it is true or not, one cannot argue that Jesus and the rest of the Bible isn't clear about it. There is only one name (or person) that saves: not Krishna, not Buddha, not Muhammad. No other person gives the ability for us to be saved other than Jesus, because he's the only one who deals with the problem we have of sin, death, and distance from God. The problem of sinfulness is solved only through the cross and resurrection. The problem of our distance from God—the challenge of our reconciliation—is bridged only through the cross and resurrection. The problem of God's wrath being on us is dealt with only through the cross and resurrection.

That's the biblical vantage point.

## The Only Way to What?

I have buried two fathers. My biological dad died when I was fifteen. He and my mother had been divorced for a few years before we got a phone call with the news that he was dying. The next day he was gone. The year after my parents were divorced, my mother married a man named Al. He raised me from the time I was nine years old: taught me how to work hard, love a woman, and be a man of integrity. He died when I was twenty-nine, on the second Sunday after we started Village Church. After preaching, I flew back that day to do his funeral, and as I sat talking with my family, we spent most of our time talking about one question: What is our destiny? Those conversations led me to preach a passage at his funeral from John 14 that tackles a question we all need answered: *If there is a heaven, how do we get there?* Most of my family aren't Christians, so it was a challenging question—just as it was for Jesus' audience—to pose to them. And the answer was even more problematic: Jesus is the *only* way. Some nodded while others looked uncomfortable.

Exclusive claims are not popular in our culture. But we need to move beyond our initial dislike for exclusivity and ask a second question. The only way *to what?* The context of John 14 answers that question. Jesus said, "In my Father's house there are many rooms," and "I go to prepare a place for you" (John 14:2–3). He was making his exclusivist claim in the context of talking about a person's destiny, about what would happen to them after they died. This is not some abstract philosophical or theological doctrine. It's a serious subject that addresses the fate of everyone who has ever lived.

Yes, Jesus was talking about heaven. Historical Jesus study has done a lot of good work in recent years to reveal a clearer picture of what Jesus meant by heaven. He was not talking about the disembodied spirit world typically envisioned, but a reembodiment: a resurrection life in a new creation (new heavens and a new earth). His vision of heaven was one of pure joy, pleasure, and delight in the presence of the most amazing, glorious person one could ever imagine—God himself.

The image Jesus used to communicate the joy of heaven here offers us a clue: heaven is a kind of *homecoming*. It fulfills and answers the deep longings in all of us. This is why Jesus used the image of a house. Home is an extremely powerful, evocative idea in the human heart and experience. We have within us a longing for home, a longing that exceeds the reality of our individual experiences of home and family.

People spend billions of dollars annually to go back to the place where they were born. They visit family and connect to their past—to their childhood, to their memories, to the comfort they experienced in those years. For me, the thought of home brings up fond memories of cottage life when I was a kid. An overflowing sense of love and excitement center on the family vacations we had. We stayed up late and spent time getting in trouble, enjoying nights by the fire.

If you have similar memories, you have a taste of what Jesus is talking about here. Even if our memories of home aren't the best, deep inside we still miss it. Yet we feel disconnected from it. And that's the problem with the longing for home. It's difficult to satisfy. It is fleeting and elusive, always just out of reach. We think to ourselves: *This year Christmas is going to be like the one I remember from my childhood— bigger than life! This year, if I make the turkey just right and set the table just like we did back then, all those feelings are going to come back and it's going to be perfect again.* And what happens? It's always disappointing. Try as we might, we cannot capture the "memory" we have, perhaps because that memory itself isn't the real source of our longing.

Our culture tries to satisfy this longing in a variety of different ways. C. S. Lewis called it a "spiritual homesickness," a sense that we were built for something that transcends our human experience. Once in a while, something pokes through our busy lives and we think, *This is what I was built for! This is what I long for more than anything!* And then, just as quickly as we felt it, it disappears. And we feel a nostalgic sadness because it's a longing we can never quite satisfy.

It may surprise you to learn that the second highest grossing movie of all time is a 2009 film called *Avatar*. It's a science fiction movie about a planet called Pandora, wherein the main character must adopt an avatar to interact with an alien species, one that is quite different from human beings. The avatar is a body he inhabits, giving him the experience of truly *being* that alien person, and in that avatar he rides dragons, visits floating islands, and encounters glowing water organisms. When *Avatar* was released, a number of articles were written about how watching the movie was affecting people. CNN ran one article called "Ways to Cope with the Depression of the Dream of Pandora Being Intangible." Thousands of people posted comments and shared testimonies after reading the story. Here are a few:

> The movie was so beautiful and it showed something we don't have here on Earth. I think people saw we could be living in a completely different world and that caused them to be depressed. That's all I have been doing as of late. Searching the Internet for more info about *Avatar*. It's so hard I can't force myself to think that it's just a movie and to get over it: that living like the Navi will never happen.

> Ever since I went to see *Avatar* I've been depressed. I can't stop thinking about all the things that happened in the film and all

of the tears and shivers I got from it. I even contemplate suicide thinking that if I do it I will be rebirthed in a world similar to Pandora and everything will be the same as an *Avatar*.

When I woke up this morning after watching for the first time yesterday the world seemed grey. It was like my whole life. Everything I've done and worked for lost its meaning. I still don't really see any reason to keep doing things at all. I live in a dying world.[4]

What's going on here? How can people be depressed about something they've never experienced, something that isn't even real? The Bible tells us that this is possible because we were made for a kind of existence that transcends what we presently see and experience. Humans were created in a garden, made to walk with God in a world where there was no sickness, death, or pain. And something innate inside us longs to get back to that reality. As C. S. Lewis famously said, "If we find in ourselves a desire that nothing in this world can satisfy, the most probable explanation is that we were made for another world." This is where the idea of heaven gains philosophical credibility. We have longings that nothing in our experience can touch, and more importantly, neither can they *justify* them or explain them. Naturalism cannot give us a reason for these longings. It makes no sense that we yearn for a perfect world. If we are just animals, there is no reason we should expect a reality like that. The biblical answer is that we were made for more, for a reality beyond what we currently see. Heaven is the "place" we seek, yes, but it also marks our origin and aim.

So what keeps us from that reality? Our sin. And that's the problem Jesus came to address. Jesus is the only one who can save us from the place where sin leads us when our debt to God remains unpaid: hell. This is why nothing else solves our deepest longings. No amount of money, power, sex, politics, work, or family can satisfy that need. Nothing in this world is an all-encompassing balm to the soul, because our restless hearts were made to find rest in God.

## Does This Claim Make Sense? Is It Rational?

Exclusivity is controversial, and most modern people reject it, but the first thing we have to admit is that being repulsed by an idea doesn't make it untrue. It just means we don't like it. We must push beyond our dislike to ask if it rings true. Does Jesus' claim line up with reality and the evidence of science, history, and philosophy? Yes, Jesus' claim to exclusivity does exactly that, far better than many of our modern, secular stories. Because while millions of people across the Western world believe that "all religious ideas are equal and all lead to some form of salvation," this belief is mistaken.

## The (Post)Modern World

The idea that all worldviews and religions are just different paths to God is the height of *hopeful idealism* versus a *philosophical realism*. Jesus and Christianity say that the inclusivist position is an unreasonable and illogical position—that two opposite ideas about God and salvation, or about anything, for that matter, can't be true at the same time and in the same way. This is sometimes called the *law of noncontradiction*. For instance, I was golfing with a guy a few months ago, and we got to talking about religion. He said, "I like religion but feel like we need to accept that all religions are true." I said to him, "That sounds really nice, but it doesn't make sense because all religions contradict each other in their basic beliefs about God, salvation, heaven, hell, and humankind." He scoffed and started to get upset: "If you say that, we'll have violence and hatred toward one another forever!"

I said, "I don't think we should abandon truth because we are afraid of what people are going to do with it. We can't settle for false realities out of fear. We wouldn't do that with science."

He doubled down by phrasing it another way: "Well what is true for one person is what is true."

I looked at him and said "You don't believe that."

"I do!" he insisted.

So I pressed him. I said, "If you asked your daughter what two plus two is, and she answered five, would you say she was right because that was her opinion?" He laughed, thought for a moment, and said, "Yes! I would be okay with that because that is her opinion!"

Now of course we all know this is absurd. Math is math. It's true and certain because it really exists and there is a right and a wrong answer. And while there are opinions and our perception of truth can vary from person to person, we can apply this to all truth claims, including those about the nature of reality, our human souls, and our future destiny. To put it simply, if the Christian view of Jesus is right, then by default the Muslim, Jewish, Hindu, and new age versions are wrong. Conversely, if any one of their versions of God is correct, then Christianity is wrong.

We can and must respect each another and each person's right to hold his or her own beliefs. But showing respect for the beliefs of others does not mean accepting that they are correct. It is nonsensical to believe in some kind of reality wherein we all are right. The truth will set us free, Jesus says, and the "truth" Jesus references is an absolute one. Our beliefs may be sincere and well-intentioned, but that doesn't make them true. My wife, Erin, reminds me of a time I came home from the grocery store with a radish when she'd sent me out on an emergency tomato run. "I appreciate that you 'tried your best,'" she said to me, "but this thing is a radish, and you're going to hate it on your burger." Metaphysical pluralism makes small talk more bearable at the barbecue, but it's still a lie. A lack of malice won't make up for incompetence.

Contradictory statements cannot both be true at the same time in the same way, even if the motive is pure and right and good. Islam says that Jesus was not God. Christianity says Jesus was and is God. Buddhism and atheists say there is no God. New age philosophy says we're all gods. They cannot all be true at the same time. And that is Jesus' entire premise. If heaven and God exist, there is one path, not a hundred different ones. And it doesn't matter what anyone *feels* about it.

Christianity is not the only worldview that claims exclusivity. Formal religions like Islam and Judaism also claim to be the only way to experience salvation. And when we really begin to dig into the details, virtually every worldview is exclusivist. Consider the so-called tolerant views of atheism and secularism that are popular with many people today. They argue that the *only* way to true freedom is the full inclusion of all people, to be loving and accepting of everyone. That is, of course, as long as you agree with *their* views on everything from sexuality to politics to the environment. If you don't fall in line and agree with the script they've written, you are cast out like a leper. And make no mistake—this is entirely a conversation about "salvation." It is about how we can be truly free in the here and now, and how to bring about the collective salvation of our souls and civilization as a whole. These worldviews have their own dogma, their prophets, their sacred texts, and their devoted followers—all the makings of a "religion."

The postmodern theory that underlies much of our contemporary way of thinking is itself built on the idea that there is no absolute truth. And while it comes across as a progressive doctrine that brings individual freedom, upon closer examination we find it is contradictory at its core. In claiming that there is no absolute truth, there is an immediate exception to that foundational belief: the truth that there is no absolute truth! The second you say, "All truth claims are true and all ways lead to God," and "Inclusivism is the right way," you end up excluding every single exclusivist worldview.

## A Final Word

Though various religions also make exclusive claims about salvation, Christianity claims it is the way to a *particular kind* of salvation. Reflecting on this, Vinoth Ramachandra notes the uniqueness of the

Christian vision of salvation. The Christian promise is not just the rescue of individual souls from earth or a vague hope to make things better or free the self or experience a state of enlightenment. It's not even the hope of going to heaven when one dies, though that is part of it. The final goal is the restoration of all creation and the affirmation that God is committed to the material world he has made (Romans 8:18–25). Ramachandra writes, "Our salvation lies not in an escape from this world but in the transformation of this world. . . . The biblical vision is unique. That is why when someone says that there is salvation in other faiths, I ask them, 'What salvation are you talking about?' No faith holds out a promise of eternal salvation for the world the way the cross and resurrection of Jesus do."[5]

The message commonly accepted—that all paths to salvation are equal and true—turns out to be a mess. And not just because it isn't logical, but because we cannot even agree on what we mean by salvation. Salvation to a Muslim is a vastly different concept than that of a Hindu or a Christian or an agnostic. Jesus doesn't claim that he is the way to whatever version of salvation a person may hold, but that he is the only way to God, to forgiveness, to reconciliation, and to ultimate pleasure and delight. Salvation in Jesus is not a disembodied spirit world or state of enlightenment, but a new heaven and a new earth, "the Great Story which no one on earth has read: which goes on forever: in which every chapter is better than the one before."[6]

# PART VIII

---

# The Problem of
# JESUS' DEATH

*"You never really understand a person until you consider things from his point of view. Until you climb inside of his skin and walk around in it."*

—HARPER LEE, TO KILL A MOCKINGBIRD

# CHAPTER 15

## What Happened: An
# APPOINTMENT
# WITH DEATH

I started going to church when I was nineteen years old. Before that I always wondered why Christians called the Friday when they gathered together to reflect on the bloody and disgusting murder of an innocent guy, "good." I didn't understand because I didn't know what his death *meant*. But the meaning of Jesus' death is what makes it good. The act itself was brutal and bloody, but the significance of that death—what it means for us and for the world—is better than good; it's great. I certainly don't have enough influence to change the name of a well-established holiday, but if I could, I would.

Believers and skeptics alike all have to face the question of Jesus' death and resurrection. If these events happened and mean what the Gospels say they mean, they are the definitive event in history. They define how God, the creator of all things, relates with humankind, and they decide the fate of every person who has ever lived. This is not an overstatement. The Gospels present these events as the pivot point from which history moves in a different direction from where it was going—the linchpin of salvation history. In this chapter and the next, we will explore (1) what actually took place around the death of Jesus, and (2) what it all *means* for us.

## Killing Jesus

There is little doubt from a historical perspective that Jesus' crucifixion happened. His death is recorded (and his resurrection alluded to) by multiple non-Christian, nonbiblical historians writing at or shortly after the time of Jesus. Josephus (AD 37–100), documented in his *Antiquities*: "About this time there lived Jesus, a wise man, if indeed one ought to call him a man. For he . . . wrought surprising feats. . . . He was the Christ. When Pilate . . . condemned him to be crucified, those who had come to love him did not give up their affection for him. On the third day he appeared . . . restored to life . . . and the tribe of Christians . . . has not disappeared."[1] Further, Thallus, an early historian who wrote a three-volume history of the Mediterranean world from before the Trojan War to the 167th Olympiad, noted, "An eclipse of the sun unreasonably . . because a solar eclipse could not take place at the time of the full moon, and it was at the season of the Paschal full moon that Christ died."[2]

All four Gospels tell us that Jesus was crucified. They don't leave the event to some vague mythological place and time. They tell us precisely when and where it happened, in Jerusalem during the reign of Pilate and Herod. They give historical markers about the Sanhedrin (a group of Jewish authorities), an earthquake, and even astrological footnotes of the day and time of year.[3] They also detail the judicial systems and torture practices used by the Roman government, both of which have been affirmed by multiple historians as accurate to that time.

## The Reasons for Jesus' Crucifixion

The question of *why* Jesus was killed is a complicated one. The Roman charge was that Jesus was a rebel leader, so they crucified him because that form of death carried both a public and political message: "We run things, you are our property, and any threat to our sovereignty will be dealt with accordingly." Jesus was not executed as a thief, as if Rome crucified common robbers, but as a rebel against the Roman

Empire. Jesus' kingdom message carried these undertones throughout his ministry: "If YHWH was at last becoming king, all other rulers, Caesar downwards, would find their power at least relativized."[4] As historians point out again and again, one of the flaws of the modern, liberal portrayal of Jesus is the unlikelihood that anyone would have wanted to crucify such an attractive and inclusive moral teacher.[5] The truth is that Jesus was seen as a threat to the empire.

The Jewish charge, as best we can tell, is based on Jesus' temple actions and his claim to be the Messiah. After his arrest, he was brought before the high priest, the chief priests, elders, and scribes for trial (Mark 14:53). Ultimately, they landed on the charge that Jesus was a false prophet leading Israel astray who needed to be killed for his theological statements. These were not small crimes. Jesus was advocating "an agenda which involved setting aside some of the most central and cherished symbols of the Judaism of his day, and replacing them with loyalty to himself."[6] Who did Jesus think he was? Such a threat to the public, to the innocent lives of Jews just trying to follow the ways of God in the world, must be silenced. The verdict had already been decided long before Jesus' formal trial. John documented several private reasons the Jews wished to kill Jesus: "The chief priests and the Pharisees gathered the council and said, 'What are we to do? For this man performs many signs. If we let him go on like this, everyone will believe in him, and the Romans will come and take away both our place and our nation'" (John 11:47–48).

John highlighted two fears that drove the Jewish leaders to kill Jesus in cold blood, though they never stopped to consider he might be telling the truth. They were so blinded by working *for* God that they never saw God when he finally showed up.

## How Jesus Was Killed

### FLOGGING

The question of how Jesus was killed is a little more straightforward. The Gospels tell us that after multiple *illegal* trials (held at night, in secret) the Romans "scourged" or "flogged" him (Matthew 27:26). We tend to pass over this detail rather quickly, but we should not. Flogging was horrific. They tied Jesus' hands to a post and beat his entire body with a multitailed leather whip that had pieces of bone and metal attached to the ends.

They slashed Jesus' back, flipped him over, and slashed his stomach, torso, legs, arms, neck, and face, with the pieces of bone grabbing his skin and tearing it off. A flogging might rip out ribs or even parts of the intestines and could itself be fatal. The prophet Isaiah, speaking hundreds of years before this event, said that Jesus, as the Messiah, would have an appearance so marred that he would be beyond human resemblance (Isaiah 52:14). The Gospels tell us that Jesus was so weakened after his flogging that someone else had to carry his 150-pound crossbeam to the place where he would be crucified (Matthew 27:32).

## CRUCIFIXION

The Gospels tell us that after Jesus was flogged, he was crucified (Matthew 27:38–44). Crucifixion was a punishment invented by the Persians in 500 BC, and the Romans were using it at the time of Jesus to kill revolutionaries and enemies of the state. It was ultimately outlawed in the Roman Empire around AD 300 when Constantine ended the practice as a punishment for crimes. It had been developed as one of the most painful forms of torture humankind has known. The victim was hung, arms stretched out and oftentimes broken, by taking five- to seven-inch metal spikes and driving them through the hands and feet to fasten the victim to a wooden post. It would occur in a public space, most often with the victim naked, giving the opportunity to nail even his penis to the post. And the cross wasn't a nice, clean crossbeam like we see on modern churches. Timber was really expensive in the ancient world, so they would reuse the same beams. Many men before Jesus would have died on his crossbeam, and it would likely have been covered with the spit, blood, feces, and urine of dying men before him.[7]

The pain of crucifixion was so horrific they invented a word to describe it—*excruciating*—from the Latin word X, which means "out of," and *cruciare*, which means "cross": a pain like the pain of crucifixion. As C. S. Lewis pointed out, death on a cross was so horrific the cross did not become common in art until the fourth century when all who had seen one used had died. Victims would die a slow and painful death, passing in and out of consciousness. Most died of asphyxiation, suffocating to death because they lacked the strength to lift their heads and give their lungs space to expand. The Gospels tell us Jesus was on the cross for about six hours (Matthew 27:45).

History affirms that Jesus was killed on a cross. In his book *The Evolution of God*, secular journalist Ronald Wright says, "We can be pretty sure the Crucifixion happened, in part because it made so little theological sense. . . . Throughout history, gods had been beings to whom you made sacrifices. Now here was a god that not only demanded no ritual sacrifices from you but himself made sacrifices—indeed the ultimate sacrifice—for you."[8]

## But What Does It Mean?

The cross is the symbol that came to represent Christianity throughout history. The early church could have used other symbols. They could have used the crib to emphasize God becoming human through being born of a virgin. They could have used a fishing boat, which Jesus often used as a pulpit, to emphasize his teaching ministry. They could have used a towel to emphasize his humble servitude. But they didn't choose any of these. Instead, they chose a cross. Why? Because this is the center of the Christian message. Without the cross, the ministry of Jesus is a series of nice ideas about God and life, but it doesn't solve anything. Christianity proclaims that something meaningful happened when Jesus died. Something that changes reality and how we relate to God, our Creator.

Mark Driscoll points out that the cross is like a multifaceted jewel—brilliant in the way it sparkles from many different angles. He summarizes several different things the cross accomplishes, all of which have a deep meaning in the history of the church:

- Christus Victor—Jesus defeats Satan and demons.
- Redemption—the cross "buys us back" from the slavery of death and sin.
- New Covenant Sacrifice—Jesus is our sacrifice and forgives our sins so that we are forgiven and can forgive others.
- Gift Righteousness—accomplishment of Christ gets applied to us.
- Justification—because of Jesus' work, we are declared righteous in the law court of God.
- Propitiation—the cross satisfies God's wrath and thus turns his relationship to us into favor.
- Expiation—Jesus' sacrifice not only forgives our sins, but also the sins that have been done to us.
- Christus Exemplar—the cross is our example for life and how we live it.[9]

All of these are crucial to the meaning of Christianity for our lives and for the world at large. And while all of them are significant, there are a few that are worth exploring further because they are foundational to understanding what God was doing in the death of Jesus Christ.

## Atonement for Sin

Speaking of the death of Jesus, Matthew provided this detail: "From the sixth hour there was darkness over all the land until the ninth hour" (27:45). It's a phrase we might just pass over. Hidden in it is another indication of what this death means. Historians tell us that at the ninth hour of the day of Passover (when Jesus was killed), the Jews would gather to offer up their daily sacrifices for the atonement of sin. We know the gospel writers don't waste words; they want us to see that this whole ordeal is really an offering—indeed *the* offering. It is the ultimate and final sacrifice to atone for sins. This is why the veil in the temple was torn in two as Jesus died and declared, "It is finished" from the cross (John 19:30). The writer of Hebrews declared that Jesus' sacrifice meant that never again do sacrifices need to be provided for human sin: "But as it is, he has appeared once for all at the end of the ages to put away sin by the sacrifice of himself . . . having been offered once to bear the sins of many" (9:26–28). Theologian Herman Bavinck pointed out the priestly significance of this idea, saying, "In his dying, Jesus was not only a witness and a guide, a martyr and a hero, a prophet and a king. He was above all active in it as a priest. It is his high-priestly function which in his death comes out into the foreground the most. His dying was a *sacrifice* freely given to the Father by him."[10]

## Jesus, Our Substitute

I loved attending college. I was excited to be there. I was a focused student, and I studied hard, worked hard, and looked forward to being a pastor one day. During my first year of college, I wrote a paper for a class and received a good grade. My best friend at the time—who was a bit of a slacker—came to me one day and asked if he could "borrow" the paper. He was writing on the same topic, and he wanted it for inspiration and direction. I loaned it to him because I'm an amazing—and naive—friend.

As you can guess, he ended up rewriting my entire paper word for word, handing it in, receiving a great grade for it, and then moving on with life. He never told me he had done any of this. And his plagiarism would probably have gone unnoticed forever, except for the fact that he abruptly developed a conscience. I received a call from him one morning just after this happened: "I copied your paper, but then I felt really convicted about it, so I told my teacher about it all today. I am so sorry."

As I listened to all of this, my entire future as a pastor flashed before my eyes: "Don't you get expelled for plagiarism? What if they kick me out of school, you idiot?" He assured me that I would be fine—the consequences surely wouldn't be that extreme. And even so, he swore he would *never* tell anyone I was the one who had given him the paper. A few days later, he was told to appear before a school tribunal who would determine his fate. When he told me this, I knew I was finished. But he insisted I was fine: "It doesn't matter what they do to me; they can torture me, suspend me, charge me, whatever. . . . I'll never tell them your name! And anyway, they aren't going to care about *you*. Stop being so self-centered. It will be all about me cheating; they likely won't even care who gave it to me."

I told him he had better not give me up. Ever.

The day of the meeting, I prayed and fasted (likely for the first time). He arrived to the meeting and found there was not a single smiling face in the group. It was all business. And there was only one question the committee cared about: "*Who gave you the paper?*"

"I'm sorry, but I'm not going to tell you," he declared. "I told him I wouldn't ever tell."

One of the professors raised his eyebrows and said, "You told *him*? Okay, well, we know the person who wrote the paper is from last semester's class, and now we know it's a him. How long do you think it's going to take us to narrow down who it is?"

"It was Mark Clark!" The guy who claimed he'd suffer torture for me didn't last three minutes.

I barely slept, awaiting their phone call. Day one passed. Then day two and day three. I checked my email. My phone. No emails. No calls. Nothing. And then, just like that, the semester was over. I got my grades and life went on as if nothing had happened.

But something had.

You see, during that first year of college, I'd become close with the head of the New Testament department. He was, and still is, the best teacher I've ever had; his name is Stephen Thomson (or, as we students called him, Stevie-T). Stephen had become my mentor and friend. When he heard about what happened and that my friend and I were going to be kicked out of school, he went to the tribunal and fought for us. And I didn't know it at the time or for a long time afterward. But that didn't change the fact that in the fall of 2001, someone went to bat for me and stood in my place. He took the heat from the tribunal so I wouldn't feel it. And it was an amazing gift.

This is the first hint of what the cross is all about: Jesus going to bat for us, taking the heat so we don't have to take the condemnation that's justly coming our way. As John Stott so wisely pointed out, sin is us substituting ourselves for God, while salvation is God substituting himself for us.[11] And this is the message hidden in Jesus' teaching in Mark 10: "The Son of Man came not to be served but to serve, and to give his life as a ransom for many" (v. 45). Jesus came to our world to do a task. And what was that task? To give his life as a ransom for people. This sums up the reason he had to die. He came as a substitute sacrifice, "a ransom for many."

# CHAPTER 16

## What It Meant:
# THE VICTORY
# OF GOD

I recently sat with a fellow pastor and friend who leads one of the largest churches in Canada. It's comprised of thousands of people and campuses that stretch across different cities and provinces. He asked me for some honest critique, so I looked up from my salad and right away knew my answer. "I've been listening to your churches' sermons online for three years, and you never talk about sin, hell, or the wrath of God; you never talk about the cross or call people to repent of their sin and believe in the crucified and risen Jesus. Why is that?"

He laughed and said, "Because no one wants to hear that stuff anymore—so why drive them away? At least we are talking about Jesus! We try to come at people with a fresh angle because no one wants to hear about a bloodied guy on a cross being punished by his father like some divine cosmic child abuse. No one wants to hear about the 'wrath of God' as if God is angry. We preach about following Jesus instead. Like, we focus on the Gospels versus the Epistles [the books of the New Testament in letter form—most of which were written by Paul]."

Aside from this being a really terrible approach to the New Testament—as if the Gospels and the Epistles present something different or contrary to one another (they don't)—I couldn't help but think of the words of preacher Martyn Lloyd-Jones: "There are many who preach about the Lord Jesus to no effect, and we can see why. They have no doctrine of sin; they never convict or convince people of sin. They always hold Christ before men and say that that is enough.

But it is not enough: for the effect of sin upon us is such that we shall never fly to Christ until we realize that we are poor and helpless."

Sin is what keeps us from having a connection with the God of the universe. Sin is why Jesus paid a price, suffering on the cross. It is what Jesus sets us free from in the resurrection. If we aren't preaching what Jesus did to defeat sin and trusting in what he has done, then we aren't Christians. The atonement for sin is what the cross—and the cross alone—accomplished.

To dig at this further, I asked my friend to explain, in his understanding, the gospel. He smiled and said, "The gospel is his kingdom, discipleship, joining God's program, and the redemption and renewal of creation."

"No." I said. "That is not the gospel."

He laughed, and said, "Check, please!"

I explained, "You're talking about things that are true because the gospel is true. You're talking about the *trajectory* and the *implications* of the gospel, but none of that stuff *is* the gospel. Discipleship, kingdom living, and social justice are *results* of the gospel but not the gospel itself." I wrote on a piece of paper "Means" and "Trajectory." Then I explained. "The means of salvation—in other words, how salvation comes about in a person's life—and the trajectory of salvation—where it goes and what it produces in a person's life—are two different things. Trying to equate them is like saying the solution to a sickness is to get better. It's not. The solution to a sickness is medication or surgery; the trajectory of that working on you is that you get better. Mistaking one for the other can have devastating consequences."

"I would remind you, brothers, of the gospel I preached to you . . . ," Paul said at the end of 1 Corinthians, "For I delivered to you as of first importance what I also received: that Christ died for our sins in accordance with the Scriptures, that he was buried, that he was raised on the third day in accordance with the Scriptures" (15:1–4). That is the gospel. Any talk of discipleship or renewal of creation flows from the cross; it's impossible without the power of Jesus' death for our sins.

Similarly, Reformer Martin Luther identified Romans 3:21–28 as the heart of the entire biblical story: "All have sinned and fall short of the glory of God" (3:23). Jesus had to die because we're sinful and separated from God. We were made in God's image, made to enjoy God's glory and to reflect it in the world. This is the story of Genesis 1–2, of Adam and Eve in the garden walking with God in a perfect and purposeful relationship. But that's just the beginning of the story; because in Genesis 3 they sinned, we bear the consequences of that sin today. They succumbed to the temptation of not being happy with the good God had given them and wanted to be gods themselves. And that same sin is now ingrained in each one of us. It's what the Bible calls a "sinful nature" and psychologists call a "false self."

Luther, in his commentary on the Ten Commandments, pointed out that the first commandment—"Thou shalt have no other gods before me" (Exodus 20:3)—is intentionally first. Not only is it the highest priority, but it is also the one commandment we break every time we break any of the other commandments, every time we sin. For example, whenever we murder or lie or cheat, it is because we are prioritizing ourselves over God. I can't tell you how often people walk up to me, ask if I received an email or text message I have zero recollection of reading, and I say, "Oh yes, it was wonderful, thank you!" What is happening in these moments when I lie? I don't want to look bad. My reputation takes priority over the truth—over trusting that if I am truthful, God will handle the outcome.

In sinning, that original relationship with God was broken. There are all kinds of consequences that come from our being out of sync with the One we were made to be in relationship with, but the most profound may be our detachment from true love. The other day I was reading something inspired by Father Thomas Keating, a Trappist monk in the Cistercian order. He was arguing that as children we all need an appropriate amount of three things for healthy psychological grounding: (1) power and control, (2) affection and esteem, and (3) security and survival. As we mature, we tend to overidentify with one of these programs for happiness and subsequently become spiritually and developmentally sick, or imbalanced.[1]

At the same time I was reading this, I was also reading Genesis 3, and the two ideas came crashing together in an interesting way. I saw how these same basic needs rose to the surface of human desires after the fall. God gave Adam and Eve limited power and control because they weren't mature enough to deal with having all knowledge. He gave them affection and esteem as a good Father and also established this between the two of them. And even after they sinned and fell from his grace, he covered them (security) as they faced the harsh realities of life outside the garden (survival).

Did God abandon them? No. God promised to deal with their sin in what scholars call the *protoevangelium* ("the first gospel"): "I will put enmity between you and the woman," he said to Satan, "and between your offspring and her offspring; he shall bruise your head, and you shall bruise his heel" (Genesis 3:15). God promised there would one day be an offspring of the woman (Christ) who would crush the serpent's head, thereby claiming victory over him and defeating his influence over all of creation. Curiously, this victory would happen in the context of the serpent biting the victor's heel—harming the very person who would destroy him. The destruction of the serpent would happen not only at the same moment as the victor was bit, but in the act of being bit.

Centuries later Paul described this moment in his letter to the Colossians: "By canceling the record of debt that stood against us. . . . This he set aside, nailing it to the cross. He disarmed the rulers and authorities and put them to open shame, by triumphing over them in him" (2:14–15). On the surface, the rulers and authorities of the world appeared to be killing Jesus; however, if you pull back the veil, you see that behind it all was the ancient enemy of the human race, Satan. And at the cross, Satan, sin, and death were being defeated, just as Jesus was dying. The fatal wound from the serpent was also the climactic victory for Jesus. For the serpent's head to be exposed and crushed, however, the offspring had to become exposed as well. Jesus knew this from the beginning. He had to allow evil to do its worst to him if he wished to put it out of commission. And he knew it would hurt.

That's what was happening at the cross.

And God's plan for redeeming people works. It's the only thing that works. The famous psychologist M. Scott Peck pointed this out: "There are dozens of ways to deal with evil [in our lives] and several ways to conquer it. All of them are facets of the truth that the only ultimate way to conquer evil is to let it be smothered within a willing, living human being. When it is absorbed there like blood in a sponge or a spear into one's heart, it loses its power and goes no further. . . . Whenever this happens there is a slight shift in the balance of power in the world."[2] Indeed.

God established the sacrificial system in the Old Testament, instructing the Israelites on exactly how and when to atone for their sin through the shedding of animal blood. In the end, however, these sacrifices were shadows of something that would one day come and do what they could not. They were preparatory. This is what the Passover celebration anticipated and the Lord's Supper remembers. In all four gospels, Jesus went into an upper room with his disciples, scandalously took the most symbolic Jewish meal—the Passover feast—and made it about him. "This is my body [and later my blood] which is given for you. Do this in remembrance of me" (Luke 22:19), he said as he passed the cup for them all to drink. Jesus was giving the ancient meal new meaning, teaching that the Passover had been pointing to him all along. He was the prophet like Moses, leading the people of God on a new exodus and then, not from the slavery of Egypt or the Roman Empire, but from the ancient enemy of sin and death. It is only through him, through faith in what he has accomplished by his death and resurrection, that true freedom can be found.

N. T. Wright says that Jesus didn't go to Jerusalem to preach but to die. Jesus believed that the messianic woes were about to burst upon

Israel as the prophets had said they would in "the day of salvation," and knew that he had to take the curses and condemnation upon himself, suffering for the sins of his people: "In the Temple and the upper room, Jesus deliberately enacted two symbols, which encapsulated his whole work and agenda. The first symbol said: the present system is corrupt. . . . It is ripe for judgment. But Jesus is the Messiah, the One through whom YHWH, the God of the world, will save Israel and thereby the world. And the second symbol said: this is how the true exodus will come about. This is how evil will be defeated. This is how sin will be forgiven."[3]

I met with a woman a short time ago whose husband had cheated on her with their close friend. "What do you most want right now?" I asked her. "I want that woman to suffer. I want him to suffer." In other words, "I want blood." That's how many of us would feel. But we also know that if grace is a thing, we should forgive people when they wrong us, even when they violate the marriage covenant, as hard and gut-wrenching as that may be. We know if life is going to flourish again, forgiveness must take place. But how? Saying, "Just move on" or "Forgive them in your heart," doesn't really work, because a real thing happened that deserves punishment.

Only Christianity provides an explanation as to how forgiveness is possible and justice can be satisfied. The beautiful news is that this woman got her blood. Jesus shed his blood for people who should die for their own sins. I told her, "Jesus shed his blood for your husband and his sins, and as a result he has forgiven him and redeemed him from his sinful way of life if he trusts in Christ." That didn't mean that her marriage could be saved or that any marriage can be saved (it has the potential to be because of Jesus' sacrifice), but whatever the thing was that was going to have to die doesn't have to die anymore because Jesus died in its place. We begin to see how expansive the cross is! Oh, how I cherish its reality for me, for my family, for the world—and for you. Because even if we don't always see it, it solves our deepest need. If God had perceived our deepest need to be entertainment, he would have sent an

entertainer; if he saw it to be economic, he would have sent an econo-
mist; if political, a politician; but he perceived it to be sin and alienation
from him and others, resulting in our death, so he sent a Savior.[4]

## Propitiation

Years ago, theologian J.I Packer wrote "Were I asked to focus the New
Testament message in three words, my proposal would be adoption
through propitiation, and I do not expect ever to meet a richer or more
pregnant summary of the gospel than that."[5] The reason this rings true
is staggering. In the book of Romans, Paul described Jesus as the One
"whom God put forward as a propitiation by his blood" (3:25), and
it was this verse that led the reformer Martin Luther to identify this
text as the center of Christianity. Ironically, this is now, perhaps, the
most neglected view of the cross in the modern church. The reasons
become clear once we understand what *propitiation* means. The word
is used four times in the New Testament (Romans 3:25; Hebrews 2:17;
1 John 2:2; 4:10) and isn't exactly part of our daily vernacular. Many
translations of the Bible interpret the word by explaining it rather than
translating the Greek word, because they want modern readers to
understand what it means. For instance, the NIV interprets it as a "sacrifice of atonement." Unfortunately, that doesn't fully capture what
the word means, only getting at half the idea of propitiation. Yes, we
need a sacrifice to atone for our sins, but this emphasizes the benefit
for us. It's about how the sacrifice travels in our direction.

The second and missing part of this translation emphasizes how
the sacrifice relates to *God*. The word *propitiation* in the ancient
world meant something that satisfied or appeased the wrath of God
(or the gods). It meant something that turned wrath or anger into
favor, making what was harmful into something "propitious" (literally,
"favorable"). When the cross is described as a propitiation, it tells us
God was angry and wrathful because of sin and that anger and wrath
needed to be satisfied.

And now we begin to see why this doctrine is neglected in the modern world. The notion that God is angry and wrathful and will bring judgment on the world is not popular. We prefer to talk about God's love and grace, but even more than that, we bristle against the suggestion that we're somehow accountable before God, deserving of God's anger and judgment. We view ourselves as naive or imperfect but not malicious or evil. Yet this modern sense of the self is directly at odds with the biblical view. Paul, along with other biblical writers, says our natural state is sinful. Jesus said that murder, adultery, slander, and sexual immorality are not pressed upon us by outside forces. Instead, they come from a place we all must own: "out of the heart" (Matthew 15:19). There really is something wrong with us. We stand against God in so many ways that he can't ignore them and they must be dealt with. God's anger against such things is just and right, even evidence of his love. It is God's love for the right, the good, and the beautiful that makes it impossible for him to ignore human sin or sweep it under a rug. Every sin must be dealt with, and God is a true and impartial judge.

A good parent is angry when his or her child misbehaves. Good parents understand that morality is not something that can be left to individual choice. We all tend toward selfishness, and collectively that leads to the evil in this world. A good parent corrects behavior and instills values and a love for what is good, true, and beautiful in a child. The parent who ignores a child's misaligned behavior is the one who is not showing love to that child.

Do you ever get angry? Do you believe in standing against injustice? Do you argue with your spouse? Disagree with your boss? Get frustrated with your kids? We all have an innate sense of justice built within us. A few years ago, I was driving down my road and was about to turn left, when a guy came out of nowhere. He drove up my left side, speeding up as he got nearer, and almost T-boned my car. He could have killed me for sure if I had not swerved off the road at the last second. As soon as he passed me, I turned the car back onto the road, and instead of moving on with my day and thanking the Lord I hadn't been killed, I began to follow him, pressing down hard on my horn—for probably ten minutes straight. Erin was in the car with me yelling, "He is going to kill us! Road rage is a real thing! What are you doing?"

What *was* I doing? Bringing justice into the world! He couldn't get away with what he had done to me! You don't cut *me* off and almost kill me. This deep desire for justice to be done simmers in all of us. It comes from being made in God's image. We get angry when we see injustice because God gets angry when he sees injustice. If your kid gets bullied or made fun of at school, what do you do? You demand justice! You want the bullies to be kicked out of school and their parents brought up on charges! You want blood. And that's you, with all your imperfect knowledge. Imagine what it's like for God, who can see our full intent and knows all the minute details of our selfish hearts. The more you love someone, the *angrier* you're going to be when you see them hurt themselves or others.

Anger and wrath are not the opposite of love; indifference is. God sees the way the world is, and it angers him. If he wasn't filled with love and goodness, he wouldn't care. And if he wasn't angry at the state of the world, he wouldn't be worth worshiping, either. This is where we see the meaning of the cross. Because how can humanity satisfy God's wrath at sin, at the sheer amount of injustice in the world throughout all human history? We get just a taste of God's anger at sin in the legitimate anger of the Old Testament prophets who threatened judgment on Israel and the world. And over and over humankind makes the same mistakes, bringing greater judgment on ourselves as we thumb our noses at God. Even in pagan cultures there was an awareness that sacrifices were necessary, that something had to be done to turn the anger of the gods into favor. We see this in the story of the Old Testament prophet Jonah. A storm was raging, and the men said to Jonah, "Call out to your god! . . . Come, let us cast lots, that we may know on whose account this evil has come upon us" (1:6–7). Once they determined it was Jonah who was the focus of this evil, they said, "What shall we do to you, that the sea may quiet down for us?" Jonah answered honestly: "Pick me up and hurl me into the sea; then the sea will quiet down. . . . So, they picked up Jonah and hurled him into the sea, and the sea ceased from its raging. Then the men offered a sacrifice to the LORD and made vows" (Jonah 1:11–16).

The sense these pagan men had was accurate. When men and women commit moral evils, there is a need for justice, and that justice demands satisfaction. This is what the cross is all about. It's about Jesus going into the depths of human sin and drowning in that ocean so we don't have to, turning God's legitimate anger into favor and bringing calm waters. John put it this way: "Whoever believes in the Son has eternal life; whoever does not obey the Son shall not see life, but the wrath of God remains on him" (John 3:36). Like a tsunami of destruction, the wrath of God is coming, and we can hide behind the cross of Christ and let it hit him in our place, or stand out in the open, hoping to hold our own record up as protection. Spoiler alert: if we choose the latter option, the wave will smash us in its devastating fury.

Some may say, "Yes, I get that I must believe, but I still have doubts!" That's okay. And it's another beautiful part of the Christian gospel. If you reach out and grab a branch as you fall from a cliff while also doubting that the branch can hold you, will it affect whether it can? No. And that's true for faith in the work of Jesus. "It is not the strength of your faith but the object of your faith that saves you. . . . It is not the depth and purity of your heart but the work of Jesus on our behalf that saves us."[6]

The cross challenges everything human beings have developed to secure their own atonement and salvation. And again, the Christian concept of God as a trinity, one being of three persons, is unique. Consider that religions throughout history have sacrificed children to appease the wrath of false gods. Yet God demanded neither our blood nor the blood of *our* children, but instead "put forth" his own Child. What God offers is the opposite of paganism, and it is far from barbaric. God comes himself and sacrifices himself to satisfy his own wrath. He himself pays the debt.

Many times in pastoral counseling I have sat with people who bear the long-term scars—be they physical or emotional—of bad parenting. "My dad hit me." "My mom abandoned us." "Dad's anger fell on me." "I just can't forgive it." So many scenarios causing years of unresolved pain. I get that. It is hard bearing the weight of a bad parent. And children are too young and innocent to bear that weight. My dad was a nightmare. He couldn't keep a job; he was verbally abusive to my mother; he drank too much; and he abandoned my brother and me in our most formative years (I was nine). He died when I was fifteen, without giving us the chance to confront any of his wrongs toward us. I hold them against him still to this day. But I need to recognize the deep reality of the cross. Jesus' Father laid on him the iniquity of *us* all (Isaiah 53:6). Jesus bore not his own sin, but ours—sins laid upon him that he didn't deserve. His Father abandoned him in his weakest, loneliest, and most vulnerable moment. And because that is true, my father, in the end, didn't need to pay for his sins against me. Jesus paid for them on his behalf. Jesus was his sacrifice as much as he was mine, so I need to be willing to let it go. It doesn't happen immediately. It can take time. But it is possible because of the cross.

## Magic Wands and Debt

Recently I was reading *The Jesus Storybook Bible* to my middle daughter, Hayden. We were reading the story of Jesus' crucifixion, and I saw something I'd never considered before. The author, Sally Lloyd-Jones, makes the point that Jesus could have come down from the cross if he had wanted to. After all, he'd fed five thousand people and walked on water. And it dawned on me: What if all those stories of miracles and impossible deeds were a preamble to the real climax? What if they pointed to the cross as the true and better miracle? Maybe all the miracles are recorded to make us appreciate *the cross* that much more. Because it is true—no one *took* Jesus' life from him. He laid it down of his own accord. The only one keeping him on that cross was him.

Skeptics ask, "Why did Jesus have to go to the cross in the first place? Why didn't God just decide that everyone is forgiven, wave a magic wand, and move on?" If you owe a ten-thousand-dollar debt to the bank, there are a couple of things that can happen. You can go in and pay it, or someone else can pay it for you. But one of those two things *must* happen. The bank is not going to hit Delete on your loan with a phone call or wishful thinking, for there is a *real debt* to be paid. It's not a fantasy or an idea. As the saying goes, "There is no free lunch. Somebody has to pay."

On the cross, God offered himself for us. As Herman Bavinck said,

God lays aside his wrath, changes his disposition towards the sinner, forgives the transgressions, and admits him again to his presence and fellowship. And the forgiveness is so perfect that it can be called a blotting out (Isaiah 43:25) . . . or as casting of the sins into the depths of the sea (Micah 7:19). The atonement obliterates the sins so completely that it is as if they never were committed. It banishes wrath and causes God's face to shine upon his people in Fatherly favor and good will.[7]

## Opening the Gift

So God has given us this gift of his Son for our forgiveness. But it doesn't make a difference to us personally unless we take that gift—his promise of forgiveness, salvation, and a new life—and trust him personally. God is "the justifier of the one who has faith in Jesus" (Romans 3:26), Paul said, and so our standing before God is entirely dependent on whether we trust Jesus' work. What he has done and the meaning behind those actions is a gift, but no gift can be enjoyed until it is opened, and we open this gift by believing in faith that what Jesus has done and said is true and real for our lives.

For some of you, the issue might not be whether the gift is real. You may be someone who has heard about the gift, but you don't believe you are worthy of opening it. *My sins are too many. You don't know what I've done. You don't know what I continue to do. You don't know what I keep from my kids, from my spouse, from my boss. I'm a bad person. Jesus' grace isn't flexible enough to accept me with my flaws.* I get that, and I feel the same way sometimes. But I want you to know that Jesus had people like us in mind when he was dying. Because the truth is that none of us are worthy of this gift. That's what grace is all about. It's not just free; it's undeserved.

Consider the people who nearly beat Jesus to death and then crucified him. These were people who literally spat on him, nailed him to the cross, and laughed in his face. What did Jesus say about them? That they would never experience his love? That the cross was for everyone except them? Nope. Are you ready for this? In the face of those horrible people, he said, "Father, forgive them, for they know not what they do" (Luke 23:34). Do you think your sins are worse than spitting in the face of God and laughing as he is tortured and killed? If Jesus Christ could forgive those people at that moment, he can forgive anybody of anything. None of us are worthy. We all have sinned. And that's the beauty of the cross. It's God's undeserved gift.

In *Good Will Hunting*, there's a scene where Robin Williams's character explains to Will that he has spent his whole life pushing away the people who love him in order to save face. He accuses Will of hiding behind his intelligence instead of embracing relationship. And then he presents himself as someone offering to help—a friend. As Will sits and listens in silence, Williams's last line is both haunting and inviting. I leave it with you to consider as it applies to the work of Christ on your behalf.

"Your move, chief."

# PART IX

# The Problem of
# THE
# RESURRECTION

*The dread of something after death, the*
*undiscovered country, from whose bourn no*
*traveler returns.*

—SHAKESPEARE, *HAMLET*

# CHAPTER 17

## The Evidence: Why the Resurrection
# LIKELY DID HAPPEN

Tiger Woods was the greatest player ever to play the game of golf—that is, until injuries, personal scandal, four back surgeries, the loss of his father, loss of his sponsors, and loss of his fans made him unable to play the game that had defined his life. Everything he knew and loved suddenly evaporated. He had no skill. No health. No family. Then, in May 2017, following back-fusion surgery, he was arrested for a DUI with high levels of pain medications in his system. His mug shot went viral—a fitting picture of a life that had fallen from the heights of fame, fortune, and athletic prowess to rock bottom. Every major sports commentator agreed that Tiger would never win another PGA golf tournament.

When asked in multiple interviews if Woods could ever again challenge today's golf superstars, analyst Brandel Chamblee, did not mince words: "No, is the short answer. Tiger's competitive career is over . . . the body, the technique, the psychological, the scandal, the chipping yips. Nobody comes back from anything like what Tiger is trying to come back from. . . . If you do an internet search of the greatest sports comebacks from injury, you'll get a litany of injuries. The one thing you will not get is a bad back followed by great athletic achievement." Tiger had always chased his idols Jack Nicklaus and Sam Snead. Nicklaus held the most major championship titles (eighteen), and Snead the most tour wins (eighty-two). Of all the records Tiger had dreamed of breaking since he was a little boy chipping around the house, these were the only two he cared about. He was so close, but he had not accomplished his dream. On the day of his arrest, he had won fourteen majors and seventy-nine tour wins.

Shane Ryan wrote a piece for *Golf Digest* in July 2015 titled "Tiger Woods Is Totally, Completely, Unequivocally, and Utterly Done," which conveyed what most of the world, and anyone who followed golf, really believed: "Is Tiger Woods done?" he asked. "Today I am pleased to report that I have a definitive answer. Yes. Tiger Woods is finished. . . . Tiger Woods being done is a metaphysical truth. There will never be another moment, from now until the sun burns up the earth . . . when Tiger Woods will be a good golfer again. . . . If there is a golfer in the future who wins 15 majors, he will beat Tiger Woods by exactly one major. Tiger Woods is done."[1]

And yet I am writing the words of this chapter the day after Tiger Woods has just won his fifteenth major championship, the 2019 Masters Tournament. At the time of this writing, he has also tied Sam Snead's record of eighty-two tour wins.

Simply amazing. You could almost call it a miracle.

Woods's return to golf is being called the "greatest comeback in sports history." Every major newspaper across North America carried the story of his Masters win on the front page. Twenty-three percent of American televisions that were on during Masters Sunday in 2019 were tuned in to see if Tiger could do it. And he did. The story yesterday was "Tiger is done." The story today is "Tiger is back." I cried like a baby as I watched him walk up the eighteenth fairway, and then cried again when he clutched his kids after the win. An ESPN video about Tiger's fight to come back—produced before the Masters—put it perfectly: "Honestly, anyone *not* going for him this week is broken inside. It might sound strange, but he *deserves* to win. He deserves at least one more major."

Why would someone say this? No one in the context of sports

*deserves* to win. We all know they have to earn it. But everybody loves a comeback story. It's part of being human, something hardwired into our psyche. We connect to stories of success, to be sure, but we connect even more to those who achieve success after tasting failure in an emotional, visceral way. We cheer for the person who rises out of it, climbing out of hell one inch at a time. Even more than wanting a perfect hero, we want heroes who have come up *through* pain and defeat to arrive out the other side. They have the scars to show for it.

In *The Last Jedi*, there is a scene where Yoda offers a lesson in leadership to a frustrated, tired, and failed Luke Skywalker:

> **Luke:** I'm ending all of this. The tree, the text, the Jedi. I'm
> going to burn it down. . . . It is time for the Jedi Order
> to end.
> **Yoda:** Time it is. For you to look past a pile of old books. . . .
> Skywalker, still looking to the horizon. Never here, now,
> hmm? The need in front of your nose.
> **Luke:** I was weak. Unwise . . . I can't be what she needs me
> to be.
> **Yoda:** Heeded my words not, did you? Pass on what you
> have learned. Strength, mastery. But weakness, folly,
> failure also. Yes, failure most of all. The greatest teacher,
> failure is. Luke, we are what they grow beyond. That is
> the true burden of all masters.

To teach and be a true Jedi master, one must pass on the lessons of failure. How do you struggle through deep pain and come out the other side better and stronger, ready to take on the world? We connect to this at a soul level, whether it is Luke Skywalker or Tiger Woods, because God has written this story on our hearts. Why? Because in creating us he knew he would one day come and fulfill that longing for bringing victory from the jaws of defeat in the death and subsequent resurrection of his Son, Jesus.

## That Time I Tried to Drown Myself

I first encountered the reality of death when I was eight years old. We had a cat named Scooter who got sick, and I overheard my parents saying they were going to "put him down." *Put him down?* What was that? Didn't sound good.

So I ran out of the cottage we were staying at and ran straight into the lake. I then began to repeatedly dunk my head into the water in an attempt to drown myself in protest. My family walked out to see what I was doing and then quickly grew bored and headed back inside. After about ten minutes of demonstrating my objections this way, I gave up and went in for dinner. A couple of days later, Scooter was dead.

My second run-in with death was my own father. As I shared earlier, my parents had divorced when I was a kid. One day, at the age of fifteen, I received a phone call from the hospital telling me my father had died from lung cancer. He was forty-seven years old. I stood over his casket and asked myself the deep questions of life, realizing I didn't have any answers.

Both of these experiences brought me to the same harsh realization: death is final. It's irreversible. This past week I conducted a funeral for a fifty-eight-year-old man, and as I stood over his open casket, I found that my brain had a difficult time accepting that he was dead. I half expected him to sit up and start talking to me as he had so many times before. Our eyes see the face of a deceased loved one, and we don't have a category that explains why the lips aren't moving and the lungs aren't expanding. We struggle to grasp the concept that *life* just isn't there anymore. And that's why we cry and mourn. Studies show that the thing we miss most about someone once they have died is their *presence*. Their seat at the dinner table is no longer occupied. Their side of the bed is empty, the bedcovers still pulled up over the pillow. The house is quieter.

Christianity has something amazing to say about the finality and the hopelessness of death. Of all the problems raised by the person of Jesus that we have explored in this book, the problem of death and the promise of Jesus may be the most important—because Jesus offers us something truly unbelievable: hope. And more than just an extension of life as we know it, eternal hope. A deep hope that gives us life and reverses the tragedy of death in the most beautiful way.

God lost his own Son—maybe some of you reading these pages have faced that loss yourself. A close friend had a son who was hit by a car and killed as a young teen. Another had a son who was shot and killed in a case of mistaken identity while housesitting. The stories of loss are endless. Almost too much for the heart to bear.

How do those who have suffered the death of a loved one still find strength to get up in the morning? For those who believe Christianity is true, it's easier. The faith we have talked about in this book is not sentimental or something they cling to as a crutch. They had already believed in the truth of Christianity and the unique way it embraces suffering because they had studied it and come to see the person of Jesus and his work as legitimate. And that belief led to real trust in the word of Jesus—his promise of future resurrection. It put steel in their spine and helped them face the day as the world collapsed around them. More than any other religion or worldview, Christianity is founded on hope. We believe this life—and death—is not the end. As Tolkien wonderfully said, everything "sad is going to come untrue." The irreversible can be reversed. Christianity says this without slipping into either sentimentalism ("I don't want to face the hardships of real life") or cold logic ("The resurrection is for study by biblical scholars—it doesn't apply to me"). The Christian life is both historic facts and life-changing personal application. Or to put it another way, Christianity is not only true, it is the most hopeful option in the marketplace of ideas. And that's all because of the resurrection of Jesus from the dead.

## Why You Should Picket My Church on Easter

I am a pastor, and this means that every Easter Sunday I preach about the resurrection of Jesus to a roomful of people, some of whom were brought (or sometimes dragged) to church by family or friends. Our church attendance is usually 25 percent greater on Easter Sunday, and I always end up saying the same thing: that I want them to understand the *scandal* of Jesus' resurrection. You see, while I'm glad they woke up, put on their nice pants, and stopped by before heading over to Aunt Marge's for a turkey, if the resurrection is real, it should change everything. It's the single most important event in history and should lead all of us to entirely rethink our lives. There are only two plausible and acceptable reactions to the resurrection. We can picket the church because the resurrection is a lie and the celebration is a waste of time, or we can accept that it is true and give our lives entirely over to Jesus. As C. S. Lewis said, "Christianity, if false, is of no importance, and if true, of infinite importance. The only thing it cannot be is moderately important." The resurrection can never be a nice suburban tradition. It's not an easy, comfortable, and pleasant truth that allows a nod and a yawn. Easter is a scandal—a real problem for us—from start to finish.

I didn't always believe Jesus' resurrection was true. As I said, I didn't walk into a church until I was nineteen years old, and even then I only stayed because there were pretty girls around. I am someone who only believes things when I have the necessary evidence for them. So when someone presented Christianity to me as a teenager, I wanted to know more. What was the evidence for it? How was it different from other worldviews? How was it better than the atheism or agnosticism I currently accepted, or the Hindu or Wiccan religions my friends practiced? At first I thought the conversation was about what Jesus taught in comparison to what those religions taught. I figured Christians were trying to say that Jesus had better ideas and was a better teacher than Muhammad or Buddha. But the more I studied, the more I realized that this wasn't just about teachings or concepts. It was about something that happened: a historical moment that, if proven false, meant the entire belief system fell apart. And I found this fascinating. It made Christianity vulnerable but also unique among the other options.

Buddhism and Hinduism, for example, are *otherworldly*. They are about "states of consciousness" and "enlightenment"—metaphysical, abstract, spiritual teachings. Judaism and Islam center around the study and practice of *law* (the Torah, the Mishnah, and the Qu'ran respectively). These religions are about living according to a particular interpretation of authoritative texts and teachings. And while Christianity has aspects of the otherworldly and the practice of law, ultimately it all comes down to an event—a verifiable moment in history. Christianity could not survive if it was only about Jesus' teachings, as good as those are. Even his death, as heroic as that was, could not sustain the faith by itself. It's a good example of sacrifice, but it becomes a sad and tragic story if you take out the resurrection. Jesus had plenty of good years ahead of him, and he could have used that time to accomplish great things.

Today you can visit the tomb for the founders of almost every major religion. You can visit the grave site for Abraham in Hebron, Palestine. Thousands of people visit the tomb of Buddha every year in India and the burial place of Muhammad in Medina. I spent thousands of dollars and flew halfway around the world to visit the tomb where people think Jesus was buried, and guess what. It was empty!

But it was a beautiful emptiness.

Christianity is vulnerable, because if a person were to find the bones of Jesus, we would have proof that Christianity is wrong. More than "not quite accurate," it would be fully wrong—a colossal error. And I'm not the only one to say this. The apostle Paul came to the same conclusion. He said that if the resurrection didn't happen, Christians are the most pitiful people on earth (1 Corinthians 15:17–19). Why? Because they are fools who have staked their lives on a lie. You can't say, "Yeah, but there are still so many other great ideas within Christianity that we should keep being Christians." No. The whole thing is built on a moment that either happened or it didn't.

Even if you haven't accepted that Christianity is true yet, I hope you find something intriguing about that. I do. Other religions have little vulnerability. They don't put their claims out there for you to test. They play it safe. But Christianity is confident that the resurrection really happened. It goes all in and bets all the chips on a historical event—a miracle. It invites historians, scientists, philosophers, and regular Joes to investigate it. Because Christians know that when they do, what they find will change everything. We know that when they do, they will come face-to-face with the answer of all answers—Jesus really did rise from the dead! And if that is true, it vindicates and validates everything God says about himself, the world, and you and me.

This is why Christianity is "good *news*." It's not fake news; it's about something that happened—a reported event. And it's not asking our opinion. It's like listening to the six o'clock news and learning there is a car accident on your route home from work. The anchor isn't giving you the information in order to get your thoughts or see how you feel about it. He is reporting what happened. *This happened, and because it happened, you should take a different route home.*

## The Resurrection

Not only does the historical evidence point to the death of Jesus, but it also points to his resurrection from the dead. Various people throughout history have claimed to see dead people. For the most part, we chalk this up to eating some bad pizza or being delusional. When I began looking at the claim of the resurrection as a skeptic, the question that pressed on me was, *Why did anyone start believing this about Jesus in the first place?* Why did anyone write it down (and why didn't it get challenged?) Why did a whole group of people claiming to be "eyewitnesses" declare they saw the resurrected Jesus? Why were they willing to die for it? Why did they start an entire movement with this as the central claim at the cost of their own lives? We know all of these to be historical facts. So *why* did Christianity become a movement if the founder was killed after three years of teaching?

There must have been something more, something other than

the teachings of Jesus and an invitation to live a good, moral life. Something grabbed ahold of these men and women to convince them that Jesus was worth the risk. This "something" couldn't have been his death alone, because others had died after making the same messianic claims without inciting the same world-changing movement. If you study the hundred years on either side of the life of Jesus, you'll find that several Jewish teachers claimed to be the Messiah: movements grew up around them, Rome killed them as revolutionaries, and then one of two things happened. In some cases, the movement died. Everyone went home sad and defeated. In other cases, someone else took the supposed Messiah's place, usually a brother or cousin, to carry on the work. But here is what *never* happened. No one else ever claimed that their leader was now *alive again*, had appeared to his followers, and continued to teach and urge his followers to carry on his mission in his name. That's just crazy.

And that's why Christianity is such a scandal. It is also why scholars, both conservative and liberal, agree that the resurrection claims of the early church are legitimate. The claims are unprecedented; no one's worldview was set up to say or believe what the early church professed. Nothing suggests that a movement would arise based on a claim that a person would rise from the dead. In fact, the beliefs of the ancient world actually countered that idea. In the ancient world, there was Judaism and paganism (which, from a Jew's perspective, was everything outside Judaism). To the pagan mind, there was no such thing as resurrection. The Greco-Roman worldview, influenced by Plato and Homer, held that there was a spirit world (the world of Plato's forms—the most influential idea in the history of philosophy) and a physical world. The spirit world was seen as perfect, pure, and good, and was filled with beauty, truth, and pleasure. In contrast, the physical world was seen as "fleshly," destructive, limiting, and filled with pain, death, and sadness. The whole point of life was to graduate from this world—"to shuffle off this mortal coil," as Shakespeare put it—and proceed into a world of disembodied spiritual bliss: "Popular opinion would attempt to bring the dead back if that were possible, but this would be a mistake . . . [for death was] seen as something to be desired. . . . The reason people do not return . . . is that life is so good [in the spirit world]; they want to stay, rather than return to the world of space, time and matter."[2]

In one of Aeschylus's stories, *The Eumenides*, Apollo makes this clear: "Once a man has died, and the dust has soaked up his blood, there is no resurrection." Resurrection was derided as something bad or wrong in pagan thought and was not permitted, even in myth. When Apollo tries to bring a child back from death, Zeus punishes him with a thunderbolt (Pindar, *Pythian Odes*, 3:1–60). According to the pagan world, not only did resurrection not happen, but no one wanted it to.

Judaism had a different view, but it, too, was unlikely to lead to the claims of the early Christians. The Jews believed resurrection was going to happen, but at the end of time. And even then it was going to be a collective, not just an individual, event. That is, the whole nation of Israel would be resurrected on the last day. They thought in terms of national movements (think of the blessing and cursing of Deuteronomy 31–33). One day, at the end of time, God would judge the world and resurrect Israel to a new world of eternal life and blessing, and everyone else to eternal judgment and punishment (Ezekiel 36–37; Daniel 12:1–3).

Judaism said resurrection would happen to a large nation of people at the end of time, and paganism said that even if it could happen, they wouldn't want it to! This is why N. T. Wright has said, "Christianity was born into a world where its central claim was known to be false," or as I am arguing, unwanted.[3] It didn't fit into anyone's paradigm. Even in the gospel stories, we find the disciples skeptical of the resurrection. They arrive at the tomb, and their first reaction is to assume that someone must have moved or stolen Jesus' body. As Craig Blomberg points out, "Stories of resurrections are actually comparatively rare and can take various forms, including metaphors.

But nowhere in any ancient mythology or folklore do we ever find even the claim that an indisputably human individual who died within the living memory of others was raised bodily, much less seen in physical form on many different occasions by hundreds, who then boldly and widely spread the word about the experiences among their contemporaries."[4]

This odd claim is an anomaly—a challenge to the thinking of the ancient world. And as I began to understand how unlikely it was for Christianity to have developed and spread, I began to explore its legitimacy in the early days of my spiritual journey. The deeper I looked, the more I found.

So much more.

## Evidence and Objections

Let's consider five types of evidence for the resurrection.

- The *medical* and *historical* evidence that Jesus really did die. Given who he was and how good Romans were when it came to killing, we should reject the claim that he just "swooned" in and out of consciousness and then woke up later.
- The evidence of the *missing body*. A body should have been easy to find (and Rome would have wanted to).
- The evidence of the *appearances*. Hundreds of people claimed to have seen the resurrected Jesus after his death (1 Corinthians 15:1–5).
- The evidence of the *empty tomb*, with the *grave clothes*.
- The evidence of the *rise of the early church*. The growth of the Christian movement was historically unprecedented in its fervor and speed.

Admittedly, none of these by themselves proves anything, nor are they sufficient in arguing for the resurrection. An empty tomb, for instance, might simply confirm the age-old practice of grave robbery. But when we consider all of these evidences together, we have "a sufficient condition" for the emergence of the early Christian belief that Jesus really did rise from the dead.[5] This is what historians do. They evaluate the evidence and see where it points—inferring the best explanation through inductive reasoning.[6] And what they find here is that this fascinating, crazy claim fits in exactly where the evidence of history leads.

Throughout history there has been great skepticism regarding the resurrection. I'll touch on a couple of popular challenges or objections raised against it. For anyone wanting further information on this topic, I explore several of these resurrection challenges in depth in my earlier book, *The Problem of God*.

## OBJECTION 1: JESUS DIDN'T REALLY DIE

Most scholars and historians write off this suggestion outright. Trusted first-century historians tell us that Jesus was killed.[7] When scholars consider the historical context of the Roman Empire and the way the Romans treated criminals, they conclude that the idea that Jesus just passed out and walked away from his crucifixion is untenable. After all, if there was one thing the Romans knew how to do, it was kill people! Remember, crucifixion was a very common practice. These soldiers didn't put guys up on crosses and take them down only to have them head home a few days later. Jesus didn't wake up, dust himself off like some kind of Monty Python scene ("*Whoa. That was close*"), and then just walk away. The idea that the Romans messed up the killing of Jesus does not hold up under historical scrutiny.

## OBJECTION 2: THE BODY WAS STOLEN

Perhaps Jesus' disciples were involved in an elaborate hoax and stole Jesus' body. This isn't an original idea—as I mentioned above, it was the first thing the disciples themselves thought when told that Jesus had been raised. "They have taken the Lord out of the tomb, and we don't know where they have put him!" Mary said to a roomful of disciples after she saw the empty tomb (John 20:2). If you are slow to believe that Jesus was raised from the dead, then you are in good company. That's what the disciples first believed!

Four factors lead historians and critics to conclude that the resurrection narratives are legitimate.

- *Multiple attestations.* The Gospels alongside multiple New Testament letters all relate the story with various levels of detail.
- *Dissimilarity.* The differences between the resurrection stories in the Gospels (such as the number of angels at the tomb) speak to the fact that the writers didn't get together and make sure that their stories were exactly the same, but wrote them as they wanted to write them, as eyewitnesses telling their side of the story.
- *Embarrassment.* The accounts include counterproductive content that would have made the early church look bad.
- *Coherence.* The four independent accounts establish certain shared facts: the empty tomb, the appearances, and the disciples' belief that Jesus was raised from the dead.[8]

## Women and a Homicide Detective

In addition, the Gospels tell us that women were the key eyewitnesses to the resurrection. If the early church was making up a story, they didn't choose the best witnesses to convince people their story was true! In that culture women were not even allowed to testify in a court of law because their testimony was considered untrustworthy. Josephus wrote, "Let not the testimony of women be admitted, on account of the levity and boldness of their sex."[9] Women were treated as second-class citizens in first-century culture, yet amazingly, in all the resurrection narratives in the Gospels, the first people to arrive at the empty tomb and serve as witnesses to the resurrection are women.

Lastly, and perhaps most convincing, is the need to explain why the disciples would create such an elaborate hoax and then be willing to die for it. Lots of people die for lies they think are true. But who dies for a lie they know isn't true—for something they made up? As E. P. Sanders asks, "Without the resurrection, would Jesus' disciples have endured longer than did John the Baptist's? We can only guess, but I would guess not."[10] The historian is forced to some interesting questions. "We must ask," says Wright, "why and how did the early disciples, shattered as they had been by the crucifixion of their master, regroup and go out and face persecution for declaring that in him the hope of Israel had quite literally come to life? Why did they organize themselves and act in the way that they did, and why did they begin very early on to worship Jesus, and to include him in Jewish-style monotheistic formulae? . . . There were no other groups in the ancient world [doing so]." The answer, Wright says, has to do "with the belief that Jesus had been raised from the dead; the historian is bound to ask whether we are forced to reject [this answer]."[11]

J. Warner Wallace, an ex-homicide detective, points out that when you are looking for the real explanation for what happened in a situation like the resurrection, or a murder, you must always resist conspiracy theories because true conspiracies are rare. They are extremely hard to pull off. He says successful conspiracies share a few common characteristics: a small number of conspirators, thorough and immediate communication, and little-to-no pressure applied on the people or the story. None of these characteristics apply to Christianity and the resurrection. Jesus appeared to more than five hundred people after his resurrection, who then spread the news widely. The early church possessed no way to quickly communicate among those people. And the highest level of pressure was applied to discourage them from sharing this news—torture and murder. Based on the best historical evidence we have, here is what happened to the original disciples of Jesus: Andrew was crucified in Patras, Greece; Bartholomew (aka Nathaniel) was flayed to death with a whip in Armenia; James the Just was thrown from the temple and then beaten to death in Jerusalem; John died in exile on the island of Patmos; James the Greater was beheaded in Jerusalem; Luke was hanged in Greece; Mark was dragged to death by a horse in Alexandria, Egypt; Matthew was killed by the sword in Ethiopia; Matthias was stoned and then beheaded in Jerusalem; Peter was crucified upside down in Rome; Philip was crucified in Phrygia; Thomas was stabbed to death with a spear in India.

The rise of the early church is a phenomenon that baffles historians. Overnight a group of poor peasants started to claim something completely against their own worldview, something they were willing to die for. Christianity grew from a group of twelve disciples to over thirty-three million people in just 350 years, and by AD 400 more than half of the entire population of the Roman Empire were Christians.[12] Why did it grow so fast? People saw Christianity as life-changing and legitimate. Jesus' followers died *because* they claimed that they had seen Jesus rise from the dead. They were persecuted and tortured and told to recant this claim, but they refused. They weren't dying for a set of metaphorical religious teachings or "principles of life" taught to them by a dead sage but for what they knew had happened to Jesus *after* he died. If Jesus really rose again, then everything he taught was vindicated. It was true! His teachings were an anchor of hope, especially his promises of eternal life. As Jesus said to his followers, "Whoever believes in me, though he die, yet shall he live, and everyone who lives and believes in me shall never die" (John 11:25–26). His followers took this promise to heart. They weren't afraid of being sawn in half, stretched apart, thrown to the lions in gladiatorial arenas, or stoned to death in the street. They never recanted their testimonies, and that conviction, courage, and hope caused the gospel to spread very quickly in the ancient world.[13] The most skeptical critic must posit some mysterious X factor to get the movement going. The New Testament claims that X factor is the resurrection. As C. F. D Moule of Cambridge concluded, the birth and rise of the church remains an unsolved mystery for any historian who refuses to take seriously the only explanation offered by the church itself.[14]

# CHAPTER 18

# Our Own Resurrection,
# IN THIS LIFE
# AND THE NEXT

Not everybody believes in the resurrection, of course. People generally fall into one of two camps when it comes to the question of Jesus rising from death: celebration or skepticism. We see both in the resurrection account in John 20. Many people are like John and Peter—they see, believe, and celebrate it (John 20:4–10). Others, however, are like Mary and Thomas—they hear of the empty tomb, immediately doubt it, and try to come up with alternative explanations (John 20:13–15, 25). The early church wasn't composed of a bunch of naive, myth-believing, ancient simpletons who didn't know any better. When Mary heard the claim that Jesus had risen from the dead, she didn't say, "Okay, great! Let's start a new religion!" She pushed back: "They have taken the Lord out of the tomb, and we do not know where they have laid him" (John 20:2).

It's funny that modern skeptics think they have come up with smart, alternative explanations to the empty tomb of Jesus by saying that people came and stole the body, when we literally see that this is the explanation of the first woman who walked into the empty tomb. "Someone must have stolen the body. That's what my logic tells me."

She didn't get it, so God sent some angels to dissolve her skepticism. That didn't work, so Jesus himself showed up, and she pushed back against him too (John 20:15). This woman was anything but gullible. And later the disciple Thomas also refused to believe: "Unless I see in his hands the mark of the nails, and place my finger into the mark of the nails, and place my hand into his side, I will never believe" (20:25). One thing caused both of these skeptics to become believers in Jesus: seeing him. Jesus appeared to Mary and spoke with her; eight days after Thomas declared he would never believe, Jesus appeared to him. It's as if Jesus knew that every skeptic reading these words would demand proof before believing. And once Thomas finally proclaimed his faith, Jesus said these beautiful and haunting words: "Have you believed because you have seen me? Blessed are those who have not seen and yet have believed" (John 20:29).

## What All This Has to Do with Us

But what does this have to do with us? The Bible offers a robust and important answer to that question. In the resurrection, Jesus is "revealed to be the Son of God" (i.e., the King/the Messiah; Romans 1:4). The "gospel climax, the theological point that receives the most emphasis in the Bible's own descriptions of the gospel, is that *Jesus is the Christ, the king.*"[1] This is only true because the resurrection is true. And the Christian life is presented as a life given over to Jesus, not just to a "belief" that he existed or that he said what the Bible records him as saying. Giving your life to Christ means *obedience to him as King.*

The reality of the resurrection means that everything Jesus said is true. His statements about reality are correct. His insights into the human condition are accurate. His predictions and promises are trustworthy. As we set our faith on the rock of the resurrection, our "faith" *in* him and "faithfulness" *to* him (Revelation 2:13) defines our lives. Without it we would still be in our sins (1 Corinthians 15:3–58). This is why we can say the resurrection (along with the cross) was God's means of saving us and setting us free. Jesus "was raised for our justification" (Romans 4:25), and through it we are united with Christ (Romans 6:5) and raised with him in the present (Colossians 2:12). In other words, Bavinck was right when he contended,

The benefits of Christ would never reach us if he had not been raised from the dead. . . . A Jesus who died would be enough for us if Christianity were nothing more than a doctrine for us to grasp with our mind, or a moral prescription and example to follow. But [it] is something very different and much more than that. . . . His work is not done at the point of his death and burial. . . . What good would a treasure of valuables do us if it remained always beyond our reach and was never put into possession? What good would a Christ do us, who had died, for our sins, but who had never been raised for our justification?[2]

Of course, the question is rhetorical. There would be no benefit to a dead Christ. The gateway to the benefits of the work of Christ in his life and death is the resurrection. It is this foundational event that provides the way into the Christian life and life in the Spirit. "The Spirit of him who raised Jesus from the dead dwells in you" (Romans 8:11).

## You Only Live Twice

The resurrection is not something that just happens to Jesus; it is something that will be experienced—at some point in the future—by everyone who has ever lived. We will experience the resurrection in one of two ways: unto *life* or unto *judgment* (John 5:28–29). The resurrection unto judgment is the experience of those who don't trust in Jesus for salvation. They are bodily raised to live the rest of eternity in the context of spiritual death, at a distance from goodness, pleasure, community, God, love, and grace. The resurrection "unto life" is bodily life in the presence of God and his new creation: a life of love, grace, peace, delight, community, and pleasures forevermore.

Our lives today and everything we do with them will echo in eternity. If we ignore the reality that Jesus rose from death and fail to embrace the promised hope God offers, we remain on a trajectory set in motion by the first human sin. Our lives will be cut off from the future purposes of God, serving as a reminder of his justice. Those who remain in their sin will be engulfed by emotional and spiritual pain. If you trust what Jesus has done and shape your whole life around it, everything good you have done and are doing will be invested in what the Bible calls a "new heaven and new earth" (Revelation 21–22). You will live in a resurrected, glorified state for all eternity.

J. R. R. Tolkien was often accused of writing "escapist" literature, stories that enabled people to forget the real world. His answer to the charge was always the same: it depends on that from which one is escaping! We view the flight of a deserter and the escape of a prisoner differently. "Why should a man be scorned if, finding himself in prison, he tries to get out and go home?" The hope of Christianity is not a vague spiritual bliss in a disembodied world. You may have thought about heaven in this way and wondered why you can't get an appetite for it—it sounds like a prison or a real snooze fest! The spiritual vision of heaven in the clouds is not something that inspires us because we were not made for that kind of life. You and I were made *physical*, for life in this material world God created, and God intends to keep it that way in a better version of what we currently know and experience.

That is what you innately feel inside yourself. And the resurrection of Jesus is the historic proof that this place, that state of pure love and joy, actually exists. "In my Father's house are many rooms. If it were not so, would I have told you that I go to prepare a place for you? And If I go and prepare a place for you, I will come again and will take you to myself, that where I am you may be also," Jesus said (John 14:2–3). The promise of Jesus changes everything, if it is true, and the resurrection is the proof that Jesus will keep his promise. That is why the early church could die without cowardice and fear, and why you can face death in the same way.

All of you reading this have stories to tell of lost loved ones, battles with sickness and cancer. Even if you don't believe the resurrection is true, I'd argue that you should want it to be. Why? Because it presents the vision our hearts long for, a life beyond sickness and pain and sadness. There is life beyond car accidents and lung disease and tumors. This life we live today is not the end. If you trust in Jesus, not even your death is the end. "I am the resurrection and the life," Jesus said. "Whoever believes in me, though he die, yet shall he live" (John 11:25). That is the great hope of the Bible.

Our culture's mantra, "You only live once" (YOLO) is wrong. You live twice. We live once, temporally, for seventy or eighty years. Then we die, spend some time in an intermediate place—paradise or hades—and then we experience resurrection, the start of a second life, or what one scholar calls "life after life after death."[3] Some will rise to "eternal punishment," but the righteous to "eternal life" (Matthew 25:46). D. L. Moody's words will certainly hold true: "One day you will read in the paper that I am dead. Don't believe it for a second, for in that moment, I will be more alive than I have ever been."

Years ago, C. S. Lewis pointed out that the New Testament talks far more about what the resurrection means for our lives than simply documenting that it happened to Jesus. The biblical documents that dive into what the resurrection means (the New Testament letters) were written first, many years before the Gospels themselves. "The miracle of the Resurrection, and the theology of that miracle, comes first: the biography comes later as comment on it"[4] Lewis said. I think there is something to that. Lewis went on to say,

> When modern writers talk of the Resurrection they usually mean one particular moment—the discovery of the Empty Tomb and the appearances of Jesus . . . . The Story of that moment is what Christian [defenders] now chiefly try to support and sceptics chiefly try to impugn. But this almost exclusive concentration on the first five minutes or so of the Resurrection would have astonished the earliest Christian teachers. . . . The Resurrection to which they bore witness was, in fact, not the action of rising from the dead but *the state of having risen*.[5]

The resurrection is an event, but it is also *who Jesus is now*. And that reality—that Jesus is alive right now as you are reading this book—demands a response from every person. What should we do about that? Jesus was not just a man resurrected two thousand years ago; he is the resurrected Lord and the ascended King. He *was* a thirty-year-old, poor Jewish peasant two millennia ago, but he isn't that today. No longer is he a victim of death and torture; he is now the victorious and risen King. Revelation tells us that he has complete control of the universe, he knows all and sees all, and is perfect in all his ways, ruling over all things at all times and bringing God's purposes in creation to completion at the appointed time (Revelation 1:12–20).

If the resurrection is true, it was the beginning of something new—a new creation. A new chapter opened up in the universe. Cosmic history, yes, but also a new chapter for Jesus. After his resurrection, he spent several weeks teaching his disciples and preparing them for his departure. He returned to the glory he once had, but in a different mode than he once had it, as the human ruler of God's universe. Upon taking his position on God's throne, he poured out the greatest gift ever given, the very Spirit of God, his gift to the church, his bride. And the Bible records the ongoing acts of Jesus through his church, demonstrating that though Jesus left our world, he is still present and actively involved in the day-to-day affairs, ordering all that happens according to God's purposes, until the day he returns.

The resurrection of Jesus means we, as human beings, don't need to keep flailing and floundering under the burden of religion. We don't need to keep setting the fires so the gods will relent, or make the trek, or set out on the pilgrimage so we can earn our way. Jesus fell and stumbled with a cross on his back for us. Religion crushed him so it wouldn't have to crush us. The fire was kindled and directed toward him on the cross, and God's anger was satisfied. He made the trek down a dusty road with a beam on his back in our place. He took the ultimate pilgrimage for us, down from heaven to earth and back, so we wouldn't ever have to.

Christianity says God came down the mountain to us. And his coming introduces a new way of life for those who will receive his words and his gift of God's Spirit. "Just as Christ was raised from the dead by the glory of the Father, we too might walk in newness of life," Paul said (Romans 6:4). The resurrection was about Jesus, yes, and about God, yes, and about how he was reconciling the world to himself, yes, but it is also about us. It is about you walking and living in a new way. Temptations and identities that once ruled us and ruined us may still be there, but they no longer control our lives, our marriages, and our money. Lies we once told ourselves dissipate in the light of new truths. Relationships once thought dead and gone can blossom again. Sickness can be overcome. Guilt banished. Shame buried, left behind like grave clothes.

Christianity is not a story of lives being unmade; it's about lives being remade. This event in Jesus' life has everything to do with us. It means something. It means we can be free. It means the things we blame ourselves for, the weight on our souls, can be buried in Christ. It means we live on the other side of death and powerlessness. It means all of this for those who trust Jesus as their Lord, Savior, and treasure, both in the present and in the future. "What is sown is perishable; what is raised is imperishable. It is sown in dishonor; it is raised in glory. It is sown in weakness; it is raised in power" (1 Corinthians 15:42–43).

There is a new way to be human. Such is the hope, and the future adventure, of Christianity. And it's why we can wake up tomorrow and face the day, even when those we love may not. That dark day two thousand years ago can only be called Good because of what happened on the following Sunday morning, an event that gives us a tantalizing clue to the riddle of the universe and life itself. Author Philip Yancey reminds us that our whole lives are lived, in a sense, on that Saturday before, "the in-between day with no name." Right now, today, as we live, it's Saturday on planet Earth, and when we decide to follow the crucified and risen Jesus, our lives reflect something interesting out to that world. We begin a new day and have a completely different perspective on everything, including the pain and trials of life in a Saturday world. We are looking forward to the next great event that we know is coming, because the last great event has already happened. Jesus rose, and he is coming again, and this is the truth that gets us out of bed in the morning. It helps us smile when there is nothing to smile about and gives us hope in the face of death itself. Yancey concludes his book on Jesus with these words: "I know a woman whose grandmother lies buried under 150-year-old live oak trees in the cemetery of an Episcopal church in rural Louisiana. In accordance with the grandmother's instructions, only one word is carved on her tombstone: "Waiting."[6]

Indeed.

# Notes

## INTRODUCTION

1. Mark Buchanan, *Your God Is Too Safe: Rediscovering the Wonder of a God You Can't Control* (Colorado Springs: Multnomah, 2001), 33.

2. C. S. Lewis, *Mere Christianity* (London: Collins, 1952), 54–56.

## CHAPTER 1: DID JESUS REALLY EXIST?

1. John Gray, *Seven Types of Atheism* (New York: Farrar, Strauss and Giroux, 2018), 14–15.

2. Bertrand Russell, *Why I Am Not a Christian and Other Essays* (New York: Simon and Schuster, 1957), 16.

3. Gerald Massey, quoted in Tom Harpur, *The Pagan Christ: Recovering the Lost Light* (Toronto: Thomas Allen, 2004), 20.

4. N. T. Wright, *Jesus and the Victory of God*, Christian Origins and the Question of God, vol. 2 (Minneapolis: Fortress, 1996), xvi.

5. Bart D. Ehrman, *Did Jesus Exist? The Historical Argument for Jesus of Nazareth* (New York: HarperOne, 2013), 2.

6. Edwin Yamauchi, "Jesus Outside the New Testament: What Is the Evidence?" in *Jesus Under Fire: Modern Scholarship Reinvents the Historical Jesus*, ed. Michael J. Wilkins and J. P. Moreland (Grand Rapids: Zondervan, 1996), 212.

7. I. Epstein, *The Babylonian Talmud*, vol. 3 (London: Soncino, 1935), cited in Gary Habermas, *The Historical Jesus: Ancient Evidence for the Life of Christ* (Joplin, MO: College Press, 1996), 203.

8. Lee Strobel, *The Case for Christ* (Grand Rapids: Zondervan, 1998), 87.

9. Michael J. Wilkins and J. P. Moreland, "Introduction: The Furor Surrounding Jesus," in *Jesus on Trial: Modern Scholarship Reinvents the Historical Jesus* (Grand Rapids: Zondervan, 1995), 3.

10. N. T. Wright, quoted in Craig L. Blomberg, "Where Do We Start Studying Jesus?" in *Jesus Under Fire*, ed. Wilkins and Moreland, 31.

11. Richard Bauckham, *Jesus and the Eyewitnesses: The Gospels as Eyewitness Testimony* (Grand Rapids: Eerdmans, 2006), 39.

12. Bauckham, 39.

13. Bauckham, 309.

14. Hans Stier, quoted in Blomberg, "Where Do We Start Studying Jesus?" in *Jesus Under Fire*, ed. Wilkins and Moreland, 34.

15. Bart D. Erhman, *Misquoting Jesus: The Story behind Who Changed the Bible and Why* (New York: HarperCollins, 2007), 55.

16. Norman L. Geisler and Ronald Brooks, *When Skeptics Ask: A Handbook on Christian Evidences* (Grand Rapids: Baker Books, 1990), 107.

17. N. T. Wright, *The Resurrection of the Son of God* (Minneapolis: Fortress, 2003), chaps. 18–19.

18. I. Howard Marshall, *I Believe in the Historical Jesus* (Grand Rapids: Eerdmans, 1977), 24.

## CHAPTER 2: WHAT JESUS WAS ALL ABOUT

1. Mark Driscoll and Gerry Breshears, *Vintage Jesus: Timeless Answers to Timely Questions* (Wheaton, IL: Crossway, 2007), 12.

2. Driscoll and Breshears, 11.

3. R. T. France, *The Gospel of Matthew* (Grand Rapids: Eerdmans, 2007), 6.

4. N. T. Wright, *Jesus and the Victory of God*, Christian Origins and the Question of God, vol. 2 (Minneapolis: Fortress, 1996), 14.

5. Quoted in Rikki E. Watts, *Isaiah's New Exodus in Mark*, Biblical Studies Library (Grand Rapids: Baker Academic, 1997), 29.

6. Wright, *Jesus and the Victory of God*, 6.

7. Wright, 23.

8. N. T. Wright, *The New Testament and the People of God* (Minneapolis: Fortress, 1992).

9. N. T. Wright, *The New Testament and the People of God* (Minneapolis: Fortress, 1992), 284.

10. G. B. Caird, *Jesus and the Jewish Nation* (London: Athlone Press, 1965), 20–22.

11. See James D. G. Dunn, *Jesus Remembered*, Christianity in the Making, vol. 1 (Grand Rapids: Eerdmans, 2003), 287; Wright, *New Testament and the People of God*, chap. 9.

12. Wright, 476.

13. Quoted in John P. Meier, *A Marginal Jew: Rethinking the Historical Jesus, Volume 2: Mentor, Message, and Miracles*. The Anchor Yale Bible Reference Library (New Haven, CT: Yale University Press: 1994), 237.

14. Mortimer Arias, *Announcing the Reign of God: Evangelization and the Subversive Memory of Jesus* (Eugene, OR: Wipf and Stock, 2001), 8.

15. Dunn, *Jesus Remembered*, 383.

16. Meier, *Marginal Jew*, 239.

17. Ben F. Meyer, *The Aims of Jesus*, Princeton Theological Monograph Series (Eugene, OR: Pickwick, 2002), 136.

18. Scot McKnight *A New Vision for Israel: The Teachings of Jesus in National Context* (Grand Rapids: Eerdmans, 1999), 118.

19. Philip Yancey, *The Jesus I Never Knew* (Grand Rapids: Zondervan, 1995), 182.

20. Wright, *Jesus and the Victory of God*, 191–92.

21. David Rhoads, Joanna Dewey, and Donald Michie, *Mark as Story: An Introduction to the Narrative of a Gospel* (Minneapolis: Fortress, 1999), 79.

22. Wright, *Jesus and the Victory of God*, 429.

23. Simon Gathercole, "The Gospel of Paul and the Gospel of the Kingdom," in *God's Power to Save*, ed. Chris Green (Nottingham, UK: Inter-Varsity, 2006), 138–54.

24. Arias, *Announcing the Reign of God*, 21.

25. Jim Wallis, quoted in Arias, *Announcing the Reign of God*, 50.

26. Wright, *Jesus and the Victory of God*, 257.

## CHAPTER 3: WHAT ARE THE GOSPELS?

1. N. T. Wright, *The New Testament and the People of God* (Minneapolis: Fortress, 1992), 384.

2. Craig L. Blomberg, "The Historical Reliability of the New Testament," in William Lane Craig, *Reasonable Faith: Christian Truth and Apologetics* (Wheaton, IL: Crossway, 1994), 294.

3. D. A. Carson, *The Gospel according to John*, The Pillar New Testament Commentary (Leicester: Apollos, 1991), 203.

4. Ben F. Meyer, *The Aims of Jesus*, Princeton Theological Monograph Series (Eugene, OR: Pickwick, 2002), 183.

5. Craig L. Blomberg, "Where Do We Start Studying Jesus?" in *Jesus Under Fire: Modern Scholarship Reinvents the Historical Jesus*, ed. Michael J. Wilkins and J. P. Moreland (Grand Rapids: Zondervan, 1996), 37.

6. A. N. Sherwin-White, quoted in Blomberg, 37.

7. Wright, *New Testament and the People of God*, 379.

8. Wright, 379–80.

9. Wright, 416.

10. Craig Blomberg, "Historical Reliability of the New Testament," 219.

## CHAPTER 4: CAN WE TRUST THE GOSPELS?

1. John P. Meier, *A Marginal Jew: Rethinking the Historical Jesus, Volume 2: Mentor, Message, and Miracles*. The Anchor Yale Bible Reference Library (New Haven, CT: Yale University Press: 1994), 168–177.

2. Irenaeus, *Adversus haereses* 3.3.4, quoted in Lee Strobel, *The Case for Christ* (Grand Rapids: Zondervan, 1998), 24.

3. Craig L. Blomberg, "Where Do We Start Studying Jesus?" in *Jesus Under Fire: Modern Scholarship Reinvents the Historical Jesus*, ed. Michael J. Wilkins and J. P. Moreland (Grand Rapids: Zondervan, 1996), 28.

4. Blomberg, 31–32.

5. Blomberg, 18.

6. Michael W. Holmes, "From Original Text to Initial Text," in *The Text of the New Testament in Contemporary Research*, eds., Bart D. Ehrman and Michael W. Holmes (Leiden: Brill, 2012), 674.

7. Gerd Thiessen, quoted in N. T. Wright, *The New Testament and the People of God* (Minneapolis: Fortress, 1992), 423.

8. James D. G. Dunn, *Jesus Remembered*, Christianity in the Making, vol. 1 (Grand Rapids: Eerdmans, 2003), 211.

9. Dunn, 211.

10. Dunn, 779.

11. Hans Stier, quoted in Blomberg, "Where Do We Start Studying Jesus?" in *Jesus Under Fire*, ed. Wilkins and Moreland, 34.

12. N. T. Wright, *The Resurrection of the Son of God* (Minneapolis: Fortress, 2003), 612.

13. Wright, *Resurrection of the Son of God*, 612.

14. Darrell Bock, *The Gospel of Luke, vol. 1, Luke 1:1–9:50)*, Baker Exegetical Commentary on the New Testament (Grand Rapids: Baker Book House, 1994), 283.

15. All of the historical analysis of these and many other events are fully explained in Josh McDowell, *The New Evidence That Demands a Verdict* (Nashville: Thomas Nelson, 1999), 63–64.

16. Richard Bauckham, "The Gospels as Eyewitness Accounts," in *Jesus and the Eyewitnesses* (2nd ed.) (Grand Rapids: Eerdmans, 2017).

17. Millar Burrows, *What Mean These Stones?* (New York: Meridian Books, 1957), 1.

18. Urban C. von Wahlde, "Archaeology and John's Gospel," in James H. Charlesworth, *Jesus and Archaeology* (Grand Rapids: Eerdmans, 2006), 560–66.

19. McDowell, *The New Evidence That Demands a Verdict*, 68.

20. Craig L. Blomberg, *Can We Trust the Bible?* 68.

21. Josh McDowell, *The New Demands a Verdict* (Nashville: Thomas Nelson, 1989), 36–37.

22. Blomberg, "Where Do We Start Studying Jesus?" 28. Italics added.

23. Josh McDowell, *The New Demands a Verdict*, 36–37.

24. Mark Clark, *The Problem of God: Answering a Skeptic's Challenges to Christianity* (Grand Rapids: Zondervan, 2017), 74–75.

25. C. S. Lewis, *Christian Reflections*, ed. Walter Hooper (Grand Rapids: Eerdmans, 1967), 155.

26. Huston Smith, *The Soul of Christianity: Restoring the Great Tradition* (San Francisco: HarperSanFrancisco, 2005), xvii.

## CHAPTER 5: MORE THAN A TEACHER

1. Eric Mason, "Breaking Free from Strongholds," Best Sermon Ever Series, Mars Hill Church, September 8, 2013.

2. Mason, "Breaking Free from Strongholds."

3. Jordan Peterson, *12 Rules for Life: An Antidote to Chaos* (Toronto: Random House, 2018), 164–166. Italics original.

4. Peterson, 167.

5. Mircea Eliade, quoted in Jordan Peterson, "Biblical Series IV: The Psychology of the Flood."

6. Jordan Peterson, "Biblical Series IV: The Psychology of the Flood."

7. David Foster Wallace, "This Is Water (Full Transcript and Audio)," *fs* (blog), accessed August 13, 2020, https://fs.blog/2012/04/david-foster-wallace-this-is-water/. Italics added.

8. James K. A. Smith, *You Are What You Love: The Spiritual Power of Habit* (Grand Rapids: Brazos, 2016), 41–46.

9. Smith, 25.

10. Gordon T. Smith, *Evangelical, Sacramental and Pentecostal* (Downers Grove, IL: IVP Academic, 2017).

11. Lev Shestov, *Athens and Jerusalem*, trans. with an introduction by Bernard Martin (New York: Simon and Schuster, 1968), 393.

## CHAPTER 6: THE THREEFOLD INVITATION

1. N. T. Wright, *The New Testament and the People of God* (Philadelphia: Fortress, 1992), 123.

2. Timothy Keller, *King's Cross: The Story of the World in the Life of Jesus* (New York: Dutton, 2011), 104.

3. Keller, 104–106.

4. Jan David Hettinga, *Follow Me: Experience the Loving Leadership of Jesus* (Colorado Springs: NavPress, 1996), n.p.

5. Hettinga, n.p.

6. Warren Carter, *Matthew and the Margins: A Sociopolitical and Religious Reading* (New York: Orbis Books, 2000).

7. Hettinga, *Follow Me: Experience the Loving Leadership of Jesus* (Colorado Springs: NavPress, 1996), 17.

8. Hettinga, 168.

9. Timothy Keller, *Center Church: Doing Balanced, Gospel-Centered Ministry in Your City* (Grand Rapids: Zondervan, 2012), 66.

10. Thomas Chalmers, "The Expulsive Power of a New Affection."

11. Chaim Potok, *The Chosen* (New York: Ballantine Books, 1967), 271.

12. Malcolm Gladwell, *Outliers: The Story of Success* (New York: Little, Brown, 2008 ), PAGE.

13. John Piper, *What Jesus Demands from the World* (Wheaton, IL: Crossway, 2007), PAGE.

14. John Piper, *What Jesus Demands from the World* (Wheaton, IL: Crossway, 2007), 17.

15. Dallas Willard, *The Great Omission: Reclaiming Jesus's Essential Teachings on Discipleship* (New York: HarperOne, 2006), 14.

16. The question "Who is Jesus Christ for us today?" is Bonhoeffer's, quoted in Stackhouse, the quote that follows is Stackhouse, see John G. Stackhouse Jr., *Making the Best of It: Following Christ in the Real World* (Oxford: Oxford University Press, 2008), 3.

## CHAPTER 7: COUNTERFEIT GODS

1. A. W. Tozer, quoted in Randy Alcorn, *Money, Possessions and Eternity* (Carol Stream IL: Tyndale House, 2003), xv.

2. Brian J. Walsh and Sylvia C. Keesmaat, *Colossians Remixed: Subverting the Empire* (Downers Grove, IL: InterVarsity, 2004), n.p.

3. Wendell Berry, "Christianity and the Survival of Creation," in *Sex, Economy, Freedom and Community: Eight Essays* (New York: Pantheon Books, 2008), 114–15.

4. John Francis Kavanaugh, *Following Christ in a Consumer Society: The Spirituality of Cultural Resistance* (Maryknoll, NY: Orbis Books: 1981), 99.

5. John Piper, "Putting My Daughter to Bed Two Hours after the Bridge Collapsed," Desiring God, August 1, 2007, https://www.desiringgod.org /articles/putting-my-daughter-to-bed-two-hours-after-the-bridge-collapsed.

6. J. R. R. Tolkien, *The Fellowship of the Ring* (Boston: Houghton Mifflin Harcourt, 2012).

7. Piper, "Putting My Daughter to Bed."

8. See John Piper, *Don't Waste Your Life* (Wheaton: Crossway, 2003), 45–46.

## CHAPTER 8: THE EXCLUSIVE POWER OF A NEW AFFECTION

1. Thomas Chalmers, "Expulsive Power of a New Affection."

2. Chalmers, "Expulsive Power of a New Affection."

3. John Piper, *God Is the Gospel: Meditations on God's Love as the Gift Himself* (Wheaton, IL: Crossway), 2005), 15.

4. Piper, *God Is the Gospel*, n.p.

5. Jonathan Edwards, *Religious Affections*, Vol. 2 (New Haven: Yale University Press, 1959), 249–50.

6. Jonathan Edwards, quoted in John Piper, "Love Is the Main Thing in Saving Faith," *Desiring God*, February 29, 2016, https://www.desiringgod. org/articles/love-is-the-main-thing-in-saving-faith.

7. Edwards, quoted in Piper, "Love Is the Main Thing."

8. Piper, "Love Is the Main Thing."

9. Stephen Dubner and Steven D. Levitt, *SuperFreakonomics: Global Cooling, Patriotic Prostitutes and Why Suicide Bombers Should Buy Life Insurance* (Toronto: HarperCollins, 2009), 206–7.

10. Bernard of Clairvaux, Sermon 83.4–6.

11. David Bentley Hart, *The Experience of God: Being, Consciousness, Bliss* (New Haven, CT: Yale University Press, 2013), 240-42.

12. Explained similarly to this in Timothy Keller, *Center Church* (Grand Rapids: Zondervan, 2012), 68.

13. Timothy R. Jennings, *The God-Shaped Brain: How Changing Your View of God Transforms Your Life* (Downers Grove: InterVarsity, 2017), 9–10.

14. Jennings, 27.

15. Jennings, 27.

16. Andrew Newberg, and Mark Robert Waldman, *How God Changes Your Brain: Breakthrough Findings from a Leading Neuroscientist* (New York: Ballantine, 2009), 111.

17. Albert Einstein. Written statement, September 1937, 70.

18. George Eman Vaillant, quoted in Jonah Lehrer, *A Book about Love* (New York: Simon and Schuster, 2016), 43.

## CHAPTER 9: THE ODD PROBABILITY THAT MIRACLES ARE REAL

1. Max Planck, quoted in Lee Strobel, *The Case for Faith* (Grand Rapids: Zondervan, 2000), 58.

2. C. S. Lewis, *Miracles*, in *The Complete C. S. Lewis Signature Classics* (New York: HarperOne, 2007), 303.

3. Lewis, 303.

4. Lewis, 304.

5. Dinesh D'Souza, *What's So Great about Christianity?* (Washington, DC: Regnery, 2007), 187.

6. D'Souza, 187.

7. Alvin Plantinga, *Where the Conflict Really Lies: Science, Religion and Naturalism* (New York: Oxford University Press, 2011), 121.

8. Lewis, *Miracles*, 341.

9. John C. Polkinghorne, *Science and Providence: God's Interaction with the World* (Philadelphia: Templeton Foundation Press, 2005), 64.

10. Lewis, *Miracles*, 343.

11. Lewis, 353, 423.

12. Lewis, 353, 423.

13. Lewis, 436.

14. Lewis, 436.

15. Lewis, 388.

16. Richard Lewontin, "Billions and Billions of Demons," *New York Review of Books*, January 1997, 28.

17. Nancy Pearcey, *Total Truth: Liberating Christianity from Its Cultural Captivity* (Wheaton, IL: Crossway, 2004), 170–71.

18. Craig S. Keener, *Miracles: The Credibility of the New Testament Accounts*, 2 vols. (Grand Rapids: Baker, 2011), 1:129.

19. David Skeel, *True Paradox: How Christianity Makes Sense of Our Complex World* (Downers Grove, IL: InterVarsity, 2014), 37.

20. Marilyn Schlitz, quoted in Lee Strobel, *The Case for a Creator* (Grand Rapids: Zondervan, 2004), 252.

21. Polkinghorne, *Science and Providence*, 68.

22. Peter Kreeft and Ronald K. Tacelli, *The Handbook of Christian Apologetics* (Downers Grove, IL: InterVarsity, 1994), 107. Italics in the original.

23. Alvin Plantinga, *Where the Conflict Really Lies*, 29.

24. Dinesh D'Souza, *What's So Great about Christianity?* 179.

25. John Polkinghorne, *Science and Providence*, 55.

26. David Hume, quoted in D'Souza, *What's So Great about Christianity?* 184.

27. Dinesh D'Souza, 184.

28. Craig Keener, *Miracles*, 1:237–38.

29. John Earman, quoted in Plantinga, *Where the Conflict Really Lies*, 95.

30. Gwyn Owen, "Enigma Number 1647," *NewScientist*, May 18, 2011, https://www.newscientist.com/article/mg21028132-400-rewriting-the-textbooks-the-periodic-turntable/.

31. Plantinga, *Where the Conflict Really Lies*, 94–96.

32. Plantinga, 113.

33. Herman Bavinck, *The Wonderful Works of God: Instruction in the Christian Religion according to the Reformed Confession* (Glenside, PA: Westminster Seminary Press, 2019), 52–53.

34. G. K. Chesterton, "The Ethics of Elfland," *Orthodoxy* (House of Stratus, 2001), 41.

35. Richard Swinburne, "Evidence," 198.

36. For this see Alister McGrath, *The Twilight of Atheism: The Rise and Fall of Disbelief in the Modern World* (New York: Doubleday, 2004).

37. Norman L. Geisler and Ronald M. Brooks, *When Skeptics Ask: A Handbook on Christian Evidences* (Grand Rapids: Baker, 2013), 73.

38. William Lane Craig, quoted in Strobel, *Case for Faith*, 65.

39. Cited in Norman Geisler and Frank Turek, *I Don't Have Enough Faith to Be an Atheist* (Wheaton, IL: Crossway, 2004), 205–6. Hume's argument is as follows: (1) Natural law is by definition a description of a regular occurrence. (2) A miracle is by definition a rare occurrence. (3) The evidence for the regular is always greater than that for the rare. (4) A wise man always bases his belief on the greater evidence. (5) Therefore, a wise man should never believe in miracles.

40. Keener, *Miracles*, 1:108.

41. D'Souza, *What's So Great about Christianity?* 188.

42. D'Souza, 188.

43. Bavinck, *Wonderful Works of God*, 50, italics mine.

44. Quoted in Bavinck, 52.

## CHAPTER 10: JESUS' MIRACLES: SIGNS AND THE DAWNING OF A NEW WORLD

1. Craig Blomberg, *Can We Still Trust the Bible? Or Jesus Under Fire*, 181.

2. John P. Meier, *A Marginal Jew: Rethinking the Historical Jesus, Volume 2: Mentor, Message, and Miracles.* The Anchor Yale Bible Reference Library (New Haven, CT: Yale University Press: 1994), 619.

3. James D. G. Dunn, *Jesus Remembered*, Christianity in the Making, vol. 1 (Grand Rapids: Eerdmans, 2003), 670.

4. Rudolf Bultmann, *Jesus* (Berlin: Deutsche Bibliothek, 1926), 159.

5. N. T. Wright, *Jesus and the Victory of God*, Christian Origins and the Question of God, vol. 2 (Minneapolis: Fortress, 1996), 187.

6. John Dominic Crossan, *Historical Jesus: The Life of a Mediterranean Jewish Peasant* (San Francisco: HarperSanFrancisco, 1991), 311.

7. C. S. Lewis, *Christian Reflections*, Walter Hooper, ed. (Grand Rapids: Eerdmans, 1967), 273.

8. Paul Meier, *Marginal Jew*, 630, italics mine.

9. N.T. Wright, *Jesus and the Victory of God*, 188.

10. James D. G. Dunn, *Jesus Remembered*, Christianity in the Making, vol. 1 (Grand Rapids: Eerdmans, 2003), 667.

11. Dunn, 691.

12. Dunn, 691.

13. Dunn, 692.

14. Meier, *Marginal Jew*, 567–68.

15. Herman Bavinck, *The Wonderful Works of God: Instruction in the Christian Religion according to the Reformed Confession* (Glenside, PA: Westminster Seminary Press, 2019), 54.

16. Meier, *Marginal Jew*, 618.

17. Robert H. Stein, *Jesus the Messiah: A Survey of the Life of Christ* (Downers Grove, IL: InterVarsity, 1996), 143.

18. Craig S. Keener, *Miracles: The Credibility of the New Testament Accounts*, 2 vols. (Grand Rapids: Baker, 2011), 1:19.

19. Wayne Grudem, *Systematic Theology: An Introduction to Biblical Doctrine* (Grand Rapids: Zondervan, 1994), 356.

20. Robert Farrar Capon, quoted in Philip Yancey, *The Jesus I Never Knew* (Grand Rapids: Zondervan, 1995), 170.

21. Bavinck, *Wonderful Works of God*, 54.

22. Jürgen Moltmann, quoted in Yancey, *The Jesus I Never Knew*, 183.

23. Yancey, 170.

24. Craig A. Evans, *Fabricating Jesus: How Modern Scholars Distort the Gospels* (Downers Grove, IL: InterVarsity, 2006), 141.

25. Yancey, *The Jesus I Never Knew*, 182.

26. Bavinck, *Wonderful Works of God*, 53–54.

27. Bavinck, 55.

28. Wright, *Jesus and the Victory of God*, 191–93.

29. Wright, 429.

30. Wright, 429. See also Scot McKnight *A New Vision for Israel: The Teachings of Jesus in National Context* (Grand Rapids: Eerdmans, 1999), 93.

31. D. A. Carson, "The Purpose of Signs and Wonders in the New Testament," in *Power Religion: The Selling Out of the Evangelical Church?* ed. Michael Scott Horton (Chicago: Moody Press, 1992).

32. John Woodhouse, quoted in Grudem, *Systematic Theology*, 360–70.

33. B. Joseph Pine II and James H. Gilmore, *The Experience Economy:*

*Competing for Time, Attention, and Money* (Boston: Harvard Business Review Press, 2019).

34. Pine and Gilmore.

35. C. S. Lewis, *The Voyage of the Dawn Treader* (New York: Harper Trophy, 1952), 108–09.

36. J. R. R. Tolkien, *The Lord of the Ring: The Return of the King* (Boston: Houghton Mifflin, 1965), 310.

## CHAPTER 11: THE MASTER STORYTELLER

1. N. T. Wright, *The New Testament and the People of God* (Minneapolis: Fortress, 1992), 123.

2. Wright, 123.

3. Christopher Booker, *The Seven Basic Plots: Why We Tell Stories* (New York: Continuum, 2004), 1–6.

4. Christopher Booker, *The Seven Basic Plots*, 3.

5. Booker, 3.

6. Booker, 698.

7. Josephus, *Antiquities of the Jews* 18.63.

8. James D. G. Dunn, *Jesus Remembered*, Christianity in the Making, vol. 1 (Grand Rapids: Eerdmans, 2003), 696.

9. James D. G. Dunn, *Jesus Remembered*, 697–98.

10. N. T. Wright, *Jesus and the Victory of God*, Christian Origins and the Question of God, vol. 2 (Minneapolis: Fortress, 1996), 170.

11. Wright, *Jesus and the Victory of God*, 178–79, 181.

12. Klyne Snodgrass, *Stories with Intent* (10th anniversary ed.) (Grand Rapids: Eerdmans, 2018).

13. Jason Rhode, "Watch the Throne: How *The Crown* Explains the Ongoing American Obsession with Britain's Upper Crust," *Paste*, November 21, 2016, https://www.pastemagazine.com/articles/2016/11/watch-the-throne-why-do -we-like-the-crown.html.

14. Dietrich Bonhoeffer, quoted in John G. Stackhouse Jr., *Making the Best of It*, 117.

15. Brian J. Walsh and Sylvia C. Keesmaat, *Colossians Remixed: Subverting the Empire* (Downers Grove, IL: InterVarsity, 2004), 82.

16. Humphrey Carpenter, *J. R. R. Tolkien: A Biography* (Boston: Houghton Mifflin, 2000), 151.

17. Carpenter, 147.

18. Humphrey Carpenter, *The Inklings: C. S. Lewis, J. R. R. Tolkien, Charles Williams and Their Friends* (London: HarperCollins, 2006), 43.

19. Christopher Booker, *The Seven Basic Plots*, 6.

20. Christopher Booker, *The Seven Basic Plots*, 33.

21. Christopher Booker, *The Seven Basic Plots*, 48.

22. Booker, 87.

23. There are three other story types or plots. The first is **The Quest**, examples of which include *Pilgrim's Progress* and *Raiders of the Lost Ark*.

    *The protagonist goes to a strange land and, after overcoming the threats it poses, returns with experience. Along the way there is priceless treasure worth any effort to achieve but also many obstacles and temptations.* The quest in the prodigal son, as in many quest stories, isn't necessarily a journey to find a literal treasure, but for the ever-elusive "good life" (pleasure, status, and reputation). This question leads the younger brother on a journey to a "far country" (Luke 15:13), where he falls into temptation and squanders everything, like an ancient telling of *The Wolf of Wall Street*. In traditional quest stories, the central character feels he *can't* stay at home (think Frodo leaving the Shire) and is driven from the safety of family out into the world by the quest itself. Upon reaching the far country, the younger brother faces many challenges he must overcome: famine, poverty, reckless living, and heartless people (vv. 14–16). At this time, the priceless treasure changes to security and a new understanding of the good life, and consequently, so does his destination. His journey back to the father begins, where all of these things await him.

    The challenges continue at the halfway mark. The younger son has to overcome his own doubts and fears in order to retrieve the treasure (vv. 18–19). He also faces, in somewhat Shakespearean fashion, the pushback and disdain of his older brother, who almost ruins his retrieving of the treasure (vv. 28–30). Ultimately, he attains the treasure after his long journey home, and his story ends, as Booker says, "with the picture of a Renewed Life that has a trajectory into the future" (vv. 23–24).

Another story type is **Comedy**, as featured in *Much Ado About Nothing* and *The Princess Bride*.

This is a story wherein the conflict becomes more and more confusing but is at last made plain in a single clarifying event; the resolution of some conflict is made, paving the way for reconciliation and celebration. The main character discovers who he is meant to pair off with—his true "other half"; before this realization, he seems "lost and incomplete . . there is division, separation, or loss, [but] Families shall be united, lost objects found" (Christopher Booker, *The Seven Basic Plots*, 87).

In the Prodigal Son recognition of the younger sons 'other half' (I would content in this story it is presented as the father himself, without whom the son has lost his identity) is the main crux on which the story turns. This becomes an essential part of his self-discovery, and when this is realized and the two are once again brought together, it is literally explained as the "lost" being "found" (v. 24). All of this comes after a confusing and tragic time of poverty and hunger, which is resolved through the single climactic event of the son's return to his father where, as Booker says, there is reconciliation and celebration (vv. 20–21).

Irony is, of course, a central part of all Comedy, and The Prodigal Son is full of it. The son wants to eat the food of an animal that he himself, as a Jew, was not even allowed to eat (v. 16). The father runs out to meet his son as he approaches (v. 20), an action that would have been shameful for him to perform, for, "distinguished Middle Eastern patriarchs did not run. Children might run. . . But not the paterfamilias, the dignified pillar of the community. . . He would not pick up his robes and bare his legs like some boy" (Timothy Keller, *The Prodigal God*, 22). And yet this one does, bringing shame on himself in order to lift the shame another brought on his family (similar to what Jesus himself does of course). The father also continues to double down on his extravagant treatment of the Younger Son, spending more of the family fortune—killing the fattened calf and throwing a party—on him even though he has already given away much of his fortune.

**Tragedy** completes the story types, illustrated by such works as *Romeo and Juliet* and *Anna Karenina*.

*The story contains a major character with one major character flaw,*
*or great mistake, which is ultimately his undoing. His unfortunate end*
*evokes pity at his folly and the fall of a fundamentally "good" character.*
Booker describes the situation of the main character at the beginning of
a Tragedy as one that cries out for a change. The main character then
receives some kind of call, which thrusts him out of his dissatisfying state
and into the adventure that is supposedly going to transform his life. We
as an audience are made to feel uneasy, and the call could often be more
aptly described as a temptation. This is because Tragedy stories frequently revolve around a tragedy of the Divided Self rather than an external
enemy hovering around some aspect of the character's personality. This
Divided Self situation often creates a downward life spiral. Again, as if
describing the opening verses of Jesus' story, Booker says of Tragedy: "We
have already become aware that there is one part of [a character], one
desire, one appetite, which is nagging at them to the point where the
urge to gratify it is building up into an overwhelming obsession." In every
instance "we are aware that what their obsession is drawing them into is
something which violates and defies convention or duty or standard of
normality" (*The Seven Basic Plots*, 173–74). Every part of the son's request for the property defies Jewish convention and standards of normality. It would have been like telling his Father that he wishes he was dead,
and that he only wants his money, not a relationship.

Booker says of the plot of Tragedy: "We have seen people, possessed by some egocentric fantasy of love or power, gradually separating
themselves from everyone around them, more and more submerged in
the darkness which springs from their own split, disordered psyche, until
finally the violent rejection they have shown to others turns in on themselves. But we have also seen how it is possible for this downward spiral
into darkness to be reversed . . for the hero or heroine to begin to knot
together again, within themselves and with others around them, so that
light is again breaking in on their darkness" (*The Seven Basic Plots*, 192).

The tragedy of Jesus' story is that the son disrupts the family
through his actions: sleeping with prostitutes, working with pigs, etc.
Other aspects of Tragedy are present in the story as well: the older
brother never re-unites with the family in the end because of his
judgment of the younger brother (vv. 29–30). But this tragedy, as with
many, has an upside to it. In his book exploring the Prodigal Son story,
Timothy Keller says: "The father could not just forgive the younger

son, somebody had to pay! The father could not reinstate him except at the expense of the elder brother. . . There was no way for the younger brother to return to the family unless the older brother bore the cost himself" (*The Prodigal God*, 84–85). Cast out of the family, so that another may join it; a cruciform pattern, pointing to Jesus own tragedy itself, which was for the saving of the world.

## CHAPTER 12: THE MEANING OF JESUS' PARABLES

1. Ernest Becker, *The Denial of Death* (New York: Free Press, 1973), 198.

2. N. T. Wright, *Simply Christian: Why Christianity Makes Sense* (New York: Harper One, 2006), 61.

3. Seth Stephens-Davidowitz, *Everybody Lies: Big Data, New Data, and What the Internet Can Tell Us about Who We Really Are* (New York: HarperCollins, 2017), 157.

4. Stephens-Davidowitz, 157.

5. Francis Schaeffer, "The God Who Is There," in *The Francis A. Schaeffer Trilogy: The Three Essential Books in One* (Wheaton, IL: Crossway, 1990), 110.

6. Mark Sayers, *The Disappearing Church* (Chicago: Moody, 2016), 16–32.

7. As quoted in Timothy Keller, *The Meaning of Marriage: Facing the Complexities of Commitment with the Wisdom of God* (New York: Penguin, 2011), 97.

8. As quoted in Keller, 97.

9. Darrell Johnson, *Discipleship on the Edge: An Expository Journey through the Book of Revelation* (Vancouver, BC: Regent College Publishing, 2004).

10. Thanks to Darrell Johnson, who shared this insight in private conversation. He served as a missionary in the Philippines for many years and talked to many elders of villages about this story, who across the board believed that this was what the younger son was deserving.

## CHAPTER 13: RETHINKING GOD

1. Craig L. Blomberg, "Where Do We Start Studying Jesus?" in *Jesus Under Fire*, ed. Michael Wilkins and J. P. Moreland (Grand Rapids: Zondervan, 1995), 18.

2. Dan Brown, *The Da Vinci Code* (New York: Doubleday, 2003), 233–34, italics in the original.

3. J. I. Packer, *Knowing God* (Downers Grove, IL: InterVarsity, 1979), 45.

4. Ben Witherington III, *Paul's Narrative Thought World: The Tapestry of Tragedy and Triumph* (Louisville: Westminster John Knox, 1994), 181: "The term *kurios* occurs in the LXX over nine thousand times, and in over six thousand of these occurrences it is used in place of the proper name of God—Yahweh."

5. Bruce Longenecker, "On Israel's God," 34: "Paul incorporates Jesus into his own reformulation of the Shema. . . . Non-Christian understandings of God . . . were themselves to be superseded since they failed to incorporate the most critical aspect of God—his christomorphic sovereignty." See also N. T. Wright, *The Climax of the Covenant: Christ and the Law in Pauline Theology* (Minneapolis: Fortress, 1993), 132. Wright calls this reshaping a "Christianized *Shema*."

6. James D. G. Dunn, *Christology in the Making* (Philadelphia: Westminster, 1980), 180.

7. I. Howard Marshall, *The Origins of New Testament Christology* (Downers Grove, IL: InterVarsity, 1990), 106. Italics mine.

8. Word and Wisdom are linked in Jewish tradition. The parallel structure in Wisdom of Solomon 9.1–2 is a good example: "O God . . . who has made all things by your word [*en logo sou*], and by your wisdom [*te sophia sou*] has formed humankind." For more on Wisdom Christology see Richard J. Bauckham, *God Crucified: Monotheism and Christology in the New Testament* (Grand Rapids: Eerdmans, 1998), 26; Dunn, *Christology in the Making*, chaps. 6 and 7; Ben Witherington III, "Christology," in *Dictionary of Paul and His Letters*, ed. G. F. Hawthorne and R. P. Martin (Downers Grove, IL: InterVarsity, 1993), 103; Seyoon Kim, *The Origin of Paul's Gospel* (Eugene, OR: Wipf and Stock, 2007), 135n3; Marinus de Jonge, *Christology in Context: The Earliest Response to Jesus* (Philadelphia: Westminster, 1988), 194–99, and Gordon D. Fee, *Pauline Christology: An Exegetical-Theological Study* (Grand Rapids: Baker, 2007), 102–5, 599–619.

9. C. S. Lewis, *Mere Christianity* (London: Collins, 1952), 56.

10. Walter J. Burghardt, *Still Proclaiming Your Wonders* (Ramsey, NJ: Paulist, 1984), 140.

11. Jacob Neusner, *A Rabbi Talks with Jesus: An Intermillennial, Interfaith Exchange* (New York: Doubleday, 1993), 30.

12. Neusner, 30.

13. Ben Witherington III, *The Christology of Jesus* (Minneapolis: Fortress, 1990), 276.

14. N. T. Wright, *Jesus and the Victory of God*, Christian Origins and the Question of God, vol. 2 (Minneapolis: Fortress, 1996), 257.

15. Mark Driscoll and Gerry Breshears, *Vintage Jesus: Timeless Answers to Timely Questions* (Wheaton, IL: Crossway, 2007), 18.

16. Adolf Schlatter, *The History of the Christ: The Foundation for New Testament Theology*, trans. A. J. Kostenberger (Grand Rapids: Baker, 1997).

17. T. W. Manson, *Teaching of Jesus: Studies of Its Form and Content* (Cambridge: Cambridge University Press, 1939), 211.

18. Timothy Keller, The Timothy Keller Sermon Archive (New York City: Redeemer Presbyterian Church, 2013).

19. Keller, Sermon Archive.

20. Jürgen Moltmann, *The Trinity and the Kingdom* (Minneapolis: Augsburg Fortress, 1993), 115.

21. Moltmann, 115.

22. Everett Fox, *The Five Books of Moses* (New York: Schocken Books, 1995), 273.

23. J. R. R. Tolkien, *The Lord of the Rings: The Return of the King* (Boston: Houghton Mifflin, 1965), 305.

24. N. T. Wright, *What Saint Paul Really Said: Was Paul of Tarsus the Real Founder of Christianity?* (Grand Rapids: Eerdmans 1997), 67–72. Wright focuses primarily on 1 Corinthians 8:1–6; Philippians 2:5–11; and Colossians 1:15–20. See also Wright, *Paul*, 91–96; Wayne Meeks, *The First Urban Christians: The Social World of the Apostle Paul* (New Haven, CT: Yale University Press, 2003), 165–70. See also Dunn, *Christology in the Making*, 182.

25. G. B. Caird, *The Language and Imagery of the Bible* (London: Duckworth, 1980), 51.

26. N. T. Wright, *The New Testament and the People of God* (Minneapolis: Fortress, 1992), 472–76.

27. Wright, *New Testament and the People of God*, 472–76.

28. Wright, *Jesus and the Victory of God*, 660–61.

29. Witherington, *Paul's Narrative Thought World*, 181.

30. Timothy Keller, *Making Sense of God* (New York: Viking, 2016), 236–37.

31. Cornelius Van Til, *An Introduction to Systematic Theology* (Nutley, NJ: Presbyterian and Reformed, 1974), 1–2.

32. Ravi Zacharias, *Jesus among Other Gods: The Absolute Claims of the Christian Message* (Nashville: Thomas Nelson, 2000), vii, 3–4.

33. Zacharias, vii, 3–4.

34. A quote from the film, *The Village* (written and directed by M. Night Shyamalan).

35. Richard Bauckham, *New Testament Theology: The Theology of the Book of Revelation* (Cambridge: Cambridge University Press, 1993), 159.

36. Emil Brunner, quoted in Donald Bloesch, *God the Almighty* (Downers Grove, IL: IVP Academic, 1995), i.

## CHAPTER 14: THE ONLY WAY

1. Martin Buber, quoted in Mark Sayers, *Disappearing Church: From Cultural Relevance to Gospel Resilience* (Chicago: Moody, 2016), 51.

2. Sayers, 32.

3. Sayers, 75.

4. Jo Piazza, "Ways to Cope with the Depression of the Dream of Pandora Being Intangible," CNN, January 11, 2010, https://www.cnn.com/2010 /SHOWBIZ/Movies/01/11/avatar.movie.blues/index.html.

5. Vinoth Ramachandra, *The Scandal of Jesus* (Downers Grove, IL. InterVarsity, 2001), 24.

6. C. S. Lewis, *The Last Battle* (New York: Harper Trophy, 1956), 211.

## CHAPTER 15: WHAT HAPPENED: AN APPOINTMENT WITH DEATH

1. Josephus, *Antiquities of the Jews* 18.63–64.

2. Thallus, quoted in Julius Africanus, *Chronography*, 18.

3. Matthew 27:45–54.

4. N. T. Wright, *Jesus and the Victory of God*, Christian Origins and the Question of God, vol. 2 (Minneapolis: Fortress, 1996), 544.

5. James D. G. Dunn, *Jesus Remembered*, Christianity in the Making, vol. 1 (Grand Rapids: Eerdmans, 2003), 784.

6. Dunn, 548.

7. Martin Hengel, *Crucifixion: The Ancient World and the Folly of the Cross* (Philadelphia: Fortress, 1977), 86–88.

8. Robert Wright, *The Evolution of God* (New York: Back Bay Books, 2009), 245–46.

9. Mark Driscoll and Gerry Breshears, *Death by Love: Letters from the Cross* (Wheaton, IL: Crossway, 2008).

10. Herman Bavinck, *The Wonderful Works of God: Instruction in the Christian Religion according to the Reformed Confession* (Glenside, PA: Westminster Seminary Press, 2019), 331.

11. John Stott, *The Cross of Christ* (Downers Grove, IL: InterVarsity, 1986), 160.

## CHAPTER 16: WHAT IT MEANT: THE VICTORY OF GOD

1. Thomas Keating, quoted in Christopher L. Heuertz, *The Sacred Enneagram: Finding Your Unique Path to Spiritual Growth* (Grand Rapids: Zondervan, 2017), 22.

2. M. Scott Peck, quoted in Philip Yancey, *The Jesus I Never Knew* (Grand Rapids: Zondervan, 1995), 204.

3. N. T. Wright, *Jesus and the Victory of God*, Christian Origins and the Question of God, vol. 2 (Minneapolis: Fortress, 1996), 609–10.

4. This idea is attributed to D. A. Carson.

5. J. I. Packer, Knowing God (London: Hodder and Stoughton, 1973), 239.

6. Timothy Keller, *The Reason for God: Belief in an Age of Skepticism* (New York: Penguin, 2018), 245.

7. Herman Bavinck, *The Wonderful Works of God: Instruction in the Christian Religion according to the Reformed Confession* (Glenside, PA: Westminster Seminary Press, 2019), 338–39.

## CHAPTER 17: THE EVIDENCE: WHY THE RESURRECTION LIKELY DID HAPPEN

1. Shane Ryan, "Tiger Woods Is Totally, Completely, Unequivocally, and Utterly Done," July 17, 2015, https://www.golfdigest.com/story/tiger-woods-is-totally-complet.

2. N. T. Wright, *The Resurrection of the Son of God* (Minneapolis: Fortress, 2003), 49.

3. Wright, 35.

4. Craig Blomberg, *Can We Still Believe the Bible?* (Grand Rapids: Brazos Press, 2014), 186–87.

5. Blomberg, 692.

6. William Lane Craig, "Did Jesus Rise from the Dead?" in *Jesus Under* Fire, ed. Michael Wilkins and J. P. Moreland (Grand Rapids: Zondervan, 1995), 143.

7. Edwin Yamauchi, "Jesus Outside the New Testament: What Is the Evidence?" in *Jesus Under Fire*, 212.

8. William Lane Craig, "Did Jesus Rise from the Dead?" in *Jesus Under* Fire, ed. Wilkins and Moreland, 162–63.

9. Josephus, *Antiquities of the Jews* 4.8.15.

10. E. P. Sanders, *Jesus and Judaism* (Philadelphia: Fortress, 1985), 240.

11. N. T. Wright, *Jesus and the Victory of God*, Christian Origins and the Question of God, vol. 2 (Minneapolis: Fortress, 1996), 111.

12. Rodney Stark, *The Rise of Christianity: A Sociologist Reconsiders History* (Princeton, NJ: Princeton University Press, 1996), 7.

13. N. T. Wright, *The Resurrection of the Son of God* (Minneapolis: Fortress, 2003), chaps. 18–19.

14. C. F. D. Moule, *The Phenomenon of the New Testament* (London: SCM Press, 1967), 13.

## CHAPTER 18: OUR OWN RESURRECTION, IN THIS LIFE AND THE NEXT

1. Matthew W. Bates, *Gospel Allegiance: What Faith in Jesus Misses for Salvation in Christ* (Grand Rapids: Brazos, 2019), 40.

2. Herman Bavinck, *The Wonderful Works of God: Instruction in the Christian Religion according to the Reformed Confession* (Glenside, PA: Westminster Seminary Press, 2019), 344.

3. N. T. Wright, *The Resurrection of the Son of God* (Minneapolis: Fortress, 2003), 31.

4. C. S. Lewis, *Miracles*, in *The Complete C. S. Lewis Signature Classics* (New York: HarperOne, 2007), 430.

5. Lewis, 430. Italics mine.

6. Philip Yancey, *The Jesus I Never Knew* (Grand Rapids: Zondervan, 1995), 275.

# The Problem of God

## Answering a Skeptic's Challenges to Christianity

*Mark Clark*

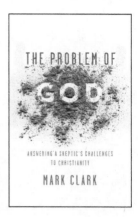

*The Problem of God* is written by a skeptic who became a Christian and then a pastor, all while exploring answers to the most difficult questions raised against Christianity. Growing up in an atheistic home, Mark Clark struggled through his parents' divorce, acquiring Tourette syndrome and OCD in his teen years. After his father's death, he began a skeptical search for truth through science, philosophy, and history, eventually finding answers in Christianity.

In a disarming, winsome, and persuasive way, *The Problem of God* responds to the top ten God questions of our present age, including:

- Does God even exist?
- What do we do with Christianity's violent history?
- Is Jesus just another myth?
- Can the Bible be trusted?
- Why should we believe in hell anymore today?

The book concludes with Christianity's most audacious assertion: how should we respond to Jesus' claim that he is God and the only way to salvation.

*Available in stores and online!*